6/25/95

To Gary —
Keep it hot!
Jenny

The

All-American

Chili

Cookbook

★ *The* ★

All-American

Chili

Cookbook

⁂

THE OFFICIAL COOKBOOK OF THE
INTERNATIONAL CHILI SOCIETY

Jenny Kellner
and Richard Rosenblatt

HEARST BOOKS · NEW YORK

It is the policy of William Morrow and Company, Inc., and its imprints and affiliates, recognizing the importance of preserving what has been written, to print the books we publish on acid-free paper, and we exert our best efforts to that end.

Library of Congress Cataloging-in Publication Data

Kellner, Jenny.
    The all-American chili cookbook : the official cookbook of the International Chili Society / by Jenny Kellner and Richard Rosenblatt.
        p.   cm.
    Includes index.
    ISBN 0-688-13693-1
    1. Chili con carne   I. Rosenblatt, Richard.   II. International   Chili Society.
III. Title.
TX749.K43 1995
641.8'23—dc20   94-24269
                                                                                    CIP

Printed in the United States of America

First Edition

1 2 3 4 5 6 7 8 9 10

BOOK DESIGN BY CAROLINE CUNNINGHAM

To our children, David and Erica, and our parents,

Kathleen and Saul and Renee

✳ *Acknowledgments* ✳

This book—indeed, the entire International Chili Society—would not have existed today had it not been for Carroll Shelby, who had the instinct, foresight, intelligence, charm, and, let's admit it, blind good luck to hold the very first World's Championship Chili Cookoff on his ranch in Terlingua back in 1967. Nor would the ICS have continued had it not been for Robert Petersen, Jim West, and Tom Deemer, whose enthusiasm and leadership on the board of governors have kept the organization vital not only through the 1970s and 1980s but through the trials and tribulations of the 1990s.

A special heartfelt "thank you" goes to ICS executive director West and his assistant, Denny Parisia, who have kept the fun in chili all these years in addition to making it possible for cookoffs to raise millions of dollars for worthwhile charities.

One of the main reasons the ICS is so much fun is because of the late C. V. Wood, Jr. (1920–1992), the man who built Disneyland, brought the London Bridge to Lake Havasu City, Arizona (yes, he did look at the reassembled structure and exclaim, "That's not the bridge I bought!"), and who with his wife, Joanne Dru, made sure every chili event he was connected with was infused with his special sense of Hollywood showmanship and gaiety.

Moreover, had it not been for Wood's organizational genius, the whole thing probably would have sputtered and died after the move from Texas to California back in 1975. Wood not only got down to the nitty-gritty and wrote the judging rules and basic guidelines for chili cookoffs, but also set up the framework that carried the ICS from its good-old-boy beginnings to its current international status.

Likewise, W. D. Ray (1934–1991), owner of the Balboa Bay Club in Newport Beach, California, and Port of the Islands in Florida, brought chilidom to a new level when he organized the first California and Florida State championships at those venues.

Lastly, we'd like to remind everyone the ICS isn't just about rules or judging criteria or cuts of meat. People are what make the ICS hum—from Shelby and Petersen and Deemer, to the advisory board members, to the cookoff chairmen and women, to the sponsors and, of course, the cooks. Without them, this book would have been very short.

We count everyone we've met along the chili trail as a friend and would like to thank them all for their friendship, interest, and support. Our deepest appreciation goes to the chiliheads of all ages who parted with their recipes, to Bill Adler for making this happen, and to our patient editor, Megan Newman.

Contents

Introduction   xi

Making Great Chili   1

ICS World's Championship Chili   17

More ICS Winners   87

Still More ICS Winners   127

ICS Guru Chili   149

Chili Appreciation Society International
   (CASI) Chili   167

Sporting Chili   187

Political Chili   217

Celebrity Chili   237

Chili by the Pros   259

Chili Appetizers   287

Not by Chili Alone — Scrumptious Sides   315

Afterburners — Delectable Desserts   337

Chili Cocktails   353

Chili Sources   371

   Recommended Chili Books   371

Magazines, Newsletters, Newspapers,

    and Pamphlets   373

Organizations   374

Events and Festivals   374

Mail-Order Sources   376

Index   381

CONTENTS

Introduction

In his megahit minibook *Life's Little Instruction Book*, H. Jackson Brown, Jr., offers as No. 13 this bit of advice: "Learn to make great chili." Like the International Chili Society, that's part of what this cookbook is all about—great chili and how to make it. The ICS defines chili as any kind of meat and spices cooked with chile peppers, but all chiliheads know chili is a good deal more than that. Chili, once ingested, becomes part of you, whether you're from Texas or Vermont, Washington State or New Mexico. With its welcoming aroma, rich flavors, and soul-satisfying warmth, it embraces all. Mention chili to the most casual chili lovers and watch their eyes light up.

Chili cuts across all borders—race, religion, socioeconomic status, or age. Anyone who's seen auto-racing legend Carroll Shelby chatting with a rookie cook nervously making his or her first batch of competition chili knows that.

That's why this book is about more than meat and spices. (OK, OK, it's also about terrific drinks and tempting appetizers and luscious desserts. We know. We wrote it.) It's mainly about people—people who love to eat chili, cook chili, and talk chili. Up and down the line they are some of the nicest, friendliest people in the world, people who would do just about anything for another chilihead. (Except divulge a secret recipe. Get too close to that handwritten scrap of paper and the owner will lovingly put out your eyes with a hot poker.)

Seriously, these are people from all walks of life and all parts of the country. From publishing magnate Robert Petersen, a member of the ICS Board of Governors, to 1993 champion Cathy Wilkey, who helps manage her husband's dental practice, to ICS official historian Ormly Gumfudgin, who got everyone's vote as the most intriguing chilihead, they are all united by a love of chili and a flair for having fun.

The majority of recipes in this book were collected from chili lovers from coast to coast, with a foray or two overseas. With such a vast array of sources and styles, it became necessary to rewrite many of them to conform to a single, workable style.

Each recipe was tested at least once (the drinks recipes were tested about, oh, five or six times each) and, if they were revised, tested again. Our thanks to our enthusiastic panel of taste testers, notably race caller Tom Durkin, who, like us, found it necessary to go out and purchase an expensive piece of exercise equipment to avoid being mistaken for the Michelin Man. So, as many recipes in this book end, enjoy!

★ A Revisionist History of Chili ★

There are as many theories about the origin of chili as there are chili recipes, and their backers can get quite rabid insisting that their pet theory is the sole correct one. Frankly, getting involved in pinning down the precise origin of the dish is something of a dead-end street, kind of like debating where meat loaf was invented or who concocted the first egg cream. (If you're not from Brooklyn, don't ask. Just fill a tall glass half-full of milk, fizz in some ice-cold seltzer, and stir in 2 ounces of Fox's U-Bet syrup. Goes great with chili.)

We do know that chile peppers, like corn, pumpkins, and potatoes, are native to the New World. Centuries ago they were incorporated into various dishes by the Indians who lived in Central and South America and the Caribbean. In fact, Montezuma was said to have started his day with a plate of plain chile peppers, which are scientifically known as capsicums but were mistakenly called peppers by explorers looking for a shorter route to the East for black pepper and other valuable spices. As the Spanish explorers spread throughout the New World, they incorporated some of the methodology used by the Indians into their own cooking, and the distant ancestors of chili took another step up on the evolutionary trail.

The earliest known recipe for a chili-like food was recorded in

INTRODUCTION

xv

1737. Susan Hazen-Hammond and Eduardo Fuss, in their dazzling book *Chile Pepper Fever: Mine's Hotter Than Yours*, report that a German-speaking Jesuit named Philipp Segesser, who moved to southern Arizona in 1732, described a stew made with Turkish peppers (chile peppers) that were placed on glowing coals, then ground up in a mortar, dumped into hot lard, and cooked with pieces of meat.

The question is, how did those long-ago Indian concoctions, that 1737 dish, and the like evolve into the chili we all know and love today? The answer, we believe, is in the powder.

Ground zero for modern-day chili is probably somewhere around San Antonio, where in the mid-1800s some unknown English settlers blended dried native spices—garlic, oregano, and *chiles pequín*, the tiny, hot peppers that grow wild in the Southwest—in a mortar and pestle to substitute for the curry powders they had used back in Britain. Once a simple chili powder blend was created for home use, it was only a matter of time before the discovery spread like wildfire, proving once again you can't keep a good recipe to yourself.

Still, the theories are often as colorful and spicy as the dish itself, and they are, in fact, distant ancestors of today's championship chili. Here are some of the most popular:

* Some hold that chili was first invented by Canary Islanders who were brought to San Antonio in the 1700s and who used local ingredients—chile peppers, wild onions, and garlic—to re-create the pungent meat dishes they had cooked in their native land.

* Another theory puts forth the proposition that chili was really invented by the *lavanderas,* or washerwomen, who followed around the nineteenth-century armies of Texas and made an amalgam of goat meat or venison, wild marjoram, and red chiles as they traveled from camp to camp.
* One story credits a native Texan who cooked for the cowboys on trail drives. In order to make fresh beef more palatable, he foraged for wild oregano, chile peppers, garlic, and onions and made a chili stew. So that he wouldn't run out, he transplanted those plants in patches of mesquite along the trails and harvested them on the next drive.
* Another version holds that settlers heading to the gold fields of California took with them "chili bricks," made by pounding beef together with lard and chile peppers, which could easily be reconstituted on the trail.
* Going way back, one source claims that chili originated with the Aztecs, who, justifiably angered at the invading Spaniards, cut them into tiny, $3/8$-inch dice and stewed them with chile peppers.
* The most fanciful tale involves a seventeenth-century Spanish nun named Sister Mary of Agreda, who entered a convent at the age of sixteen. Sister Mary, who slept a great deal, claimed she had "spirit-walked" among the Indians in the Southwest collecting recipes, including one, according to George Herter's *Bull Cook and Authentic Historical Recipes and Practices,* that called for venison, onions, tomatoes, and chile peppers. In fact, the Indians do have a legend concerning a "Lady in Blue" (who seems to have borne a striking resemblance to Sally Field) who was said to have visited their encampments at about that time.

The first recorded mass cooking of *chili con carne*—peppers with meat—occurred in the late 1800s in San Antonio. In the evenings, dozens of Mexican women who came to be known as "chili queens" would trundle wagons loaded with homemade "chili," tables, pots, colorful lanterns, and even stools for the customers to Military Plaza. From nightfall until the wee hours, by the glow from the ornate lanterns and the mesquite fires they built to heat the chili, the chili queens would ladle out bowls of red to those lured by the colorful carts and the tantalizing smells. By the mid-1890s, going downtown for a bowl of chili had become a standard Saturday night ritual, and in 1893 there was even a San Antonio "Chilley" Stand at the Chicago World's Fair. (The San Antonio Health Department finally put the queens out of business in 1943.)

All of this would have remained a quaint local custom, however, had it not been for the efforts of William Gebhardt and DeWitt Clinton Pender, two Texans who pioneered the commercialization of chili powder in the 1890s and made it easy for restaurants and home cooks to prepare chili con carne. By 1908 Gebhardt's had produced the first canned chili, and chili was on its way to becoming a national dish. Although chili consumption declined after the 1930s, when it was known as an inexpensive, substantial food, America's love for the dish was revived in the 1960s when Texan Lyndon Johnson took office. Today more than 1 billion pounds of chili are consumed in the United States each year, and a group called CHILI-USA is lobbying to have chili declared the official food of the United States.

For further reading on the origins and lore of chili, try to get your hands on Joe Cooper's ground-breaking book, *With or*

Without Beans, which is out of print. Frank X. Tolbert's book, *A Bowl of Red,* is a classic, while Bill Bridges's *The Great Chili Book* is also recommended reading.

★ An ICS History of Chili ★

Chili, as we now know it, did not exist before 1967.

That's when Carroll Shelby and Dallas attorney Dave Witts, who wanted to sell their ranch in Terlingua, Texas, first asked a PR man by the name of Tom Tierney, "What can we do to get rid of that 150,000 acres of rocks and rattlesnakes?" A couple of weeks later, no doubt over a bowl of chili and some cocktails, Tierney blurted out the words that would change so many lives: "We'll always have Paris."

No, really, what he said was "Let's hold a chili cookoff."

No one had ever heard of a chili cookoff, but it sounded like a good idea and before anyone knew it, the thing was organized and on board. Or as Shelby says, disorganized and on board.

Cooking for the Chili Appreciation Society International was Wick Fowler, legendary chief cook of that organization, which was formed in 1951 by George Haddaway. So profound a lover of chili was Haddaway that he once physically attacked a Houston chef who put Boston baked beans in his chili. The police came and, according to reports, yelled at the chef.

Set to cook against Fowler was Dave Chasen, a Los Angeles restaurateur. His chili was so popular that Elizabeth Taylor demanded it be flown to the set of *Cleopatra* when she and Richard Burton were filming in Puerto Vallarta. Chasen, however, became sick (from eating someone else's chili), but fortuitously a New York writer named H. Allen Smith had just published in *Holiday* magazine an article entitled "Nobody Knows More About Chili Than I Do," which totally defiled Texas chili. He was chosen to replace Chasen by the CASI group and a challenge was issued.

With Texas newspapermen Frank Tolbert and Fowler making a Very Big Deal about the dare in various publications, Smith could not refuse, and after a great deal of correspondence involving words such as "varlet" and "childish, semi-rumped Rotarian cracker-breakers," he arrived in Terlingua, a patch of land so desolate that Fowler once said it looked like the place they tested the first atomic bomb—after the bomb went off.

There, beginning at noon on the porch of the Chisos Oasis Saloon on the Chiricahua Ranch, Smith and Fowler stirred and spiced and simmered while about 300 friends, relatives, and strangers had a helluva good time eating and drinking (mostly drinking) while they waited to see what would happen.

What did happen was that one judge, Hallie Stillwell, voted for Smith; another, Floyd Schneider, voted for Fowler; while the third, Dave Witts, self-proclaimed mayor of Terlingua, spat out his chili, declared his taste buds were "ruint," and said they would have to do the whole thing over again next year.

"Before that, no one had even thought about making it an annual event," Shelby recalls. "Those first couple of years, there was a bunch of us who were friends and we just got together before the cookoff and asked each other, 'Well, are you going? Who's coming with you? What time are you going to get there?' and that was the beginning, and end, of organization."

The second time around, a masked *bandido* ran off with the ballot box, throwing it down an outhouse located over a mineshaft, and again there was no winner. But to the vast majority of the 700 or so fans who had trekked out to Terlingua to witness the cookoff (and in doing so, consumed 90 percent of the tequila in West Texas) it didn't matter. A year later, to the growing astonishment of the "organizers," people from all over the country were clamoring to be included in the contest, each proclaiming he concocted the finest chili in the nation. (Women were not allowed at this point.)

Joe DeFrates, who packaged chili in Illinois, heard about it on the radio, told his wife, "I've got to get in on this," and showed up to cook in 1969 against Fowler and C. V. Wood, the man who had brought the London Bridge to Lake Havasu and built Disneyland. (That was also the year Shelby and some friends tried to turn loose a herd of goats on some unsuspecting campers in the ranch house at 2:00 A.M., throwing in some firecrackers and locking the door for good measure. After some initial confusion, everyone went back to sleep.)

More than one thousand fans showed up, and some of them actually were able to recall that Woody, whose "helpers" were a bunch of very beautiful (and very friendly) Hollywood starlets, was named the first official World's Champion. Whether the judges were more impressed with his chili or his entourage will forever be lost in time.

"He actually thought he made the best chili in the world and wasn't shy about saying so," Shelby recalls, adding, "In the very early days we tried to keep the judging honest, but there were only a few judges and I'm not sure if some of them weren't unduly influenced."

After Fowler finally won in 1970, Woody returned to cook, demanding a head-to-head battle with CASI's chief cook, and won again, promptly retiring as the only undefeated World's Champion. From then on, Woody would watch the proceedings from a throne, wearing an ermine-trimmed velvet cape of his own design and carrying a scepter.

For the next couple of years, the cookoffs were sort of like an adult version of spring break. "The idea," says Shelby, "was to have fun first and worry about who made the best chili second. Woody brought in hot-air balloons, Hollywood celebrities, beautiful assistants. It became an adult Woodstock. I have fond memories of those cookoffs."

While Shelby and his band of fun-loving Californians appreciated the show-biz glamour and excitement that Woody brought to the event, Tolbert did not. The final straw came when Shelby and Wood transported a CBS camera crew on their private plane to the cookoff. Naturally, the television people interviewed Shelby and Wood, who claimed the original cookoff was their idea and all but ignored Tolbert.

Steamed, Tolbert wrote to the duo and said he was ready to quit, as it was obvious they were trying to promote something he said should be called the annual C. V. Wood Show. "Why don't you fellows stage it in California and save the freight," he suggested.

Which is precisely what Shelby and Wood did. Unbeknownst to the Chili Appreciation Society, Shelby had copyrighted the title "World's Championship Chili Cookoff" several years earlier, and in 1975 they held their own event to raise money for the Children's Hospital at Tropico Gold Mine, an abandoned mine located near Rosamond, California. Terlingua continued as a site for an annual cookoff, which later became several cookoffs going on simultaneously, as CASI factions warred over who ran which cookoff.

Unlike Terlingua, which is about eight hours from Nowhere, Rosamond is just ninety miles north of Los Angeles. Rather than a few thousand fans, the first cookoff at Tropico drew fifteen thousand people, and it became clear that the event needed more than the fond but haphazard guidance provided by Shelby and Wood.

"When we first organized the ICS to be more than just a bunch of friends having a party, we hired Jim West as our executive director," Shelby says. "Jim had an office and did something [entertainment director] for the Balboa Bay Club, a private yacht club. So our first office was at an exclusive private club on the waterfront in Newport Beach, California. We brought in sponsors like Hunt-Wesson, McIlhenny Company [Tabasco], and Pepsi. Rules and regulations were formulated and we started approaching charities and nonprofit organizations to hold cookoffs. The fun didn't change, but we put some meaning in the crazy madness that cookoffs represented. I'll bet there weren't over twenty-five cookoffs in the world at that time, and by 1994 we will have sanctioned over three hundred cookoffs throughout the United States and several foreign countries. There has been $40 million raised by these organizations from sanctioned chili cookoffs.

"Jim is still the director and credit must go to him for staying with it, but I think he will tell you, as I will, that it's an American phenomenon because chili is a creative food, and everyone thinks they can make it better than the next guy. The organization makes chili cookoffs a fund-raiser; the dish itself, fun and creative. Most of all, the thousands of chiliheads who have volunteered, starting with the first cookoff, have contributed to the growth. Another reason cookoffs have gotten so big is they are fun! Some of the early cookoffs were wilder—I was a little younger back then—but I still have as much fun as I did at the first one."

The pots of chili have gotten smaller and the prizes bigger at the celebrity-infested World's Championship, now held in the Biggest Little City in the World—Reno, Nevada—the first weekend in October. The haphazard concoctions that were so predominant at the first cookoffs (see Ormly Gumfudgin's recipe, page 162) have been replaced by chilis that are so fine-tuned in the quest for the perfect bowl of red, it is difficult to imagine further evolution.

Making

Great Chili

∾

Contrary to what a competition chili cook may have told you, making great chili is not akin to brain surgery. Before embarking on any one of these recipes, remember the following formula sent to us by Pulitzer Prize–winning author Dave Barry. Dave warned us that it might be beyond the reach of those without a deep culinary background but urged us to try it anyway, claiming it was worth the effort:

1. *Get some chili.*
2. *Get some beer.*
3. *Eat the chili and drink the beer.*

First and foremost, chili-making should be enjoyable. If you don't have a good time making chili, you take away the key ingredient—

fun. Even at the World's Championships, where cooking chili borders on a scientific procedure, the cooks don't spend all of their time huddled over their portable stoves, dropping in Tabasco with eyedroppers and timing the addition of spices to the nanosecond. They all enjoy themselves, which is what you should be doing when you make chili at home, not worrying about whether you used too much chili powder (nearly impossible) or whether you cubed your beef perfectly (who cares?).

Armed with a basic recipe—and all the recent championship chilis are pretty basic—you can hardly mess up. For example, in 1992, Ed Pierczynski got confused, put his spices in all wrong, spent the next three hours trying to correct his mistakes and still wound up with the winning bowl of red (page 78).

That doesn't mean chili should be thrown together carelessly. Top-quality ingredients and care in preparation make all the difference in the world between a ho-hum chili and chili that will put a sparkle in your eyes, a glow on your cheeks, and a few beads of sweat on your brow.

Which brings us to another key point—great chili doesn't mean incendiary chili. Any chucklehead can make super-hot chili just by throwing in a few habanero peppers or a tin of cayenne, in which case all you get is a nuclear meltdown in your mouth instead of the exquisite treat for your taste buds you were looking for in the first place. There should be some spiciness and heat. How much? It's up to you, but in the words of 1993 World's Champion Cathy Wilkey, a perfect bowl of red should leave you with a nice, smooth wave of warmth from the front of your mouth to the back of your throat.

Chiliheads may not agree on a lot of things, but they do agree that top-quality chili calls for top-quality ingredients. Strong, harsh onions, tinny-tasting "bargain-brand" tomato sauce, oversalted canned broth or fatty meat can all ruin an otherwise well-thought-out pot of chili. And not even a world-class chili cook can make a palatable bowl of red using chili powder that's been moldering away in the back of the pantry since the Ford administration. Likewise, adding stale cumin or musty oregano can produce a distinctly "off" flavor to chili.

Although we confess to once having used seven-year-old chervil in a nonrelated recipe, we generally throw out spices that have been hanging around for six months or so. They are easily (and economically) replaced with new ones from one of the excellent mail-order sources listed at the back of this book.

Many of the sources also offer a dazzling variety of pure chile powders that you can experiment with to make your own custom blend, which is a very heady experience. However, try to avoid becoming a chili snob and prattling on at cookoffs about back heat and front bite and late salt and killer cumin, because nobody will want to listen. They're all too busy having fun.

MEAT

The ICS defines true chili as any kind of meat cooked with spices and chile peppers, but the No. 1 choice is beef. Most championship cooks these days go for a cut of meat known on the West Coast as "tri-tip" and on the East Coast as "huh?" The full name is "triangle tip" and it is a wedge-shaped hunk of beef at the end of the bottom sirloin, which your butcher can cut for you if he is cooperative. If he is feeling cranky, get another butcher or substitute sirloin tip, although the expense can be prohibitive, particularly if you're just cooking for friends and not finicky judges.

In any case, well-trimmed chuck (arm, shoulder, or blade) also makes a delicious chili, as do shank crosscuts.

If you're aiming for a true Texas chili, the meat should be hand-diced into 3/8-inch cubes—which is easily accomplished by having that same cooperative butcher slice the meat into 3/8-inch-thick slabs, freezing the meat, and then dicing it while it is still partially frozen.

If all that sounds too daunting, go for coarsely ground meat, not twice-ground meat, which will turn into mush. In the Southwest butchers routinely package "chili-grind" meat, which makes wonderful chili without all the bother of hand-dicing. You can also use your food processor to grind the meat, throwing in a few 2-inch chunks at a time and using the "pulse" switch.

Turkey, chicken, venison, pork, antelope, and even rattlesnake (it tastes like chicken, if you were wondering) are all used successfully in chili, and there has been a renewed interest in using buffalo meat to prepare what is a truly authentic American dish. (See Chef John Bennett's recipe, page 267, and George Faison's recipe, page 100.)

SPICES AND OTHER STUFF

In 1968 Woody DeSilva used woodruff, the first spice mentioned in the Bible, when he cooked against Wick Fowler in Terlingua, and three years later Ormly Gumfudgin threw in a little too. No one's used it since, which is not surprising because it belongs in May wine, not chili. Moreover, great chili doesn't require an extensive array of spices, and most championship cooks will tell you their chili improved the more they took out of, not put into, the original recipe. The following are the most commonly used spices and other ingredients for cooking chili (for chiles, see page 10):

Bay leaf: Bay leaves are sometimes added to chili as a bouquet garni, and basil, which goes so well with tomatoes, is not uncommon.

Beans: Some people like them. Some people don't. Classic ICS competition chili forbids the use of beans because to judges, chili cooked with beans tastes like beans. The solution is simple: serve beans (pinto, kidney, etc.) on the side and let people add them if they want. But if a recipe doesn't call for beans and you like them, put them in. If the recipe calls for beans and you don't like them, leave them out. Overall, soaked and cooked dried beans are better than canned beans, and plain canned beans are better than already-spiced canned chili beans, which tend to be overprocessed and generally icky.

Cayenne: This is the dried, powdered form of the cayenne pepper, which is the most widely grown chile pepper in the world and which is used primarily as a heat source. Árbol and guajillo chiles are types of cayenne peppers.

Cilantro: Some cooks add fresh cilantro, an herb also known as Chinese parsley or fresh coriander, which is a key ingredient in most salsas and, along with cumin, makes Tex-Mex food taste like Tex-Mex food. Cilantro is not the hardiest of plants and is usually sold with the roots attached. You can grow it in little pots at home too. If you are addicted to its pungent flavor, as we are, try it sprinkled on top of chili, not cooked in it.

Cumin: Without cumin, there would be no such thing as chili. This musky spice is available in powdered and seed form. Many cooks like to toast the seeds in a skillet over low heat until they start to brown (about 5 minutes) and then grind them up in a spice mill.

Fat: In this day and age, many people eschew the use of saturated fats in sautéing chili meat and vegetables, preferring to use vegetable oil in place of the traditional suet, lard, or bacon grease. The sad fact is, chili is infinitely tastier when animal fats are used in cooking the beef and vegetables. If you really want to throw caution to the wind, get hold of some goose fat. It brings out the flavor of the meat to a degree you just can't get with vegetable oil. If you're concerned about your cholesterol, you might try using vegetable oil with a very little bacon grease for flavoring.

Garlic: We are of the opinion that no chili is worth eating unless it contains huge amounts of garlic. (We start with ten cloves. Big ones.) Elephant garlic is sweeter and easier to peel than regular garlic. (For a definite taste treat, use a whole head of roasted garlic and squeeze it into your chili.) Championship cooks sometimes substitute granulated or powdered garlic in their cookoff chili because judges deduct points for "visible vegetables," and unlike onions, garlic does not disappear. This can be avoided by using whole, slightly smashed cloves and then removing them before turning in one's chili for judging.

Lime juice, red wine vinegar: A dash or two in the last half hour of cooking will cut right through the greasiness and bring out the flavor of the spices.

Liquids: Chicken broth is often used instead of beef broth because its lighter flavor doesn't cover up the spices. Beer adds a nice, rich taste (the alcohol burns off, sadly), and red wine lends a wonderful flavor, although its presence darkens the chili considerably. (Serve by candlelight and no one will know.)

Masa harina: *Masa* means "dough" in Spanish and masa harina is a ground flour from dried corn that has been soaked overnight in a lime solution. It is used to thicken chili.

Onion: Onions are an integral part of chili-making. The bigger and sweeter onions—Vidalia or Walla Walla, for instance— seem to work best, especially when they are very finely diced and can disappear into the chili. If you're cooking chili at home, you can experiment using several different kinds of onions, including red onions, leeks, and scallions. Just don't let anyone see you.

Oregano: Chili cooks usually use the type of oregano known as "Mexican" oregano, which is part of the verbena family. It is used in such small amounts that we really can't detect in the finished product whether European oregano, Mexican oregano, or even marjoram, a relative of both, has been used. For that matter, we usually can't tell when it's been left out.

𝒫 a p r i k a :   Used in chili primarily for its lovely, bright red color. Hungarian paprika is spicier than paprika from Spain or Mexico.

𝒮 a l t :   Use kosher salt or sea salt.

𝒮 w e e t e n e r s :   Most championship chili cooks add some type of sweetening agent to their chili in the last hour or so of cooking in order to smooth out the rough, harsh taste of the chili powders. Brown sugar, white sugar, and honey are commonly used; Dutch cocoa, unsweetened chocolate, cinnamon, and even coffee granules have the same effect without the added sweetness.

𝒯 o m a t o e s :   Texans would have you believe that true chili contains not a single tomato. But the addition of a small (8-ounce) can of tomato sauce is almost uniform these days among championship chili cooks, who use it not only for the color but for the body it gives to chili. Home recipes often use canned tomatoes with great success, and canned diced tomatoes with chiles are a common ingredient as well—just don't let the tomatoes overwhelm the whole dish or you'll find yourself serving a batch of spaghetti sauce flavored with chili powder.

CHILI OR CHILE POWDER

Don't confuse the chili powder you see sitting in between the chervil and cinnamon on your grocer's spice display with the pure, unseasoned chile powder called for in many of this book's recipes.

To get things straight, chili refers to the dish itself; chili powder refers to a premixed blend of ingredients including cumin and garlic used to make chili; chile powder is the ground form of one or more specific types of dried chiles (such as ancho or Anaheim); chile and/or chile pepper refers to the fruit of the domesticated *Capsicum*, the genus to which all chiles belong; and chiles simply means more than one pepper as in "Give me a bunch of them little red chiles."

Commercial chili powder contains ground dried chiles but it also can contain a lot of salt, some garlic, cumin, oregano, and the ubiquitous "other spices." Of the commercial brands, Gebhardt's makes the best-quality chili powder, and of the custom blends available by mail order, Reno Red is touted by many championship cooks. The International Chili Society is also marketing its own World's Championship Chili Powder, which is a blend derived from twenty-eight years of championship recipes.

Without getting too technical, you can substitute any one of those blends for the pure powders, cumin, oregano, and so on, called for in some recipes by using it in equal measure to the total called for in the recipe. For example, if a recipe calls for 4 tablespoons California chile powder, 3 tablespoons ground cumin, 1 tablespoon paprika, 1 teaspoon garlic powder, 1 teaspoon dried oregano, and 1 teaspoon salt, substitute 9 tablespoons of the blend and adjust the seasonings to your taste (for example, add more cumin).

Most championship chili cooks customize their chili by using different amounts of pure New Mexico, California, ancho, and pasilla powders, which are available by mail order (see Mail

Order Sources, page 376) or, if one is fortunate enough to be living in the Southwest or California, in one's supermarket. The chiles are available in powdered form or in whole pods, which many cooks prefer because they grind the chiles themselves and then sieve them for a very fine, grit-free powder.

Each chile has a different flavor (Mark Miller of the Coyote Cafe has more than forty adjectives he uses to describe chiles in *The Great Chile Book*) and a different heat level. The ultimate goal is to get a perfect blend that Miller likens to a musical chord — a high, citrusy note, a deep, rich, basso profundo, and a predominant middle note. Translated into chile-ese, that could mean a tiny amount of habanero, chile pequín, or serrano for the citrus note (and the heat), some ancho or pasilla for the depth, and a lot of New Mexico or California chiles for the middle range of flavors.

Like people and snowflakes, no two chiles are alike. Even chiles harvested at exactly the same time from different parts of the same field may vary wildly in terms of heat and flavor, which is what makes cooking chili such an adventure.

To give chili a richer taste, some cooks, in addition to or in place of chile powders, use a chile paste made from the pulp of dried chiles. The whole dried pods are stemmed and seeded, then covered with boiling water and soaked for 45 minutes to 1 hour. The pulp is scraped off the skin with a knife and mashed into a paste. Alternatively, the rehydrated chiles are put into a blender with a little of the soaking water, then pureed and sieved. Several companies make commercial chile paste (see Mail-Order Sources, page 376).

The most commonly used chiles, powdered or in pod form, are California/New Mexico. A bewildering number of chiles are called

New Mexico chiles, including NuMex, Big Jim, Hatch, Anaheim, NuMex No. 9, and so on. They are red to reddish-brown, about 6 inches long, and up to 2 inches wide, with a thin skin and a pungent, earthy taste with varying amounts of heat. The milder versions are usually billed as California; the hotter are marketed as New Mexico.

Ancho and/or mulato: These have a very wrinkled, almost heart-shaped pod that is dark red, about 4 inches long, and 3 inches wide. They are the dried version of the poblano and the sweetest of all the dried chiles. They are used interchangeably, but the mulato has a chocolate taste.

Pasilla: Technically, this is the dried form of the chilaca chile, but on the West Coast the ancho chile is referred to as a pasilla. It is medium-hot, about 6 inches long and 1 inch wide, and very dark brown.

Chipotle: This is a dried, smoked jalapeño, very hot and with a lingering, smoky aftertaste. It is also available canned with a tomato-vinegar sauce and marketed as *chipotles en adobo.*

FRESH CHILES

Some cooks like the snap and lively, green taste that fresh chiles lend to a batch of chili. Sautéed along with onions and garlic, diced bell peppers are commonly found in home-style chili, while jalapeño, serrano, and the ultra-hot habanero peppers are sometimes floated in the chili to give it that late, back-of-the-throat heat.

The fresh green New Mexico, California, and poblano chiles are roasted and peeled before use. To do this, place the chiles under a flame broiler (or over a gas burner), turning frequently until they are blistered all over. Wrap in paper towels, let cool, and rub off the skins. Dry and stem before using. *Note:* As with all chiles, use caution when handling and never rub your eyes. These babies can be HOT! If you have some of those latex disposable gloves, by all means use them. If not, wash your hands thoroughly after working with chiles and, if necessary, dip them in a light chlorine solution to remove the capsaicin, which will burn the hell out of you if you're not careful.

Frozen chiles are available throughout the Southwest. Elsewhere, canned chiles are an acceptable substitute in cooking chili, as long as they are thoroughly rinsed.

✶ The Chili Pot ✶

At the end of his piece "Nobody Knows More About Chili Than I Do," H. Allen Smith gives his recipe for chili, which begins, "Get three pounds of chuck, coarse ground. Brown it in an iron kettle. If you do not have an iron kettle you are not civilized. Go out and get one."

More chili has been ruined by using the wrong pot than anything else. A flimsy stockpot with a thin base—the kind you use for boiling spaghetti—is not a proper chili pot. If you use something like that, your chili will scorch and stick to the hot spots on the bottom and you'll wind up with a batch of chili that tastes like burnt hoss flesh.

A 6½- to 8-quart pot is the size most chili cooks use for competition, whether it's an enamel-coated cast-iron French oven, an anodized aluminum saucepot, a professional-quality stainless steel pot, or even, as Smith suggested, a good old-fashioned iron kettle.

OK. Now you're ready to cook some chili!

ICS World's Championship Chili

The secret of making superior chili lies first in the
ingredients and second in the genius of the cook.
—H. Allen Smith

★ A Bowl of Red ★

Tom Russell

You don't put beans in chili
You never water good whiskey down
And never play poker with a man named Doc
On the Spanish side of town
And if you want to go peekin' at the Doctor's daughter
You better pay the old man his bread
Then it's a short ride from hell to Heaven ridin' on a bowl of red
I'm talkin' about Sweet Lorene, the chili queen
Down at number nine Pecos Street
She's got bull meat hangin' above her head
And chili peppers down at her feet
She's got an iron pot smokin' on a woodsmoke stove
Near an antique feather bed
Where it's a short short ride from hell to Heaven
Ridin' on a bowl of red
Here's the recipe:

Bull meat, crab meat, pig's feet, chicken feet
I've even seen her use a rabbit's head
Comino, oregano, cilantro, let it go . . .
Then sop it up with sour dough bread

Let it boil all day —you'll be rollin'
In the hay

Lorene keeps a man well fed
Just walk on down to number nine
Say give me a little bowl of red
Peter Piper picked a bunch of chili peppers
Tell me how many pecks did Peter Piper pick?
Then he took 'em on down to Sweet Lorene
Said I need a bowl of red real quick
She put Peter Piper's peppers in a pot on the stove
She put Peter Piper in her feather bed
And now Peter Piper's pickin' peppers all day
Just to get his daily bowl of red

After years of cooking untold gallons of chili for adoring friends at various functions, including, but not limited to, Super Bowls, Christmas caroling parties, the return of the swallows to Capistrano, and the linear conjugation of the planets, we decided to enter our first chili cookoff in 1986.

Serene in the knowledge that Jenny's chili was, indeed, the finest in the known universe, we toddled up to Fort Lauderdale with our newly purchased Coleman stove, enough canned Italian tomatoes to choke a yak, a jar of four-year-old cumin seeds, and five packages of freshly purchased hamburger meat. Loud Hawaiian shirts, a couple of bottles of tequila, a boom box with every Rolling Stones tape ever recorded, and a hand-lettered sign bearing the legend "Big J's Rock 'n' Roll Chili" were the finishing touches to what our entourage thought was a thoroughly hip entry.

The first tipoff that we had entered a strange new universe came when we found ourselves next to a chili team that had built a ten-foot-tall papier-mâché volcano belching actual smoke. They spent most of the day playing "Let's Find a Virgin to Throw in the Lava." Directly across from us was a team from a frozen dessert company that gave out "Icy Hot" chili samples from an igloo made of 2,700 white balloons. Yet another team had turned their cooking area into a military bunker adorned with a well-endowed woman clad in bits and pieces (mostly bits) of camouflage. "Rambo Chili," the sign said. "It Will Blow You Away!"

Undaunted, at the cry "Chili cooks, light your fires!" we tossed down a couple of shots, proceeded to chop up our onions and garlic, and had a great time making what we thought was a perfectly divine vat of chili.

Somehow, we made the finals table. (The judges must have been drunker than we were.) But after we stumbled into the judges' tent and checked it out, we found the chili that had kept so many friends happy for so long bore about as much resemblance to the championship chili as Rich's high school hot rod did to one of Carroll Shelby's Cobras. Our chili was thick, rich, and mild, with chunks of tomato and onion floating about; the winning chili was smooth and hot, with an overlay of freshly toasted cumin that put it light years beyond our home concoction.

Discouraged? No way. We had such a good time we couldn't wait to do it again. And again. And again. Along the chili trail we picked up pointers on how to improve our chili, indulged in a few showmanship contests (Rich demonstrated how to shoot a beer), laughed at the outrageous themes people came up with to decorate their booths, and most of all, met a whole bunch of great people.

Somewhere, way down at the end of the trail, is the World's Championship. For chili cooks, it's the Super Bowl, the Final Four, and the World Series all packed into one dizzying day. Serious business? With a grand prize of $25,000, yes. Sort of. But the pursuit of the perfect bowl of red goes beyond the addition of just the right amount of cumin and the timing of that final squeeze of lime juice. The World's Championship Chili Cookoff was conceived in glee, to guarantee all chiliheads certain inalienable rights, among them fun, frolicking, and the pursuit of that bowl of blessedness.

1st Annual World's Championship

1967, Terlingua, Texas
H. Allen Smith, Mount Kisco, New York, and Wick Fowler,
Austin, Texas (tie)

This is where it all began, a few short months after H. Allen Smith's "Nobody Knows More About Chili Than I Do" article appeared in *Holiday* magazine. Those few hundred souls attending were only allowed to bring a sleeping bag, a toothbrush, and their own liquor. Not surprisingly, nobody remembers too much about that cookoff (not even Gary Cartwright, who covered it for *Sports Illustrated*), but records reveal it was declared a tie between Smith and Fowler, who was truly one of the finest chili cooks in the known universe and no doubt suffered a serious injustice. Still, if someone had been declared a winner, it probably would have ended right there, and what would we all do on weekends? Anyway, Allen's recipe appears here, with Fowler's appearing as the winner of the 4th Annual World's Championship.

Chili H. Allen Smith

〰️

4 pounds coarsely ground
sirloin

olive oil or butter

2 cans (6 ounces each) tomato
paste, thinned with water

3 to 4 medium onions, chopped
(about 3 cups)

1 green bell pepper, chopped
(about 3/4 cup)

2 to 10 cloves garlic, minced
(to taste)

3 tablespoons commercial chili
powder (or more to taste)

1 tablespoon ground cumin

1 tablespoon dried oregano

1/2 teaspoon dried basil

1. In a 4-quart pot, cook meat in a little olive oil or butter (or a blend of the two) until no longer pink. Drain excess fat.

2. Add remaining ingredients and simmer 2 to 3 hours with the lid on.

🍴 MAKES 6 TO 8 SERVINGS

2nd Annual World's Championship

☙❦

1968, Terlingua, Texas
Woodruff DeSilva, Ontario, California, and Wick Fowler,
Austin, Texas (tie)

Once again, two competed and tied. This time Fowler's opponent was Woodruff DeSilva, the former manager of Los Angeles International Airport, who had wiped out the California competition at Tommy Friedkin's house and replaced the ill Allen (some said he got sick on his own chili). For two hours DeSilva and Wick Fowler went at it chili pot to chili pot (actually, DeSilva used a wok), and the competition got so fierce they actually crossed cooking spoons on several occasions. At one point, DeSilva, who drank copious amounts of champagne, set his gas line on fire but managed to persevere, thanks to Ormly Gumfudgin's inventive method of dousing the fire. (He also drank a lot of champagne.) After the ballots were cast, however, a masked gunman leapt up on the porch, grabbed the ballot box from chief judge Scott Carpenter, and flung it into an outhouse located over a mine shaft. DeSilva's recipe appears here, with Fowler's appearing as the winner of the 4th World's Championship.

Chili Woodruff DeSilva

5 medium onions, chopped (about 4 cups)

cooking oil

salt and black pepper to taste

4 pounds beef chuck, cut in thumbnail-sized pieces

5 cloves garlic, minced

4 tablespoons dried oregano

8 tablespoons commercial chili powder

2 tablespoons paprika

2 teaspoons dried woodruff

1 teaspoon cayenne

1 teaspoon crushed chiles pequín or dried red pepper flakes

4 dashes of Tabasco sauce

3 cans (8 ounces each) tomato sauce

1 can (6 ounces) tomato paste

water

$1/4$ cup masa harina

1. In a skillet, brown onions in a little oil, seasoning with salt and pepper. Place in a chili pot.

2. In the same skillet, cook meat until no longer pink, adding oil if necessary. Stir in garlic and 1 tablespoon oregano, then add meat mixture to chili pot.

3. In a paper bag (you can use a bowl with a tight-fitting lid, but it's not as authentic), shake together remaining oregano, chili powder, paprika, woodruff, cayenne, and crushed chiles. Add blended spices to the chili pot and cook briefly.

continued

4. Add Tabasco, tomato sauce, tomato paste, and enough water to cover. Bring to a boil, lower heat, and simmer 2 hours.

5. Cool the chili and refrigerate overnight. Reheat and stir in a paste of masa harina and a little water to thicken.

🍴 MAKES 8 SERVINGS

3rd and 5th Annual World's Championships

⟡

1969 and 1971, Terlingua, Texas
C. V. Wood, Jr., Beverly Hills, California

Woody, as he was known, loved chili cookoffs with a passion unmatched by anyone, past or present. After he retired as the undenia-BULL, undeFEETed World's Champion, Woody attended the World's Championships clad in monarchical robes with a crown of chile peppers. Surveying the goings-on from the stage at a cookoff in the mid-70s, he flung his arms wide as if to embrace the crowd and announced to ICS executive director Jim West and Sy Brockway, then with Pepsico, "By God, they're cooking for America." Chairman of the Board of McCulloch Oil, Woody never did things in a small way, and once he even tried to attend a cookoff in his own hot-air balloon (it collapsed). He could also make a mean bowl of red. When asked to rate chilies, Carroll Shelby says to this day, "Woody could stir a pot with the best of them." Here is his recipe.

Chili à la Woody

8 ounces suet, cut into cubes, or ½ cup cooking oil

5 pounds center-cut pork chops, thinly sliced

6 long green chiles, roasted and peeled

5 tablespoons commercial chili powder

4 teaspoons salt

1 tablespoon dried oregano

1 tablespoon ground cumin

1 tablespoon black pepper

2 teaspoons sugar

1 teaspoon chopped fresh cilantro

1 teaspoon dried thyme

½ teaspoon monosodium glutamate

1 cup beer

5 cups homemade or canned chicken broth

4 cans (15 ounces each) tomato sauce

1 small stalk celery, finely chopped (about ¼ cup)

2 cloves garlic, minced

4 pounds flank steak, cut in ³/₈-inch dice

3 medium onions, cut in ½-inch dice (about 2¼ cups)

2 green bell peppers, cut in ³/₈-inch dice (about 1½ cups)

1 pound Monterey Jack cheese, grated (about 4 cups)

juice of 1 lime

1. Render suet to make 6 to 8 tablespoons oil and set aside (or use cooking oil).

2. Trim fat and bones from pork chops and cut into ¼-inch dice. Set aside.

3. In a small saucepan, boil chiles 15 minutes, or until tender. Let cool, then seed and cut into $\frac{1}{4}$-inch dice.

4. In a small bowl, mix chili powder, salt, oregano, cumin, black pepper, sugar, cilantro, thyme, and MSG with the beer and stir until all lumps are gone.

5. Place chicken broth in a chili pot and add tomato sauce, celery, reserved chiles, beer mixture, and garlic.

6. In a large skillet, warm 2 tablespoons suet or oil and brown $\frac{1}{2}$ of the pork. Add to chili pot, then do the same with remaining pork.

7. In oil remaining in the skillet, brown beef, $\frac{1}{3}$ at a time, and add to chili pot. Bring to a boil, then lower heat and simmer 1 hour.

8. Add onions and peppers and simmer an additional 2 to 3 hours, or until meat is tender, stirring every 15 to 20 minutes with a wooden spoon. Remove from heat, let cool an hour, and then refrigerate 24 hours.

9. Reheat chili and stir in cheese about 5 minutes before serving. Just before serving, add lime juice and stir well.

 MAKES 12 SERVINGS

4th Annual World's Championship

ᏀᏀ

1970, Terlingua, Texas
Wick Fowler, Austin, Texas

By this time a lot of folks had gotten into the act, including Fulton Battise, a Native American; Jose Sierra, a Tigua Indian from El Paso; Joe DeFrates, the Illinois chili king; Chalio Salis, the Mexican champion; and Dick Wilcox from Fort Smith, Arkansas, as well as several women who weren't officially invited but who stood around making chili anyway. One of them was Janice Constantine of Midland, Texas, who set up her cooking area with a silver service and candelabra and cooked while accompanied by a violinist. Despite all the distractions, Fowler composed what Frank Tolbert called "a poem" of chili and won hands down.

Wick Fowler's 2-Alarm Chili

2 pounds diced beef

2 teaspoons vegetable oil

1 can (8 ounces) tomato sauce

2 cups water

1 package Wick Fowler's 2-Alarm Chili seasoning*

1. In a chili pot, cook beef in oil until no longer pink. Drain off fat. Add tomato sauce, water, and chili seasonings, then cover and simmer 1 hour 15 minutes.

2. Skim off excess fat and stir in a paste made with masa harina and a little water. Simmer an additional 15 to 20 minutes to thicken and enhance flavor.

MAKES 4 SERVINGS

* If unavailable, substitute 3 tablespoons pure New Mexico chile powder, 1 tablespoon paprika, 1 teaspoon dried oregano, 1 teaspoon ground cumin, 1 teaspoon dehydrated garlic, 1 teaspoon salt, and 1 teaspoon cayenne, plus 1 tablespoon masa harina to thicken in final 15 minutes of cooking.

6th Annual World's Championship

1972, Terlingua, Texas
Howard Windsor, Colorado Springs, Colorado

The 1972 championship, which was now a tradition, was dedicated to the memory of Fowler, who had died the previous year. Although C. V. Wood, Jr., did not compete, he made sure there was plenty of showmanship surrounding the event by bringing in mentalist Uri Geller, who went around bending watches, pens, and chili spoons. (He wasn't invited back.)

Howard Windsor's Chili

&&

1	medium onion	5 to 6	jalapeño peppers
5 to 6	large cloves garlic	1	can (35 ounces) whole tomatoes
½	cup water		
2	pounds lean beef, cut in ¼-inch dice	¼	cup commercial chili powder
1	pound pork, cut in ¼-inch dice	4	bay leaves
		1	tablespoon dried oregano
1	can (7 ounces) green chiles, Ortega brand preferred, liquid included	1	tablespoon salt
		1	teaspoon ground cumin

1. Using a blender or food processor, chop onion and garlic in water. Place in a small saucepan and cook over medium heat until softened. Place in a chili pot and add beef and pork, cooking until meat loses its red color.

2. Put canned chiles and jalapeños in the blender and puree. Add the pulp to the chili pot along with tomatoes; bring to a boil, then lower heat and simmer 20 minutes. Add chili powder, bay leaves, oregano, salt, and cumin; cover and simmer 1½ hours.

3. Remove bay leaves and simmer another 1 hour 15 minutes, adding water if necessary. Serve with or over hot pinto beans.

MAKES 6 SERVINGS

7th and 9th Annual World's Championships

1973, Terlingua, Texas
1975, Rosamond, California
Joe DeFrates, Springfield, Illinois

The genial DeFrates, whose father, Walt, had opened up a chili parlor in Springfield called the Heidelberg in the 1920s and went on to the commercial chili business, was a popular representative of the state of Illinois, which, like Texas, has chilli (note spelling) as its official state dish. DeFrates sometimes wore a stovepipe hat à la Abraham Lincoln as part of his motif. In his classic book *A Bowl of Red,* Frank Tolbert tells of the time DeFrates left the hat on the airplane after disembarking in Dallas. An hour later he bumped into a man wearing a stovepipe hat and only after a few moments did he realize it was his hat. The man gave it back. Two years later DeFrates became the first champion at the new site for the World's Championship—Tropico Gold Mine.

Chilli Man Chilli

~~

1 pound ground beef

1 package (1¼ ounces) Chilli Man Chilli Mix*

1 can (8 ounces) tomato sauce

water

dash of Tabasco sauce

1. In a heavy skillet, cook meat until no longer pink. Stir in seasoning mix and tomato sauce, bring to a boil, then lower heat and simmer 1 hour, adding water if needed.

2. Just before serving, add a dash of Tabasco.

MAKES 2 TO 3 SERVINGS

* If unavailable, substitute 1 tablespoon pure California chile powder, ½ tablespoon sugar, ½ teaspoon arrowroot, ½ teaspoon ground oregano, ½ teaspoon ground cumin, ½ teaspoon paprika, ½ teaspoon salt, ¼ teaspoon garlic granules, and ¼ teaspoon onion flakes.

8th Annual World's Championship

૭૭

1974, Terlingua, Texas
Jani Schofield-McCullough, Midland, Texas

In the spring of 1974, the mysterious hooded monk known as Father Duffy (who in actuality was a pleasant, if hard-drinking, young man by the name of Grant McNiff) approached Jim West of the Balboa Bay Club and asked if the club would be interested in holding the first cookoff ever in California. On the Thursday before Memorial Day weekend (scheduled so as not to conflict with the Indy 500), Al Dunlap won the first California State Championship and had the good luck to be included in the group of BBC chili pioneers that flew to Marfa on Carroll Shelby's plane and from there, by bus, went on to Terlingua.

Having completely demolished the liquor supply on the plane, the passengers made the bus pull over repeatedly until the annoyed driver announced he was making no more stops. Undeterred, Father Duffy made his way to the rear exit door and, with various passengers holding his rope belt to keep him from falling out into the dust, opened the door and found a lone motorcyclist following in the bus's wake. Duffy, who had been an altar boy and knew all the appropriate gestures, first blessed the motorcyclist, who flashed him the peace sign. Duffy then raised his robes and began relieving himself, whereupon the astonished motorcyclist hit the brakes and made an abrupt left turn into the sagebrush. He was never seen again. The next day, with her legendary "Hot Pants Chili," Allegani Jani became the first woman to win a World's Championship.

Allegani Jani's Hot Pants Chili

@@

2	tablespoons cooking oil	1	teaspoon sugar
4	pounds beef stew meat, ground once	1/2	can (6 ounces) beer
		1/2	cup commercial chili powder
3	onions, chopped (about 3 cups)	1	tablespoon mole paste
		1	teaspoon Tabasco sauce
salt and black pepper to taste		1	teaspoon salt
2	heaping teaspoons cuminseeds	1	quart water
		4	jalapeño peppers, chopped
6	cloves garlic, crushed	1/4	cup masa harina
1	can (15½ ounces) tomatoes		

1. In a chili pot, heat oil, add meat and onions, and sauté until browned. Drain excess fat. Season to taste with salt and pepper.

continued

2. Using a molcajete (a Mexican grinding tool) or a mortar and pestle or a blender, grind cuminseeds and garlic with a little water and add to meat.

3. In a blender, puree tomatoes, sugar, beer, and chili powder. Add to chili pot along with mole paste, Tabasco, salt, water, and chopped jalapeños. Bring to a boil, then lower heat and simmer 2½ hours.

4. At the end of the cooking time, make a runny paste of masa harina and water. Add to the chili while stirring constantly to prevent lumping. Simmer an additional 30 minutes.

MAKES 8 SERVINGS

10th Annual World's Championship

ഇഇ

1976, Rosamond, California
Rudy Valdez, Palmdale, California

After fifteen thousand people showed up at the first ICS cookoff at Tropico Gold Mine, C. V. Wood and Carroll Shelby decided they had better do something about feeding all the fans. Pancho McNiff, brother of Grant, was nominated to cater the event and duly went about acquiring a dozen brand-new slushy machines to make frozen margaritas. Unfortunately, no one told Pancho he needed to run warm water through the machines for six hours to get rid of the packing grease. As the first batch came out, Shelby happened by and said, "Boy, that looks good." Before anyone could stop him, he had taken a swig of lime-green motor oil. As the others watched in semi-horrified silence, trying not to laugh, Shelby spat the fluid out and stalked off, muttering something about the mix not being good. Nonetheless, the margarita-deprived crowd had a fine time watching Rudy Valdez, a Ute Indian who claimed to use a two-thousand-year-old recipe, win the World's Championship.

Rudy's Ancestral Chili

இ

1   pound pork shoulder, cut in ³/₈-inch dice

1   pound beef flank steak, cut in tiny cubes

1   teaspoon ground cumin

1   ripe tomato, chopped

1   clove garlic, minced

1   medium white onion, chopped (about ³/₄ cup)

6   small stalks celery, chopped (about 1¹/₂ cups)

1   can (8 ounces) green salsa, Ortega brand preferred

1   can (7 ounces) diced green chiles, Ortega brand preferred, undrained

1   teaspoon dried oregano

1   teaspoon Tabasco sauce

1   tablespoon hot pure New Mexico chile powder

1   tablespoon medium-hot pure New Mexico chile powder

1   heaping tablespoon mild pure New Mexico chile powder

salt to taste

1. In separate pans over medium-low heat, cook pork and beef for 20 minutes, seasoning each pan with ¹/₂ teaspoon cumin.

2. Meanwhile, in a 6-quart saucepan, combine tomato, garlic, onion, celery, salsa, chiles, oregano, and Tabasco. In a small bowl, make a paste of the chile powders and a little water and add to the saucepan. Bring to a boil, lower heat, and simmer 20 minutes.

3. Drain cooking liquids from the meat, reserving ¼ cup. Add meat and reserved cooking liquids to the vegetable mixture, bring to a boil, lower heat, and simmer 1½ hours, or until the meat is tender. Just before serving, season with salt.

MAKES 4 TO 6 SERVINGS

11th Annual World's Championship

❦

1977, Rosamond, California
Jay Pennington, Las Vegas, Nevada

By 1977, the World's Championship had become one of the best-attended and hottest outdoor events around. Celebrities from television, sports, and Hollywood mingled with the crowd of twenty thousand, including Peter Marshall, Ernie Borgnine, William Conrad, Joanne Dru, Levar Burton, Bobby Unser, and Tommy Lasorda. Chief scorekeeper was the great baseball umpire Emmett Ashford, who tallied up the votes and declared real-estate man Jay Pennington of Las Vegas winner of the first Nevada State Cookoff, the 1977 World's Champion.

Jay's Chili

∽

1	tablespoon cooking oil	1	can (6 ounces) tomato paste
3	medium onions, finely chopped (about 2¼ cups)	1	can (4 ounces) salsa
2	green bell peppers, finely chopped (about 1½ cups)	1	canned hot green pepper, about 3 inches long, finely chopped
2	stalks celery, finely chopped (about ¾ cup)	2	jars (3 ounces each) commercial chili powder
3	cloves garlic, minced	1	can (4 ounces) diced green chiles
8	pounds round steak, coarsely ground		pinch of dried oregano
5	cups tomato sauce		salt, black pepper, garlic salt to taste
5	cups stewed tomatoes		
5	cups water		

1. In a 10- to 12-quart pot, heat oil and add onions, bell peppers, celery, and garlic. Sauté over medium heat until onions are translucent.

2. Gradually add meat, stirring until redness disappears. Drain excess fat. Add remaining ingredients, one at a time, stirring well after each addition.

3. Bring to a boil, then lower heat and simmer 2½ to 3 hours, stirring frequently to prevent scorching. Adjust seasonings with salt, pepper, and garlic salt to taste.

MAKES 12 TO 16 SERVINGS

12th Annual World's Championship

❧

1978, Rosamond, California
LaVerne Harris, Las Vegas, Nevada

We first met LaVerne at a 1987 cookoff in the pouring rain in Clearwater, Florida, where she was gracious enough to taste our (losing) chili and offer insider's tips (more salt, less heat) and some sound advice we still follow to this day: "Cook it with lots of love," she said.

Nevada Annie's Championship Chili

❧

vegetable oil
3 medium onions, diced (about 2½ cups)

2 medium green bell peppers, diced (about 1¼ cups)
2 large stalks celery, diced (about 1 cup)

2 small cloves garlic, diced

½ small jalapeño pepper, diced (or more to taste)

8 pounds lean chuck, coarsely ground

1 can (7 ounces) diced green chiles

2 cans (14½ ounces each) stewed tomatoes

1 can (15 ounces) tomato sauce

1 can (6 ounces) tomato paste

2 jars (3 ounces each) commercial chili powder

2 tablespoons ground cumin

Tabasco sauce

½ can (6 ounces) beer

1 bottle (12 ounces) mineral water

2 to 3 bay leaves

garlic salt, salt, black pepper to taste

1. In a large pot, heat the oil, add the onions, green peppers, celery, garlic, and jalapeño, and sauté until softened. Add the meat in batches, cooking until it is no longer pink. Drain excess fate.

2. Add remaining ingredients in order up to the mineral water (pausing briefly to drink the other half of the can of beer), then add the water to cover. Add bay leaves, bring to a boil, then lower heat and simmer 3 hours, stirring often. Adjust seasonings with garlic salt, salt, and pepper.

MAKES 12 TO 16 SERVINGS

13th Annual World's Championship

⟲⟳

1979, Rosamond, California
Joe and Shirley Stewart, San Francisco, California

The victory by Joe and Shirley represented the first in a series of quasi-related chili championships, all of which began the year before when Joe and a friend, Dave Johnson, were in Reno on a business trip. Staggering into a casino, they saw a sign for a chili cookoff and thought it would be hilarious to sign up the founder of their company, Zytron Corporation, for the cookoff. It turned out that Truett Airhart was one fine chili cook and won the High Sierra Cookoff. For the World's Championship he designated the Stewarts, the Johnsons, and Carol and Dave Hancock as his helpers. The Stewarts had so much fun they decided to cook on their own with a version of Truett's recipe, and they won the High Sierra, qualifying for the 1979 World's. As they drove up to Tropico, it was raining and the wind was blowing, and they had huge hangovers and were convinced the cookoff was going to be miserable. An hour later the sun came out and they knew it was an omen—six hours later they were the new World's Champions.

Reno Red

~

3   pounds round steak, coarsely ground

3   pounds chuck steak, coarsely ground

1   cup cooking oil, preferably Wesson, or rendered fat from kidney suet

black pepper to taste

3/4   cup mild pure chile powder

6   tablespoons ground cumin

2   tablespoons monosodium glutamate

6   small cloves garlic, minced

2   medium onions, chopped (about 1½ cups)

6   dried New Mexico chile pods, stemmed, seeded, and boiled in water to cover 30 minutes, or 1 jar (3 ounces) hot pure New Mexico chile powder

1   tablespoon dried oregano, brewed like tea in ½ cup beer

2   tablespoons paprika

2   tablespoons cider vinegar

3   cups beef broth

1   can (4 ounces) diced green chiles, Ortega brand preferred

1   cup stewed tomatoes, Hunt's brand preferred

1   teaspoon Tabasco sauce

2   tablespoons masa harina

1. In a large chili pot, cook beef in oil or suet, adding black pepper to taste, until meat is no longer pink. Drain off fat, then add chile powder, cumin, MSG, garlic, and onions. Simmer 30 to 45 minutes, adding as little water as possible and stirring often.

continued

2. Remove skins from boiled chile pods and mash pulp; add to meat mixture (or, if using powder, add that to meat). Strain oregano and beer mixture through a fine sieve and add beer to meat mixture along with paprika, vinegar, 2 cups beef broth, chiles, stewed tomatoes, and Tabasco. Simmer 30 to 45 more minutes, stirring often.

3. Dissolve masa harina in remaining beef broth, add to chili, and simmer 30 more minutes, stirring often.

MAKES 12 SERVINGS

14th Annual World's Championship

1980, Paramount Movie Ranch, California
Bill Pfeiffer, Washington, D.C.

Pfeiffer, a Texan who was working for Zytron in its branch in the nation's capital, became the second person to win a World's Championship using a variation of Truett Airhart's recipe. Peter Marshall and Joe Landis filmed a special on the cookoff, which featured appearances by Robert Mitchum, Rory Calhoun, Tom Poston, Arte Johnson, Slim Pickens, and dozens of other stars. The real star was this chili.

ICS WORLD'S CHAMPIONSHIP CHILI

Capital Punishment Chili

〰️

9	tablespoons mild pure chile powder	2	pounds extra-lean pork, chili grind
1/4	cup ground cumin	1	pound extra-lean chuck, cut in 1/4-inch cubes
1/4	cup instant beef bouillon granules	2	large onions, finely chopped (about 2 cups)
2	tablespoons paprika	10	cloves garlic, minced
2	tablespoons dried oregano	1	tablespoon sugar
1	tablespoon monosodium glutamate	1	teaspoon mole powder
1	tablespoon commercial chili powder	1	teaspoon ground coriander
		1	teaspoon Tabasco sauce
2	cans (12 ounces each) beer	1	can (8 ounces) tomato sauce, Hunt's brand preferred
2	cups water	1	tablespoon masa harina
1/2	cup vegetable oil, Wesson brand preferred, or kidney suet		salt to taste
4	pounds extra-lean chuck, chili grind		

1. In a large pot, combine chile powder, cumin, beef bouillon granules, paprika, oregano, MSG, chili powder, beer, and water. Bring to a boil, reduce heat, and simmer.

continued

2. In a large skillet, heat 1 tablespoon oil or suet, add 1½ pounds of meat, and sauté until meat is lightly browned. Drain and add to the simmering spices; continue until all the meat has been browned and added.

3. Add 1 tablespoon oil to the skillet and sauté onions and garlic until softened. Add to the meat and spices and simmer 2 hours, adding water as necessary.

4. Add sugar, mole, coriander, Tabasco, and tomato sauce and simmer an additional 45 minutes. Dissolve masa harina in a little warm water to make a paste and add to chili. Adjust seasonings with salt and simmer 30 more minutes. For hotter chili, add more Tabasco.

MAKES 12 SERVINGS

15th Annual World's Championship

❧❧

1981, Hollywood Park, California
Fred Drexal, Van Nuys, California

A casual conversation in a beauty salon between Joanne Dru, wife of C. V. Wood, and Marge Everett, owner of Hollywood Park, led to the 1981 World's Championship being held at a racetrack for the first time. Fred Drexel, the California State champion, had handicapped the competition perfectly and won with his special "Butterfield Stageline Chili." On accepting his first prize of $20,000, Drexel stepped up to the mike and thanked his crew, who "chopped and stirred their hearts out." The secret of his team's success, he said, was a simple recipe, care in preparation—and a can of beer and a shot of tequila.

Butterfield Stageline Chili

ⓒⓒ

2 tablespoons vegetable oil, Wesson brand preferred

2½ pounds beef brisket, cut in 1-inch cubes

1 pound lean ground pork

1 onion, finely chopped (about ¾ cup)

salt and black pepper to taste

2 to 3 cloves garlic, minced

2 tablespoons diced green chiles

1 can (8 ounces) tomato sauce, Hunt's brand preferred

1 beef bouillon cube

1 can (12 ounces) beer

1¼ cups water

4 to 6 tablespoons mild pure chile powder

2½ tablespoons ground cumin

⅛ teaspoon dry mustard

⅛ teaspoon brown sugar

pinch of dried oregano

1. Heat oil in a large kettle or Dutch oven. Add beef, pork, and onion and sauté until meat is no longer pink. Add salt and pepper to taste.

2. Add remaining ingredients and stir well. Simmer 3 to 4 hours, stirring occasionally, until meat is tender and chili is thick and bubbly.

MAKES 4 TO 6 SERVINGS

16th Annual World's Championship

෧෨

1982, Universal Studios, Burbank, California
Bill Pfeiffer, Dallas, Texas

Pfeiffer, back in Dallas by this time, joined C. V. Wood and Joe DeFrates as the only two-time World's Champions with this new and improved version of his 1980 recipe (page 51) and raised his winnings at the World's to $40,000. By this time everyone was itching to get back to the rocks and the rattlesnakes, and the next year the championship moved back to Tropico.

La Venganza del Alamo

〜

11 tablespoons commercial chili powder, Gebhardt's brand preferred

1/4 cup ground cumin

1/4 cup instant beef bouillon granules

2 tablespoons paprika

2 tablespoons monosodium glutamate

1 tablespoon dried oregano

3 cans (12 ounces each) beer

2 cups water

1/2 cup vegetable oil, Wesson brand preferred, or rendered kidney suet

2 pounds pork from thick butterfly pork chops, cut in 1/2-inch cubes

2 pounds beef chuck, cut in 1/2-inch cubes

6 pounds beef rump, ground

4 large onions, finely chopped (about 4 cups)

10 cloves garlic, minced

1 tablespoon sugar

2 teaspoons ground coriander

1 teaspoon mole powder

1 teaspoon Tabasco sauce

1 can (8 ounces) tomato sauce, Hunt's brand preferred

1 tablespoon masa harina

salt to taste

1. In a large pot, combine chili powder, cumin, beef bouillon granules, paprika, MSG, oregano, beer, and water. Bring to a boil, lower heat, and let simmer.

2. In a large skillet, heat 1 tablespoon oil or suet, add 1½ pounds of meat, and sauté until browned. Drain off oil, transfer meat to simmering spices, and continue until all the meat has been browned and added.

3. Sauté onions and garlic in 1 tablespoon oil or suet until softened and add to spices and meat mixture. Simmer 2 hours, adding water as needed.

4. Add sugar, coriander, mole, Tabasco, and tomato sauce and simmer an additional 45 minutes.

5. Dissolve masa harina in a little water until it is pasty and add to chili. Season to taste with salt and simmer another 30 minutes. Add Tabasco for hotter chili.

MAKES 16 TO 20 SERVINGS

17th Annual World's Championship

◎◎

1983, Rosamond, California
Harold R. Timber, Taos, New Mexico

What makes this championship chili different and very tasty is the inclusion of ground pork. While diced pork lends a good flavor, it is much lighter in appearance than beef and looks, well, unattractive in a real bowl of red. The ground pork disappears into the sauce and still gives the chili an irresistible sweetness.

Harold's Chili

◎◎

7 tablespoons commercial chili powder, Gebhardt's brand preferred

2 tablespoons paprika

2 tablespoons ground cumin

1 tablespoon sugar

1 tablespoon celery salt

1 tablespoon mole paste

2 teaspoons dried oregano

1 teaspoon cayenne

1 teaspoon garlic powder

1 teaspoon monosodium glutamate

1 cup beef consommé

2 cups warm water

vegetable oil, Wesson brand preferred

2	pounds beef chuck, cut in 3/8-inch cubes	1	cup chopped green chiles
2	pounds top round, coarsely ground	2½	cups tomato sauce, Hunt's brand preferred
2	pounds ground pork butt	1	can (12 ounces) beer
3	large onions, finely diced (about 3 cups)		salt to taste
4	cloves garlic, minced (about 2 tablespoons)	2	tablespoons masa harina

1. In a small bowl, dissolve chili powder, paprika, cumin, sugar, celery salt, mole paste, oregano, cayenne, garlic powder, and MSG in consommé and warm water. Transfer to a 6-quart saucepan, bring to a boil, reduce heat, and simmer.

2. In a large skillet, using a little oil, sauté beef and pork until no longer pink. Transfer to the simmering spices, allowing fat to drain.

3. In the same skillet, again using a little oil, sauté onions and garlic until softened, then add to the saucepan along with chiles and tomato sauce. Bring to a boil, add beer, and simmer, uncovered, for 1½ to 2 hours, stirring occasionally. Turn off heat and let stand for ½ hour, skimming off any excess fat.

4. Correct seasonings with salt and stir in a paste of the masa harina dissolved in water to thicken the chili. Let stand 1 hour before serving.

¶¶ MAKES 12 SERVINGS

ICS WORLD'S CHAMPIONSHIP CHILI

18th Annual World's Championship

☾☽

1984, Rosamond, California
Dusty Hudspeth, Irving, Texas

Dusty's universally appealing chili has its roots in Texas, where her husband was the Head Chile Pepper of a local pod of CASI.

Bottom-of-the-Barrel Gang
Ram-Tough Chili

∾

1	tablespoon cooking oil, Wesson brand preferred	$\frac{1}{4}$	cup commercial chili powder, Gebhardt's brand preferred
2	pounds beef, coarsely ground	2	teaspoons ground cumin
1	can (8 ounces) tomato sauce, Hunt's brand preferred	$1\frac{1}{2}$	teaspoons salt
1	onion, finely chopped (about $\frac{3}{4}$ cup)	1	teaspoon dried oregano
		$\frac{1}{4}$	teaspoon Tabasco sauce
1	teaspoon garlic powder	$\frac{1}{2}$	teaspoon cayenne
		$\frac{1}{2}$	can ($\frac{3}{4}$ cup) beer

1. Heat oil in a small saucepan, add beef, and sauté until it is no longer pink. Drain. Add tomato sauce, onion, and garlic powder, cover, and simmer 30 minutes, stirring occasionally.

2. Add remaining ingredients, stirring well, and simmer 1 hour, adding water if necessary. Adjust seasonings and serve with side dishes of pinto beans, chopped onion, and grated Cheddar cheese. ENJOY!

MAKES 4 TO 6 SERVINGS

19th Annual World's Championship

⊙⊙

1985, Rosamond, California
Carol and Dave Hancock, Los Altos, California

Named for country singer Willie Nelson, Shotgun Willie Chili evolved when the Hancocks were roped into the chili world by (you guessed it) Truett Airhart. Cooking only in the finest resort areas (Mexico, Hawaii, Lake Tahoe), the Hancocks made it to the World's several times, finishing fifth in 1984 and winning in 1985. "All of a sudden we were celebrities," recalls Carol. "We did *Live with Regis and Kathie Lee, AM San Francisco*, the *700 Club*, blah-blah-blah. It was great." Since then Carol has made chili for school carnivals, auctions, private parties, a prospective chili franchise, classroom demonstrations, and even a couple of food producers. Here is their yummy recipe.

Shotgun Willie Chili

⊙⊙

6	dried New Mexico chile peppers		1	can (15 ounces) tomato sauce, Hunt's brand preferred
6	dried pasilla chile peppers		4	cups beef broth
1½	tablespoons dried oregano		2	tablespoons red wine vinegar
1	cup warm water		1	teaspoon Tabasco sauce
2 to 3	tablespoons vegetable oil, Wesson brand preferred		1	cup commercial chili powder, Gebhardt's brand preferred
6	pounds prime beef, cut in ⅜-inch dice or coarsely ground		2	tablespoons ground cumin
			1	tablespoon monosodium glutamate
4	medium onions, finely diced (about 3 cups)		1	teaspoon cayenne
			½	teaspoon sugar
	black pepper to taste		14	cloves garlic, crushed
				salt to taste

1. Seed and stem chile pods and boil in water for 1 hour, until pulp separates from skin. Scrape off pulp, mash into a paste, and set aside.

2. Cover oregano with 1 cup warm water and bring to a boil. Let steep like tea for 5 minutes, then strain and add broth to chile paste.

continued

3. Heat oil in a large skillet and, working in batches, cook meat until no longer pink, transferring it to a chili pot as it browns. Stir in chile-oregano mixture, then add remaining ingredients, stirring well. Bring to a boil, lower heat, cover, and simmer 2 hours, stirring occasionally.

4. Correct seasonings with salt and serve.

†¶ MAKES 12 SERVINGS

20th Annual World's Championship

☯

1986, Rosamond, California
Jim Beaty, Sespe, California

One evening over margaritas at a little Mexican restaurant in Greenwich Village, we asked Travelin' Chilihead Charlie Ward who was the finest chili cook he knew. Without hesitating, he said Jim Beaty. In 1986, Beaty (whose chili we finally had the privilege of tasting at the World's Championship several years later) beat out contestants from around the world, including a champion from the Gulf of Sidra, Lt. Comdr. Sergei Kowalchik, who held a cookoff on board his ship while stationed in the Gulf to keep an eye on Colonel Qaddafi. (Kowalchik, by the way, finished third. And Qaddafi never did get to taste any chili.)

Sespe Creek Chili

꩜

2 tablespoons vegetable oil, Wesson brand preferred

2½ pounds sirloin, cut in ⅜-inch cubes

2 small white onions, chopped

1 small yellow onion, chopped (about ½ cup)

1 can (10½ ounces) beef broth

1 can (10½ ounces) chicken broth

½ cup commercial chili powder, Gebhardt's brand preferred

2 teaspoons ground cumin

1 teaspoon dried oregano

5 cloves garlic, crushed into a paste

1½ teaspoons seasoned salt

½ cup tomato sauce, Hunt's brand preferred

2 teaspoons hot pure New Mexico chile powder (or more to taste)

½ teaspoon mole powder (optional)

1½ teaspoons monosodium glutamate

½ teaspoon ground coriander

1 teaspoon Tabasco sauce

salt to taste

1. In a large skillet, heat 1 tablespoon oil, add ½ of meat, and sauté until no longer pink. Drain off fat and transfer meat to a chili pot. Repeat with remaining oil and meat.

2. Add chopped onions, ½ can of beef broth, 1 can of chicken broth, chili powder, cumin, and oregano to chili pot. Stir well and simmer 2 hours.

continued

3. Stir in garlic, seasoned salt, tomato sauce, New Mexico chile powder, mole powder, MSG, and coriander. Simmer 20 minutes and then add Tabasco. Thin to desired consistency with remaining beef broth and correct seasonings with salt.

MAKES 6 SERVINGS

21st Annual World's Championship

∽

1987, Rosamond, California
Margo Knudson, Loomis, California

Almost as thrilling as Margo's chili in 1987 was the flyover by two F-18s just before noon. At 11:55 A.M., Lt. Comdr. Don Lewis asked the crowd to look skyward as the jets, piloted by Comdr. Rick Fessenden and Lt. Comdr. Rick Moore screamed over the cookoff in close formation. As Jim West recalls, there wasn't a dry eye in the place by the time Sherre Mesker got up and sang "God Bless America" to officially start the cookoff. Even the pilots, listening to the festivities on the ground-to-air radios, shed an emotional tear or two, as they later confessed to Mesker.

Margo's Chili

2 teaspoons rendered kidney suet or vegetable oil, Wesson brand preferred

2 medium onions, finely chopped (about 1 1/2 cups)

5 to 7 cloves garlic, minced

1/4 cup commercial chili powder, Gebhardt's brand preferred

1 tablespoon mild pure chile powder

1/2 teaspoon hot pure New Mexico chile powder

3 pounds tri-tip, cut in 3/8-inch cubes or coarsely ground

white pepper to taste

1 can (10 1/2 ounces) beef broth

3 ounces bulk sausage

1 canned green chile, minced, Ortega brand preferred

1/2 teaspoon ground coriander (optional)

1/4 teaspoon cayenne (or more to taste)

1/2 cup tomato sauce, Hunt's brand preferred

1 tablespoon dried oregano, brewed like tea in 1/2 cup beer and strained

salt to taste

1. In a small skillet, heat suet or oil, add onions and garlic, and sauté for 3 minutes. Stir in commercial chili powder and pure chile powders and mix well. Set aside.

2. In another nonstick skillet, sauté beef 1 pound at a time, adding white pepper to taste. Transfer to a chili pot and, using a little beef broth to prevent sticking, stir in the onion mixture.

continued

3. In the same skillet, sauté sausage and green chile together for 2 minutes over high heat and transfer to chili pot. Simmer meats together for about 15 minutes, stirring frequently. Drain excess fat.

4. Add coriander, cayenne, tomato sauce, and remaining beef broth and stir well. Simmer 30 minutes and add oregano tea. Simmer 2 hours or until meat is tender, stirring occasionally.

5. About 20 minutes before serving, adjust seasonings with salt and more cayenne if desired.

MAKES 6 TO 8 SERVINGS

22nd Annual World's Championship

1988, Rosamond, California
Kenton and Linda Stafford, Fillmore, California

Not only was the 22nd cookoff the closest finish in ICS history; it also featured the world's biggest pot of chili, as sponsor Pepto-Bismol created the "Titanic Bowl of Red" in a one-thousand-gallon pot shipped from Tulsa and sold the chili for charity. Father Duffy, who had taken the pledge by this time, helped officiate at the first-ever wedding held at a cookoff, uniting Hope and Monty Spurgeon in chili matrimony. Their wedding feast was based on Kenton and Linda Stafford's excellent chili.

7/8 Chili

SEASONING MIX #1:

1/2 teaspoon garlic powder

1/4 teaspoon meat tenderizer

1/4 teaspoon garlic salt

1/8 teaspoon seasoned salt

SEASONING MIX #2:

5 tablespoons commercial chili powder, Gebhardt's brand preferred

5 tablespoons pure California chile powder

1 tablespoon New Mexico chile powder

1 tablespoon pasilla chile powder

1 tablespoon ground cumin

1/4 teaspoon salt

1/4 teaspoon ground coriander (optional)

SEASONING MIX #3:

1 tablespoon California chile powder

1 tablespoon ground cumin

1 teaspoon New Mexico chile powder

1/2 teaspoon dried oregano

1/2 teaspoon garlic salt

1/4 teaspoon cayenne

CHILI:

1 teaspoon vegetable oil, Wesson brand preferred

3 pounds top sirloin, cut in 1/4-inch dice

2 cans (13 3/4 ounces each) chicken broth

3/4 cup beef broth

1 can (8 ounces) tomato sauce, Hunt's brand preferred

½ medium yellow onion, chopped (about ⅓ cup)	3 to 5 cloves garlic, minced
½ medium white onion, chopped (about ⅓ cup)	1 teaspoon Tabasco sauce (optional)
	salt to taste

1. Combine spice mixtures in 3 separate containers and set aside.

2. In a skillet, heat oil and cook meat 1 pound at a time, sprinkling each batch with ⅓ of Seasoning Mix #1. As meat loses its pink color, use a slotted spoon (to allow excess fat to drain off) to transfer it to a chili pot.

3. Add 1 can chicken broth, beef broth, tomato sauce, onions, garlic, Tabasco (if desired), and Seasoning Mix #2 to the chili pot. Mix well and simmer 1½ hours, adding remaining can of chicken broth as needed.

4. Stir in Seasoning Mix #3 and simmer an additional 1½ hours, keeping your eye on the pot from time to time. Adjust seasonings with salt if needed, and serve.

MAKES 6 TO 8 SERVINGS

23rd Annual World's Championship

❦

1989, Rosamond, California
Phil Walter, Seattle, Washington

When we first ran across Phil at the New York State Championships back in 1991, we weren't sure what to call this intent, burly, bearded guy who was doing strange things to his garlic. Jack? Mr. Tarantula? Sir? (We stuck with "Sir.") At the 1993 World's, one chemically impaired soul stopped by Phil's booth and spent twenty minutes asking really dumb questions, which Phil fielded with uncharacteristic patience while measuring out his spices. Finally, Phil snapped. "What planet are you from?" he asked the guy, who helpfully replied, "Earth, I think." Asked Phil, "Are there any more like you where you came from?" Phil and his chili are definitely one of a kind.

Tarantula Jack's Thundering Herd Buffalo-Tail Chili

❧

2 teaspoons vegetable oil

3 pounds beef, cut in small cubes

2 medium Walla Walla sweet onions, chopped (about 1¹/₂ cups)

3 large cloves garlic, minced

2 cans (10¹/₂ ounces each) chicken broth

1 can (8 ounces) tomato sauce, Hunt's brand preferred

1 can (15 ounces) tomato sauce, Hunt's brand preferred

7 tablespoons commercial chili powder, Gebhardt's brand preferred

2 tablespoons ground cumin

¹/₄ teaspoon Tabasco sauce

salt to taste

1. In a skillet, heat oil and sauté beef until no longer pink. Drain off fat. Put beef in your favorite chili pot and simmer with onions, garlic, and chicken broth for 1¹/₂ hours. Keep the lid on and your hands off!

2. Add tomato sauce, chili powder, and cumin. Stir, replace the lid, and continue to simmer until meat is tender.

3. About 15 minutes before eating time, take the lid off and enjoy the aroma of the greatest chili ever to slide into a Melmac bowl.

continued

Add the Tabasco, put the lid back on, and simmer for another 15 minutes. Add salt to taste.

4. Now it's ready to serve. Give out Pepto-Bismol samples to all small children and women who wish to eat your chili. Give your empty chili pot to the chili groupies and suggest they use new Dawn detergent to clean it up. (It's the official grease cutter of the International Chili Society.) Comb your hair, straighten your hat, and practice being modest before you receive applause or the championship trophy if your are competing in a sanctioned ICS cookoff. Serve with Pillsbury cornbread twists, cold Pepsi, and Yago Sant'Gria.

MAKES 6 TO 8 SERVINGS

24th Annual World's Championship

൭൦

1990, Rosamond, California
David Valega, Bethany, Oklahoma

In Oklahoma folks call a bowl of red "Sooner Chili," and it is a staple at tailgate parties before University of Oklahoma football games.

Backdoor Chili

$1^1/_2$ teaspoons vegetable oil, Wesson brand preferred

3 pounds beef chuck tender, cut in small cubes

2 cans ($13^3/_4$ ounces each) beef broth

1 can (8 ounces) tomato sauce, Hunt's brand preferred

4 dashes Tabasco sauce

2 teaspoons instant beef bouillon granules

$1^1/_2$ teaspoons onion powder

1 teaspoon instant chicken bouillon granules

$3/_4$ teaspoon cayenne

6 tablespoons commercial chili powder

$1^1/_2$ tablespoons ground cumin

$3/_4$ teaspoon garlic powder

$3/_4$ teaspoon white pepper

1. In a chili pot, heat oil and cook meat until no longer pink. Cover with beef broth and stir in tomato sauce and Tabasco. Add beef bouillon granules, onion powder, chicken bouillon granules, and cayenne, stir well, and bring to a medium boil. Lower heat and let bubble 2 to $2^1/_2$ hours, or until meat is tender, adding water as needed.

2. About 30 minutes before you're going to serve your guests or turn in your bowl for judging, add chili powder, cumin, garlic powder, and white pepper and simmer to achieve World's

continued

Championship Chili. As a precaution, make sure you have plenty of soothing Pepto-Bismol on hand.

3. Grab a couple of chilled bottles of Yago Sant'Gria, pop some Pillsbury cornbread twists in the microwave (they're great for dunking), and get ready to hear the praises. Try to be modest.

🍴 MAKES 6 TO 8 SERVINGS

25th Annual World's Championship

෨෨

1991, Rosamond, California
Randy Robinson, Columbus, Ohio

Randy is one of the few ICS cooks from east of the Mississippi to win a World's Championship, a banner he wears proudly. After taking the title, he wrote a long essay for the ICS newspaper on how to cook winning chili. The ideal, he said, is to cook chili that is perfectly balanced, with no unusual flavors. Other tips for competition chili cooks included setting up one's portable stove in the backyard and whipping up a batch of chili for practice, adhering to a single recipe, and checking out the judges to cook chili to their taste. In other words, what would please Ormly Gumfudgin might overwhelm an Elk. This chili, on the other hand, is an all-around winner.

Road Meat Chili

~~❧~~

SEASONING MIX #1:

3 tablespoons commercial chili powder, Gebhardt's brand preferred

1½ teaspoons garlic powder

1½ teaspoons ground cumin

1 teaspoon black pepper

SEASONING MIX #2:

¼ cup commercial chili powder

2 tablespoons ground cumin

2 tablespoons hot pure New Mexico chile powder

1½ teaspoons brown sugar

1 teaspoon garlic powder

CHILI:

1 tablespoon vegetable oil, Wesson brand preferred

3 pounds beef, cut in small cubes

8 ounces ground pork

1 tablespoon flour

1 very small onion, chopped (about ⅓ cup)

1 can (10½ ounces) beef broth

2 cans (10½ ounces each) chicken broth

1 can (4 ounces) mild green chiles, drained, seeded, and finely chopped

1 jalapeño pepper, minced

1 can (8 ounces) plus ½ can tomato sauce, Hunt's brand preferred

1 teaspoon Tabasco sauce

salt to taste

1. Combine seasoning mixtures in 2 separate containers. Set aside.

continued

2. In a large skillet, heat oil and sauté beef and pork until no longer pink. Drain and transfer to a 4-quart chili pot. Stir in flour, onion, beef broth, chicken broth, chiles, jalapeño, 1 can tomato sauce, and Seasoning Mix #1. Simmer, covered for $1\frac{1}{2}$ hours.

3. Stir in remaining tomato sauce, Tabasco, and Seasoning Mix #2. Simmer, uncovered, 45 minutes. Adjust seasonings with salt if needed.

MAKES 6 TO 8 SERVINGS

26th Annual World's Championship

1992, Scottsdale, Arizona
Dr. Ed Pierczynski, Carson City, Nevada

A family practice physician, Ed took weekends off and cooked chili from Carson City north until he qualified for the World's by winning the Canadian Championship in Vancouver. "This prescription is good for what ails ya!" he says. "It is known to cure lumbago, mange, dry rot, blind staggers, and a bad hangover." Ed loved winning the World's Championship, but as he told us the next year in Reno, it was pure hell going week to week without being able to cook competitively. He didn't repeat as champion, so 1994 found him happily cooking on the chili trail again!

Doc's Secret Remedy

∾

¼ cup vegetable oil, Wesson brand preferred

3 pounds sirloin, London broil, or tri-tip, cubed

6 ounces bulk sausage

7 ounces beef broth

1 can (8 ounces) tomato sauce, Hunt's brand preferred

1 can (6 ounces) Snap-E-Tom or other spicy tomato juice cocktail

6 ounces beer, Budweiser preferred (drink the other 6 ounces)

11 tablespoons commercial chili powder, Gebhardt's brand preferred

1 tablespoon onion powder

1 teaspoon garlic powder

2 teaspoons Tabasco sauce

1 tablespoon ground cumin

salt to taste

1. In a large skillet, heat oil and sauté beef until no longer pink. Drain well and put in your favorite chili pot. Brown sausage until well done, drain, and add to the pot along with beef broth. Bring to a slow simmer and add tomato sauce, Snap-E-Tom, beer, 6 tablespoons chili powder, onion powder, garlic powder, and 1 teaspoon Tabasco. Simmer 1½ hours, or until meat is tender.

2. Add remaining chili powder and Tabasco along with cumin, and simmer an additional 30 minutes. Adjust seasonings with salt.

MAKES 6 TO 8 SERVINGS

27th Annual World's Championship

1993, Reno, Nevada
Cathy Wilkey, Seattle, Washington

Cathy and her husband, Doug, have been on the chili trail for more than a decade—in fact, they even got married at a chili cookoff. Cathy, whose recipe was derived from Doug's Dog Breath Chili, says she has a lot of great stories from her younger days, but now that she's married and a mother, those stories are better forgotten. What she won't forget are those Friday nights before a cookoff when friends and rivals spent endless hours dicing meat in the family's kitchen in Seattle. In Reno, even as the five finalists gathered on the stage, the buzz among the cooks was that Cathy had cooked the best bowl ever. One taste of this and you'll agree.

Puppy's Breath Chili

꩜

2 teaspoons vegetable oil, Wesson brand preferred

3 pounds tri-tip or sirloin tip, cut in small pieces or coarsely ground

1 small yellow onion, finely chopped (about ½ cup)

1 can (13¾ ounces) beef broth

3½ tablespoons ground cumin

½ teaspoon dried oregano

6 cloves garlic, finely chopped, then divided in half

3 tablespoons commercial chili powder, Gebhardt's brand preferred

1 tablespoon mild pure New Mexico chile powder

6 tablespoons mild pure California chile powder

1 can (8 ounces) tomato sauce, Hunt's brand preferred

1 dried New Mexico chile pod, boiled and pureed

3 dried California chile pods, boiled and pureed

1 can (13¾ ounces) chicken broth

1 teaspoon Tabasco sauce

1 teaspoon brown sugar

juice of 1 lime

pinch of monosodium glutamate

salt to taste

1. In a chili pot, heat oil and cook meat over medium heat for 30 minutes. Add onion and enough beef broth to cover. Bring to a boil and cook 15 minutes.

continued

2. Add 1 tablespoon cumin and the oregano, reduce heat to a simmer, and add $1/2$ of the garlic. Then stir in $1^{1}/_{2}$ tablespoons commercial chili powder, $1/2$ tablespoon New Mexico chile powder, and 3 tablespoons California chile powder and simmer 10 minutes.

3. Stir in tomato sauce, pulp from the dried chiles, and remaining garlic. Add remaining beef broth and enough chicken broth for desired consistency and simmer 1 hour, stirring occasionally.

4. Add remaining New Mexico and California chile powders, commercial chili powder, and cumin and simmer for 25 minutes, stirring occasionally.

5. Turn up heat to bring chili to a slow boil and add Tabasco, brown sugar, lime juice, MSG, and salt to taste. Simmer on medium heat for 15 minutes, until it is time to turn in this championship recipe at your next cookoff or to a group of hungry chili lovers. Be sure to have plenty of Gaviscon on hand for those with weak stomachs. Keep your pot hot!

MAKES 8 SERVINGS

28th Annual World's Championship

1994, Reno, Nevada
Bill and Karen Ray, Riverside, California

This cooking duo has won more than two hundred cookoffs in twenty years, but never did they dream of actually winning the World's Championship. Well, actually, they did dream of winning the World's Championship. Frequently. That's why they kept cooking. And finally, on October 2, the Rays built as "close to a perfect pot of chili" as they ever had, and narrowly beat Missouri's Jerry Simmons to lay claim to that $25,000 grand prize. "I've been trying for twenty years to get up on this stage," said Bill Ray, who with his wife manufactures a portable pop-up canopy. "This is such a thrill I can't put it into words." Right after the cookoff Ray found himself whisked to New York where he prepared chili on the Fox network's morning show *Breakfast Time, Anytime,* and with Robin Leach on *Talking Food* on the TV Food Network, as well as enlightening millions of radio listeners in New York as to what goes into his recipe. "Thirteen tablespoons of chili powder?" asked the astonished WCBS host, Therese Crowley. "Sometimes I use fifteen," Ray informed her. And, by the way, Dr. Pierczynski got his wish, sort of. Proving his 1992 victory was no fluke, he finished fifth. But his wife, Mary, was third.

Mountain Express Chili

෩

4 tablespoons chili powder, Gebhardt's brand preferred

4 tablespoons California chile powder

3 tablespoons mild New Mexico chile powder

3 tablespoons ground cumin

2 tablespoons hot New Mexico chile powder

2 tablespoons flour

1 tablespoon pasilla chile powder

1 tablespoon garlic powder

1 teaspoon ground Mexican oregano

1 can (14$\frac{1}{2}$ ounces) whole peeled tomatoes, Hunt's brand preferred

1 can (14$\frac{1}{2}$ ounces) chicken broth

4 cups water

2 medium onions, finely chopped

1 clove garlic, pressed

4 pounds tri-tip or bottom sirloin, trimmed and cut in $\frac{1}{4}$-inch cubes

salt to taste

Tabasco sauce to taste

1. Combine all dry ingredients in a small container. Clean tomatoes of seeds and put through a sieve or chop finely. Combine tomatoes, broth, water, and dry spices in a bowl; mix well. Put into a chili pot and simmer for 30 minutes.

2. Meanwhile, in a nonstick skillet, sauté onions and garlic in a little water over low heat for 30 minutes. Drain and add to tomato sauce and simmer 30 minutes.

3. In a large nonstick skillet, cook meat until no longer pink, drain off juices, and add to chili pot. Simmer for 1½ hours or until meat is tender. Adjust seasoning with salt and add Tabasco if hotter chili is desired.

MAKES 8 SERVINGS

More ICS Winners

∞

There's no such thing as bad chili.

Some's just better than others.

—CARROLL SHELBY

1. Thou shalt have no beans in thy chili.
2. Thou shalt not make unto thee any advance preparation until thou hearest the thunderings and the lightnings and the noise of the trumpet.
3. Thou shalt not take the name of thy chief judge or thy sponsor in vain.
4. Remember the cookoff day and keep it filled with fun. Six days shalt thou labor and gather all thy meat and onions and chiles and on the seventh day thou shalt take all thy cutters and thy choppers and thy cloggers and thy fiddlers and thy Miss Chili Pepper and cook chili.
5. Honor thy cutters and thy choppers that their days may be long on thy chili team.
6. Thou shalt not kill the taste of thy chili with too much cumin or oregano or cayenne.
7. Thou shalt not commit adulteration of thy chili with garnish or rice or grits or spaghetti.
8. Thou shalt not steal every idea of every upstart winner but remain true to thine own recipe.
9. Thou shalt always bear false witness when asked about thy ingredients.
10. Thou shalt not covet thy neighbor's pot nor his spices nor his Miss Chili Pepper nor his ox nor his ass nor anything that is thy neighbor's.

—R. S. TAYLOR,
HOT TONGUE CHILI CO.,
APRIL 1987

MORE ICS WINNERS

Thousand Mile Chili

Jerry and Jean Simmons, Florissant, Missouri

"None better within thousands of miles."

Traveling around the world as a field artillery officer with the U.S. Army, Jerry Simmons and his family found the one constant thing they could easily prepare and enjoy was chili—as long as they could get New Mexico red chile powder through the mail. (Try shopping in Sydney, Australia, for chili ingredients.) Two years after retiring in 1980, Jerry entered his first cookoff and won. Jean got involved the next year and was soon followed on the cookoff circuit by daughter Jill, son James, daughter-in-law Betsy, son Jay, and his wife, Laura. Jerry, Jean, James, and Jill have all qualified for the World's at various points in their lives, with Jerry finishing second in 1994 and 1986, third in 1988, and Jean placing fourth in 1987. "The companionship and camaraderie are important," says Jerry Simmons, "but the thrill of competing and striving to make that perfect bowl of red keeps us all cooking."

SPICE MIX:

3½ tablespoons commercial chili powder, Gebhardt's brand preferred

4 teaspoons ground cumin

1 tablespoon paprika

1 tablespoon commercial chili powder, French's brand preferred

1 tablespoon cracker meal

1½ teaspoons sugar

1½ teaspoons light brown sugar

1 teaspoon mild pure New Mexico chile powder

1 teaspoon onion salt

1 teaspoon celery salt

1 teaspoon garlic powder

½ scant teaspoon jalapeño powder

¼ teaspoon dried oregano

¼ teaspoon black pepper

CHILI:

1 tablespoon bacon drippings

2 medium onions, diced (about 1½ cups)

1 cup beef broth

½ can (³/₄ cup) beer

1 teaspoon monosodium glutamate

³/₄ cup tomato sauce, Hunt's brand preferred

2 teaspoons dried beef stock base

2 cans (4 ounces each) diced green chiles, drained

2 tablespoons kidney suet

3 pounds chuck, cut in ³/₈-inch cubes

1. In a small container, mix together all spices. Set aside.

2. Heat bacon drippings in a chili pot over medium heat and sauté onions until softened. Stir in beef broth, beer, MSG, tomato sauce, stock base, and chiles. Turn up heat, bring to a boil, and stir in ½ cup of the spice mix.

3. Heat suet in a skillet over medium-high heat and sauté meat until no longer pink. Drain off fat and add meat to the chili pot. Cover and simmer 2½ hours, stirring occasionally and adding water as needed.

4. About 30 minutes before serving, add remaining spice mix and simmer, uncovered, until ready to serve.

MAKES 6 SERVINGS

MORE ICS WINNERS

Bun Burner Chili Shack

〰

Mike Austin, San Bernardino, California

*Mike, who started cooking chili in 1987, had a tremendous season in
1993 when he won the California State Championship and finished
fifth in the World's at Reno. His wife, Maria, qualified for the World's
in 1992 (her recipe follows). Actually, they used to cook together, but
their support teams got too big and they had to split up! "We have
several heroes in the chili world," says Mike, "and one is Fred Wieland,
who took the time to critique our awful chili and guide us in the right di-
rection." Nice guidance, Fred—here are two winners.*

5	pounds tri-tip or top sirloin, cut in small cubes	2	tablespoons pure California chile powder
1	large sweet onion, finely chopped (about 1 cup)	6	tablespoons ground cumin
6	cloves garlic, finely chopped	3	tablespoons extra-hot pure New Mexico chile powder
4	cans (13 3/4 ounces each) chicken broth	1	tablespoon pasilla chile powder
1	can (15 ounces) tomato sauce	2	teaspoons garlic powder
			salt to taste

1. In a large nonstick skillet over medium heat, cook meat 1 pound
   at a time, removing and setting aside when it is no longer pink.

2. Meanwhile, in a large chili pot, combine all remaining ingredients and simmer 1 hour.

3. Add meat to sauce. Cook for 2 more hours and keep covered as much as possible. Adjust seasonings. For hotter results, add more hot New Mexico chile powder.

MAKES 10 SERVINGS

Fam-Lee Affair Chili

Maria Austin, San Bernardino, California

4½ pounds tri-tip or top sirloin, cut in small cubes

1 onion, finely chopped (about ¾ cup)

½ cup California chile powder

5 tablespoons ground cumin

¼ cup hot pure New Mexico chile powder

2 canned green chile peppers, seeded, stemmed, and finely chopped

3 cans (14½ ounces each) chicken broth

1 can (8 ounces) tomato sauce

10 cloves garlic, finely chopped

salt to taste

1. In a large nonstick skillet over medium-high heat, cook meat until no longer pink. Drain off fat and set aside.

continued

2. Meanwhile, in a large chili pot, combine remaining ingredients and simmer 1 hour. Add meat to sauce and simmer an additional 2 hours.

3. Adjust seasonings. For hotter results, add more hot New Mexico chile powder or cayenne. Be careful! Say a prayer!

❧ MAKES 10 SERVINGS

Grandma Chili's Green Revenge

Loretta Logsdon, Albuquerque, New Mexico

Loretta, who makes a championship bowl of red, also loves green chili and serves it to everyone, including her grandchildren, who call her "Grandma Chili." "Now everyone calls me that," she says with a laugh. "You can't live in New Mexico without becoming addicted to the robust green chili. It is smothered on, mixed in, added to, and poured over almost anything edible. Just the aroma is an exciting jolt to the senses."

2 tablespoons vegetable oil

1 pound lean beef, cut in ½-inch cubes

1 pound lean pork, cut in ½ inch cubes

1 medium onion, coarsely chopped (about ¾ cup)

salt and black pepper to taste

1½ teaspoons garlic powder

2 tablespoons flour

2 cans (14½ ounces each) chicken broth

1 can (10 ounces) diced tomatoes

2 pounds green chiles, roasted and diced, or 4 cans (7 ounces each) Ortega brand diced green chiles, drained

1 tablespoon ground cumin

1½ teaspoons seasoned salt

pinch of dried Mexican oregano

1 teaspoon chopped fresh cilantro

1. Heat oil in a large skillet over medium heat and sauté meat and onion, adding salt, pepper, and garlic powder as meat browns. When beef and pork are no longer pink, add flour and mix in well. Cook mixture an additional 5 minutes, then add chicken broth, tomatoes, green chiles, and water, to cover (if needed).

2. Add cumin, seasoned salt, oregano, and cilantro. Bring to a boil, lower heat, and simmer 30 minutes.

3. Adjust salt and garlic powder to taste, and serve with warm tortillas.

SERVES 4 TO 6

Jazzabell's Chili

Isabel Robinson, Phelan, California
(1994 California State Champion)

The Robinson family has been cooking in chili cookoffs for 15 years, with Isabel on her own since 1988. Winning the California State Championship in 1994 was the biggest thrill of her chili-cooking career, but the icing on the cake was that her husband came in fourth and her son, sixth!

4	pounds tri-tip or top sirloin, cut in $\frac{1}{4}$-inch dice	6	tablespoons commercial chili powder, Gebhardt's brand preferred
2	cans (8 ounces each) tomato sauce	3	tablespoons pure New Mexico chile powder
2	cans ($14\frac{1}{2}$ ounces each) chicken broth	3	tablespoons ground cumin
1	medium onion, finely chopped (about $\frac{3}{4}$ cup)	$\frac{1}{4}$	teaspoon salt
10	cloves garlic, minced		cayenne to taste

1. In a large nonstick skillet, brown meat 1 pound at a time, draining off fat.

2. Place meat in a large saucepan and add tomato sauce, chicken broth, onion, garlic, chili and chile powders, cumin, and salt. Blend thoroughly, bring to a full boil, then lower heat and simmer 2 to 3 hours.

3. Adjust seasonings, adding cayenne if not hot enough.

🍴 MAKES 6 TO 8 SERVINGS

Betty Flinchbaugh's Award-Winning Chili

Betty and Dawson Flinchbaugh, Harrisburg, Pennsylvania

As chief judge of the Big Boulder Chili Cookoff and Fiddle Fest in the Pocono Mountains and judge at the World's Championships, Dawson has learned the inside scoop on what's hot and what's not. "At the World's, the chilis are all good," he says. "Things such as how well the spices permeate the meat and appearance become real important." When it comes to Betty's chili, however, Dawson gives her a perfect "10."

vegetable oil

5 pounds chuck, cut in small cubes or $1/2$ ground, $1/2$ cubed

5 tablespoons commercial chili powder, Gebhardt's brand preferred

2 cans (12 ounces each) beer

$1^1/_2$ teaspoons dried oregano

1 tablespoon ground cumin

1 tablespoon paprika

2 large onions, diced (about 2 cups)

6 cloves garlic, minced

$1/2$ large red bell pepper, diced (about $1/2$ cup)

2 jalapeño peppers, seeded and diced

1 can (4 ounces) whole green chiles, seeded, drained, and chopped

1 can (15 ounces) crushed tomatoes

1 teaspoon Tabasco sauce

1 tablespoon brown sugar

1 teaspoon red wine vinegar

1 teaspoon flour (optional)

salt to taste

1. In a large skillet, heat a little oil and brown meat with $1/2$ of the chili powder until no longer pink. Drain off fat. Meanwhile, in a large pot, combine beer, oregano, cumin, paprika, and remaining chili powder and bring to a slow boil. Add meat and simmer $1^{1}/_{2}$ hours.

2. In a large skillet, heat a little oil, sauté onions and garlic until softened, and add to chili. Add peppers, chiles, and tomatoes and simmer another $1^{1}/_{2}$ hours. Add Tabasco, sugar, and vinegar and cook another 45 minutes.

3. About 20 minutes before serving, stir in flour to thicken (if needed) and add salt to taste.

MAKES 10 SERVINGS

George Faison's Venison Chili

D'Artagnan, Jersey City, New Jersey

When it comes to meat, George Faison knows his stuff. He runs D'Artagnan, a company that purveys wild boar, free-range chickens, buffalo meat, venison, antelope, and so on, and volunteered this excellent chili. "The leaner meats and the chile puree give this recipe an authentic flavor," he says.

5   pounds venison or buffalo from the shoulder

1   carrot, finely chopped (about ⅓ cup), trimmings reserved

2   stalks celery, finely chopped (about 1 cup), trimmings reserved

2   large onions, finely chopped (about 2 cups), trimmings reserved

4   cups water

2   tablespoons duck fat or olive oil

3   pounds ground venison or buffalo

4   cans (12 ounces each) cold beer

¾   cup chile paste (recipe follows)

2   cans (8 ounces each) tomato sauce

2   tablespoons ground cumin (or more to taste)

2   whole heads of garlic, minced

1   tablespoon dried oregano

2   bay leaves

salt and black pepper to taste

1. Trim buffalo or venison and cut in ½-inch cubes. Set aside. Place meat scraps and vegetable trimmings in small saucepan, add water, bring to a boil, and skim off any scum. Simmer 20 minutes, strain, and reserve meat and stock separately.

2. Meanwhile, in a large chili pot, render duck fat, add carrot, celery, and onions, and sauté until onions start to brown. Add both cubed and ground meat and sauté, stirring frequently, until no longer pink.

3. Add beer, let foam settle, and bring to a boil. Add reserved stock, chile paste, tomato sauce, cumin, garlic, oregano, and bay leaves and bring to a boil. Lower heat and let simmer 2 to 3 hours, stirring occasionally and adding water if needed.

4. Skim off fat and adjust seasonings, adding salt, pepper, and more cumin if needed, then serve.

MAKES 10 TO 12 SERVINGS

Chile Paste

| 5 | dried ancho chiles | 3 | dried pasilla chiles |
| 4 | dried mulato chiles | 4 | dried chipotle chiles |

1. Cover chiles with warm water and let soak 30 minutes, or until softened. Drain.

2. In a food processor or blender, puree completely, adding water if necessary. Press through a fine sieve to remove seeds and pieces of skin.

MAKES ABOUT $3/_4$ CUP

A Distant Cousin to Big Jim's Hogbreath Chili

Jim Heywood, Red Hook, New York

We first met Big Jim (known as Chef Heywood to his students at the prestigious Culinary Institute of America in Hyde Park, New York) at a tiny cookoff in New York at which he and his son, Slim Tim, strolled off with all the prizes. Curious, we wandered over to his booth and picked up one of his special jars of spices, whereupon he warmly whacked us across the knuckles with a wooden spoon. Seriously, Big Jim's chili is a closely guarded secret ("Madonna couldn't get it out of me," he says), but this relative is a very close approximation. When he's not cooking chili (he's been to the World's several times), Jim teaches advanced garde manger in the CIA's Education Division.

½ cup vegetable oil

5 pounds lean beef, cut in ½-inch cubes or coarsely ground

1½ pounds large white onions, finely diced (about 3 cups)

6 to 8 cloves garlic, minced

2 cups beef broth

½ cup red wine

1 bottle (12 ounces) dark beer

1 can (28 ounces) tomato puree

4 large green fresh chiles, diced (about 2 cups)

3 to 4 jalapeño peppers, minced

1 cup mild pure chile powder

⅓ cup ground cumin

3 tablespoons dried oregano

1 teaspoon cayenne

salt to taste

Tabasco sauce to taste

1. In a large skillet, working in batches, heat oil and brown meat. Using a slotted spoon, remove meat to a large pot, leaving excess oil in the skillet.

2. Over medium heat in the same skillet, sauté onions and garlic until softened, then add to meat along with beef broth, wine, beer and tomato puree. Bring to a boil, lower heat, and cook 1 hour. Add chiles, jalapeños, chile powder, cumin, oregano, and cayenne and simmer another 1 to $1^{1}/_{2}$ hours.

3. Skim off fat and adjust seasonings, adding salt to taste. Adjust heat with Tabasco.

MAKES 10 TO 12 SERVINGS

Southwest Whiskey Chili for a Crowd

○○

James Mullin, Scottsdale, Arizona

Chili varies in different parts of the United States, says Mullin, but you will find that all four corners will agree that the following recipe is without a doubt satisfying to all palates—beans and all. It certainly was to our tasting panel's!

6   tablespoons bacon drippings

8   medium onions, chopped (about 5 cups)

2   large red onions, chopped (about 2 cups)

5   cloves garlic, minced

9   pounds beef, cut in 1/4-inch dice

4   cans (16 ounces each) dark red kidney beans, undrained

2   large green bell peppers, finely chopped (about 2 cups)

2   large red bell peppers, finely chopped (about 2 cups)

2   cans (28 ounces each) whole tomatoes, drained

2   cans (16 ounces each) tomato sauce

6 to 10 tablespoons commercial chili powder

2   teaspoons dried basil

6   bay leaves

freshly ground black pepper

2   cans (4 ounces each) chopped jalapeño peppers, drained

1   jar (4 ounces) smooth apricot preserves

Tabasco sauce to taste

paprika and salt to taste

1   heaping tablespoon brown sugar

2   cups Johnnie Walker Black (12 years old)

3   cans (16 ounces each) stewed tomatoes

1. In a really big pot, heat bacon drippings and sauté onions and garlic until softened. In batches, sauté meat until browned. Drain off excess fat.

2. Using a food processor, puree 2 cans kidney beans and add to meat along with remaining 2 cans of beans. Stir in peppers, tomatoes, tomato sauce, chili powder, basil, bay leaves, black pepper, jalapeños, apricot preserves, Tabasco, paprika, salt, and brown sugar and mix thoroughly. Add 1 cup Johnnie Walker Black and bring to a boil, then lower heat, cover, and simmer 4 hours.

3. If serving right away, stir in remaining whiskey and stewed tomatoes and heat through; otherwise, refrigerate and reheat over low heat with whiskey and tomatoes.

4. Serve with sourdough rolls cut into soup cups, and top with grated Cheddar cheese if desired.

MAKES 30 SERVINGS

Austin Red Championship Chili

○○

S. Neal Tooni, Trumbull, Connecticut

Neal, whose wife, Beth, is a talented artist, has been to the World's Championship several times and in 1993 was the first cook to represent Saratoga in Reno. Meticulous in his approach to chili, Neal and his topflight bowl of red are winners everywhere, not just at the track.

SPICE MIX:

3/4 cup plus 2 tablespoons mild pure chile powder

1/4 cup onion powder

2 teaspoons ground cumin

1 tablespoon garlic powder

2 teaspoons paprika

1 1/2 teaspoons white pepper

1 teaspoon cayenne

1/2 teaspoon black pepper

CHILI:

2 cans (14 1/2 ounces each) chicken broth

1 can (15 ounces) tomato sauce

2 tablespoons vegetable oil

4 1/2 pounds sirloin tip, cut in 3/8-inch cubes

1 1/2 teaspoons salt

spring water

1. Combine ingredients for spice mix in a container with a tight-fitting lid.

2. Heat a Dutch oven over medium-low heat. Add chicken broth, tomato sauce, and 1/3 of the spice mix. Bring to a slow boil, stirring often.

3. Meanwhile, heat oil in a large skillet over medium-high heat. Brown meat in batches, sprinkling with some spice mix and salt as it cooks. As each batch is browned, transfer to the Dutch oven with a slotted spoon. When all the beef is in the Dutch oven, cover and lower heat to a simmer.

4. Add spring water to remaining spice mix to make a paste, blending thoroughly and setting aside. Stir occasionally.

5. After meat has simmered 2½ hours, stir the spice mix a final time and add it to the Dutch oven. Simmer another 30 minutes. Adjust seasonings before serving.

MAKES 8 SERVINGS

Canadian Chili

〜

Warren Chan, Alberta, Canada

Warren started cooking chili competitively in 1983 after he tried Carroll Shelby's recipe and became intrigued with the idea of chili cookoffs. Two years later he won his first championship and went to California to represent Alberta at Tropico. It was only after he began to travel, says Warren, that he really found out what cooking chili competitively was all about. "Some of the nicest people in the world are chili cooks," he says. "In the late hours of the evening before a cookoff, in some dingy—or swanky—hotel, you can bet there will be a bunch of cooks swapping stories over a cool one. It's easy to become friends very fast."

$1\frac{1}{2}$ pounds sirloin, cut in cubes

$1\frac{1}{2}$ pounds venison, cut in cubes

$1\frac{1}{2}$ pounds pork, cut in cubes

vegetable oil

1 large onion, diced (about 1 cup)

3 to 4 jalapeño peppers, diced (about $\frac{1}{4}$ cup)

2 whole shallots, minced (about $\frac{1}{2}$ cup)

1 can (15 ounces) tomato sauce

1 can ($13\frac{3}{4}$ ounces) beef broth

10 cloves garlic, minced

3 bay leaves

1 tablespoon instant chicken bouillon granules

2 cups water

$\frac{3}{4}$ cup mild pure chile powder

$\frac{1}{4}$ cup ground cumin

2 tablespoons cayenne

$1\frac{1}{2}$ teaspoons ground oregano

1 teaspoon dry mustard

1 tablespoon hot pure New Mexico chile powder

$\frac{1}{2}$ teaspoon monosodium glutamate

$\frac{1}{2}$ teaspoon ground coriander

salt to taste

1. Heat a little oil in a large skillet over medium-high heat and brown meat 1 pound at a time. Using a slotted spoon, transfer meat to a chili pot and add onion, jalapeños, shallots, tomato sauce, beef broth, garlic, bay leaves, chicken bouillon granules, and water. Bring to a boil, then lower heat and simmer 1 hour.

2. Stir in mild chile powder, cumin, cayenne, oregano, and mustard and simmer another 30 minutes. Add New Mexico chile powder, MSG, and coriander and simmer 30 more minutes. Adjust seasonings with salt, serve, and enjoy!

🍴 MAKES 8 TO 10 SERVINGS

KATJ Chili Kats' Secret Brew

⁌⁌

Scott Brody, Mike Matlock, and Charlie Fore, KATJ Radio,
Victorville, California

*The Chili Kats swear this recipe has its roots in the chili cooked by the
San Antonio chili queens and perfected in 1950 high in the Sierras at a
cow camp called Vaquero Camp near Monitor Pass. (We'll take their
word for it.) This chili was common fare for cowboys as they moved
cattle from Carson Valley in Nevada to the high summer range in
California. The secret lies in the quality of the ingredients, when the ingredients are introduced to the chili, and the care taken while cooking.*

1½ teaspoons vegetable oil	¼ cup pure pasilla chile powder
1 medium onion, finely diced (about ¾ cup)	¼ cup pure California chile powder
4 cloves garlic, minced	3 tablespoons ground cumin
3 pounds lean chuck, cut in ⅜-inch cubes	2 teaspoons salt (or more to taste)
1 cup chicken broth	water
3 tablespoons tomato sauce	cayenne to taste
1 canned green chile, seeded and finely diced	

1. Heat oil in a skillet over medium-low heat and sauté onion and
    garlic until just beginning to soften. Turn up the heat, add meat
    cubes, and sauté until no longer pink. Drain off excess fat and
    transfer to a chili pot.

2. Stir in chicken broth, tomato sauce, green chile, chile powders, cumin, and salt. Add water just to cover meat and simmer for about 3 hours.

3. Before serving, adjust heat with cayenne and add more salt if needed.

MAKES 6 SERVINGS

The Traveling Chiliheads' Competition Chili

◎◎

Charlie and Barbara Ward, Lake Havasu City, Arizona

At last count, the Traveling Chiliheads, as Barbara and Charlie are known to the followers of their column in the ICS newspaper, have won eleven regional and state titles between them. The couple, both retired Los Angeles city officials, travel from cookoff to cookoff in their RV until each of them qualifies for the World's, which they've done every year since 1990. When they're not cooking, they're judging. And having tasted many a bowl of competition chili alongside Charlie, we can vouch he's as good a judge as he is a cook. The Wards make a mean vegetarian chili too (see next recipe).

4   pounds beef chuck, diced in pieces the size of a large pea

1   can (8 ounces) tomato sauce

1   can (13 ¾ ounces) beef broth

1   large onion, chopped fine

1   tablespoon crushed garlic

1   jar (3 ounces) commercial chili powder, Gebhardt's brand preferred

3   tablespoons ground cumin

salt to taste

1. In a large nonstick skillet over medium heat, sauté meat until no longer pink.

2. Meanwhile, in a heavy chili pot, combine tomato sauce, beef broth, and onion, bring to a slow boil, and simmer 15 minutes. Add meat, garlic, chili powder, and cumin, mix well, and simmer 2 hours, covered, adding water as necessary.

3. Before serving, adjust seasonings with salt.

MAKES 6 TO 8 SERVINGS

Vegetarian Chili

Charlie and Barbara Ward, Lake Havasu City, Arizona

1 tablespoon cooking oil

1 tablespoon margarine

2 cloves garlic, minced
(1 tablespoon)

2 tablespoons commercial chili
powder

1 teaspoon ground cumin

1/2 teaspoon dried oregano

1/2 teaspoon black pepper

1 pound green beans, cut in
1/4-inch pieces (about
2 1/2 cups)

3 large carrots, shredded
(about 1 1/2 cups)

4 to 6 stalks celery, diced (about
1 cup)

1 can (15 ounces) whole
tomatoes, diced, with juice
reserved

1/2 cup water

1 large onion, diced (about
1 cup)

1 large green bell pepper, diced
(about 3/4 cup)

1 large red bell pepper, diced
(about 3/4 cup)

2 long green chiles (Anaheim
or New Mexico), roasted,
peeled, and diced

1 can (16 ounces) red kidney
beans, undrained

salt to taste

1. In a large Dutch oven, heat oil and margarine over low heat.
   Stir in garlic, chili powder, cumin, oregano, and black pepper
   and cook, stirring, for 1 to 2 minutes.

2. Add green beans, carrots, celery, juice from canned tomatoes, and water. Stir well, cover, and simmer 10 minutes.

3. Stir in onion, bell peppers, and chiles, cover, and cook another 10 minutes.

4. Add tomatoes and kidney beans and cook 10 minutes longer. If you want to stretch the chili, add another can of beans, drained. Adjust seasonings with salt and serve.

⑪ MAKES 4 TO 6 SERVINGS

JT's Truckin' Chili

୦୨

Jerry and Patty Thomas, Sutton, Massachusetts

One of the big mysteries on the chili circuit is why Patty has put up with truck-drivin' Jerry for all these years. Not only that, she covers up for him when folks ask him for his secret chili recipe. We know he doesn't really use paprika. Now that we have the true truckin' chili, we know why Patty has put up with Jerry all these years. In fact, it's so good he carries copies of it with him on long-distance hauls and uses them to wangle his way out of speeding tickets. It's a fact that several chili-loving officers of the law have folded up their summons books when given this recipe.

2	teaspoons vegetable oil	5	tablespoons commercial chili powder
4	pounds chuck, well trimmed, cut in small cubes	2	teaspoons cayenne
2	onions, finely chopped (about 1½ cups)	8	cloves garlic, crushed
1	Italian pepper, finely diced	4	teaspoons ground cumin
1	can (4 ounces) whole green chiles, seeded, rinsed, and minced	1	teaspoon salt (or more to taste)
1	can (12 ounces) beer	3	jalapeño peppers, finely diced (optional)

1. In a large chili pot over medium heat, heat oil and sauté meat until no longer pink. Drain off fat and add onions, Italian pepper, and chiles. Cook over medium heat until vegetables are softened.

2. Stir in beer, chili powder, cayenne, garlic, and cumin. Bring to a boil and simmer 3 hours, or until meat is tender, stirring occasionally and adding water. Add salt during the last 45 minutes and adjust again before serving. For hotter chili, add diced jalapeños.

MAKES 6 TO 8 SERVINGS

Jim Parker's Competition Chili

Hard Times Cafe, Alexandria, Virginia

Jim cooks and brother Fred judges, although never at the same cookoff!

1	teaspoon vegetable oil	1	can (13 3/4 ounces) beef broth
3	pounds beef, cut in 3/8-inch cubes	1	can (8 ounces) tomato sauce
1/2	teaspoon salt	1/4	teaspoon dried oregano
2	teaspoons garlic powder	3	teaspoons ground cumin
1	tablespoon onion powder	1	tablespoon paprika
5	tablespoons mild pure chile powder	1/2	teaspoon jalapeño powder
		1/4	teaspoon cayenne

1. In a chili pot, heat oil and begin cooking meat over medium-high heat. As it begins to lose its pink color, stir in salt, 1 teaspoon garlic powder, and the onion powder. When meat is no longer pink, stir in 2 tablespoons chile powder, the beef broth, and enough water to cover. Add tomato sauce and simmer 2 hours, or until meat becomes tender.

2. Stir in remaining chile powder, oregano, cumin, paprika, jalapeño powder, cayenne, and remaining teaspoon of garlic powder. Cover and continue to simmer for another hour.

MAKES 6 TO 8 SERVINGS

Bill Neale's Chili

Bill Neale, Dallas, Texas

Bill is one of the folks who was around for the first one at Terlinguaback in 1967. An artist, he did the posters for the early cookoffs, some of which go for as much as $1,000 now. We know people who'd pay that much for a recipe as good as his.

3	pounds beef, cut in ¼-inch dice	1	tablespoon paprika (optional)
		1	tablespoon dried oregano
1	can (15 ounces) tomato sauce	1	tablespoon ground cumin
1	onion, chopped (about ¾ cup)	1	teaspoon cayenne
		1	teaspoon salt
1	clove garlic, minced	6	red chiles pequín (optional)
4	heaping tablespoons mild pure chile powder	1	teaspoon Tabasco sauce
		2	tablespoons flour

1. In a nonstick skillet, sauté beef in batches until no longer pink. Transfer to a chili pot and stir in tomato sauce, onion, garlic, chile powder, paprika, oregano, cumin, cayenne, and salt. Add water to cover meat by an inch, bring to a slow boil, and simmer 2 hours, adding more water only if needed. If desired, float chiles pequín in the chili to lend extra heat.

2. Remove chiles pequín and add Tabasco. Make a paste of flour and water and stir into the chili to thicken. Simmer another 30 minutes.

MAKES 6 SERVINGS

Truett's Mother Lode Chili

꩜

Truett Airhart, Houston, Texas

Truett has a tendency to blend in wherever he goes. At first glance you'd never take him for the founder of Zytron or some of his other wildly successful ventures. Nor would you take him for one of the world's great unsung chili cooks. Variations of his basic recipe have won more than $100,000 in chili cookoffs since he first stirred a pot of competition chili back in 1979. We are pleased and privileged to include his recipe here for just plain good eatin' at home.

8	dried New Mexico chile pods
5	pounds coarsely ground chuck
1/4	cup rendered kidney suet
	black pepper to taste
2	onions, chopped (about 1 1/2 cups)
2 1/2	teaspoons cuminseeds, crushed with a rolling pin
1/2	cup commercial chili powder
3	cloves garlic, put through a garlic press
2	tablespoons monosodium glutamate
1	can (13 3/4 ounces) chicken broth
1	teaspoon dried oregano, steeped in 1 cup warm water and strained
8	ounces Velveeta cheese
	salt to taste

1. Stem and seed chile pods, place in a saucepan, cover with water, and simmer for 30 minutes. Strain, reserving the water, and puree in a blender. Press through a sieve to remove pieces of skin and set aside.

2. Working in batches, heat suet in a skillet over medium heat and sauté meat until it is no longer pink, seasoning with black pepper. Remove with a slotted spoon, allowing fat to drain off, and put into a chili pot. Stir in onions, cuminseeds, chili powder, garlic, and MSG. Adding reserved chile water to prevent scorching, cook 10 minutes, stirring constantly.

3. Stir in the chile puree, chicken broth, and $\frac{1}{2}$ of the oregano water, and cook another 45 minutes. Stir in remaining oregano water and cook another 45 minutes, adding water as necessary.

4. Before serving, stir in Velveeta cheese and allow to melt through the chili. Add salt to taste.

MAKES 10 SERVINGS

Award-Winning New York Chili

୧୨

Jonathan Levine, New York City

When we first ran into Jonathan, he was wandering around a cookoff in upstate New York wearing a beanie hat with a propeller, Bermuda shorts, and black socks with sandals. Nice hat, we told him. Little did we know he is one of the great chiliheads of this or any other generation. A wine enthusiast and a world-class bridge player, Jonathan works for the New York City Board of Education when he's not running chili cookoffs in the Northeast. One of his great regrets as an Advisory Board member of the ICS is that he can't cook competitively. If he could, this is what he'd make.

5	pounds first-cut brisket or top-grade chuck, cut in thumbnail-sized pieces
2	teaspoons vegetable oil
2	medium onions, chopped (about 1½ cups)
6	cloves garlic, minced
¼	cup cayenne
½	cup commercial chili powder
3	tablespoons mild pure chile powder
1½	heaping teaspoons ground cumin (made from toasted cuminseeds)
1	heaping teaspoon ground coriander
1	heaping teaspoon dried oregano
1	can (28 ounces) whole tomatoes, crushed with your hands, liquid reserved
½	pound ground chuck
	salt to taste

1. In a Dutch oven over medium heat, cook meat in oil until no longer pink. Stir in onions, garlic, cayenne, chili and chile powders, $1/_2$ teaspoon cumin, coriander, oregano, and tomatoes with liquid. Bring to a boil, lower heat, and simmer 3 hours, adding water as needed.

2. Stir in ground chuck and cook until brisket is tender and chili is thickened, about 1 more hour. About 15 minutes before serving, stir in remaining 1 teaspoon cumin and adjust seasonings with salt.

MAKES 8 SERVINGS

Silverado Saloon Chili

Ron and Sherre Mesker, Woodinville, Washington

*Ron and Sherre are better known in chili circles as Renegade Red and
Silverado Sherre, the singer. One of the most vivid memories Ron has of the
many World's Championships they've attended is from 1991, when the final
one was held at Tropico Gold Mine. The evening before the cookoff, Ron
bumped into C. V. Wood in the breezeway at the Antelope Valley Inn and the
two chatted for a few moments before being joined by Sherre and Joanne Dru,
Woody's wife. As Ron recalls it, Woody suddenly put his arm around Ron's
shoulder and said, "How did two ugly old boys like you and me end up with
such beautiful women? Guess the good Lord is just taking care of us." Woody's
warmth and good humor will always stay with the Meskers.*

3 large sweet onions, chunked	1 tablespoon pure New Mexico chile powder
14 medium cloves garlic	
6 pounds tri-tip, cut in cubes	2 tablespoons pasilla chile powder
3 teaspoons commercial chili powder	
	1/2 cup California chile powder
1 can (13 3/4 ounces) beef broth	1/2 cup commercial chili powder, Gebhardt's brand preferred
1 can (13 3/4 ounces) chicken broth	
	2 1/2 scant tablespoons ground cumin
1 teaspoon brown sugar	
1 teaspoon salt	1/2 teaspoon cayenne
1 teaspoon white vinegar	1 can (8 ounces) tomato sauce
1 tablespoon monosodium glutamate	1/4 teaspoon black pepper

1. In a blender puree onions and garlic. Drain.

2. In a large nonstick skillet, brown meat $^1/_3$ at a time with $^1/_3$ of the onion-garlic puree and 1 teaspoon chili powder. Transfer meat to a chili pot as it loses its pink color.

3. Meanwhile, in a saucepot, combine all remaining ingredients and bring to a slow boil. Lower heat and simmer 30 minutes.

4. Add sauce to meat mixture and simmer 1 hour, adding more broth if needed. Adjust seasonings, adding more cayenne or salt if desired, and serve.

MAKES 12 SERVINGS

Still More ICS

Winners

Each of us knows that his chili is light-years beyond other chili in quality and singularity; each of us knows that all other chili is such vile slop that a coyote would turn his back on it.

—H. ALLEN SMITH

Each year at the ICS World's Championship, the American Spice Trade Association awards its Golden Chili Pepper medal to the cook whose recipe makes the best use of spices. Here are the winners.

Bottom-of-the-Barrel Gang Mid-South Heat Wave Chili, 1994 winner

୭୨

Richard Knight, Lebanon, Tennessee

Knight is the first two-time Golden Chili Pepper winner, having won in 1991 with a deliciously different recipe.

1/3 cup commercial chili powder	1/2 teaspoon cayenne
1 tablespoon ground cumin	1/8 teaspoon black pepper
1 tablespoon garlic powder	1/8 teaspoon white pepper
2 teaspoons onion powder	2 1/2 pounds ground beef
2 teaspoons paprika	1 can (13 3/4 ounces) beef broth
1 teaspoon dried oregano, crushed	1 can (8 ounces) tomato sauce
	1 cup water
1/2 teaspoon salt	3/4 cup beer

1. In a small container combine the dry ingredients; set aside.

2. In a large nonstick saucepan sauté the ground beef, stirring frequently, until crumbly. Drain off excess fat; stir in reserved spice mixture and cook, stirring constantly, about 1 minute.

3. Stir in beef broth, tomato sauce, water, and beer; bring to a boil, reduce heat, and simmer, covered, 1 hour or until thickened.

MAKES 4 TO 6 SERVINGS

Tokyo Tom's Banzai Chili, 1993

Winner

୭୨

Robert Stillborn, Alberta, Canada

SPICE MIX:

4	teaspoons onion powder
1	tablespoon paprika
2	teaspoons salt
1½	teaspoons dried thyme, crushed
1½	teaspoons celery salt
1½	teaspoons garlic salt
1½	teaspoons white pepper
1	teaspoon dry mustard
1	teaspoon dried oregano
½	teaspoon cayenne
½	teaspoon ground cardamom
pinch of ground nutmeg

CHILI:

1	tablespoon vegetable oil
4½	pounds ground beef
⅓	cup mild pure chile powder
⅓	cup instant minced onion
1	tablespoon ground cumin
2	teaspoons instant minced garlic
1	teaspoon ground black pepper
1	teaspoon salt
⅛	teaspoon cayenne
1	bay leaf
1	can (29 ounces) tomato sauce
1	can (13¾ ounces) beef broth

continued

STILL MORE ICS WINNERS

131

1. Combine all ingredients for spice mix and store in a tightly covered container.

2. Heat oil in a large saucepan, add beef, and cook, breaking up meat as it loses its pink color, about 5 minutes. Drain off liquid.

3. Add chile powder, onion, cumin, garlic, black pepper, 1 teaspoon spice mix, salt, cayenne, and bay leaf; stir until beef is coated. Stir in tomato sauce and beef broth and simmer, covered, 1 hour.

4. Adjust seasonings and remove bay leaf before serving.

MAKES 6 TO 8 SERVINGS

Buns Burner Chili, 1992 winner

Bob Griffith, Garden Grove, California

In the years he's competed in chili cookoffs, Bob has garnered more than four dozen awards. His hot tip? "Simmer the different spices awhile so they all come together and develop a smooth, robust flavor."

1/3 cup instant minced onion

1 teaspoon instant minced garlic

1/2 cup water

2 1/2 pounds coarsely ground chuck

8 ounces country pork sausage

1/2 cup commercial chili powder

1 can (13 3/4 ounces) chicken broth

1 can (8 ounces) tomato sauce

2 tablespoons ground cumin

1 teaspoon dried oregano

1/2 teaspoon salt

1/4 teaspoon ground coriander

1/4 teaspoon white pepper

1/8 teaspoon cayenne

1 bay leaf

1. Combine onion, garlic, and water in a cup and let stand until softened, about 10 minutes.

2. Meanwhile, in a large nonstick skillet, cook chuck and sausage until meat is no longer pink, about 5 minutes. Drain off fat.

3. Drain onion-garlic mixture and add to meat along with chili powder; cook until meat is coated, about 1 minute. Transfer meat to a chili pot and stir in chicken broth, tomato sauce, cumin, oregano, salt, coriander, white pepper, cayenne, and bay leaf. Simmer, covered, about 1 hour.

MAKES 4 TO 6 SERVINGS

Miami Heat Chili, 1991 winner

Richard and Carol Knight, Coral Gables, Florida

The Knights are part of a twelve-member team called "The Bottom-of-the-Barrel Gang," which has been competing in chili cookoffs since the mid-1970s.

5	teaspoons vegetable oil	$1/_2$	teaspoon dried oregano,
1	pound round steak, cut in		crushed
	1-inch cubes	$1/_2$	teaspoon paprika
1	pound boneless chuck steak,	$1/_8$	teaspoon cayenne
	cut in 1-inch cubes	$1/_8$	teaspoon black pepper
3	tablespoons commercial chili	1	can (15 ounces) tomato sauce
	powder	1	can (12 ounces) beer
1	tablespoon ground cumin	$1^1/_2$	cups water
1	tablespoon instant minced		
	garlic		

1. Heat 2 teaspoons oil in a Dutch oven until very hot. Add meat a few pieces at a time and cook, stirring, until browned on all sides; remove to a plate and repeat until all the meat has been cooked.

2. Add remaining 3 teaspoons oil to the pot and stir in chili powder, cumin, garlic, oregano, paprika, cayenne, and black pepper; cook, stirring, for 1 minute. Remove from heat and stir in

tomato sauce, beer, water, and reserved meat. Bring to a boil, lower heat, and simmer, covered, about 2 hours, or until meat is tender, stirring occasionally. Serve with cooked pinto beans, chopped onion, jalapeño peppers, and grated Cheddar cheese.

MAKES 4 TO 6 SERVINGS

Buzzard Breath Chili, 1990 Winner

George Anderson, Giessen, Germany

George is a retired Air Force master sergeant who hails from White Salmon, Washington, but now lives in Germany, where his wife, Starr, teaches in an American school. A full-time house husband, he has taken a decade to fully develop his chili recipe, which took the British Isles cookoff in 1990.

SPICE MIX:

- 3/4 cup chili powder
- 2 tablespoons ground cumin
- 4 1/2 teaspoons garlic powder
- 1 teaspoon dried oregano, crushed
- 1/2 teaspoon ground nutmeg
- 1/2 teaspoon curry powder
- 1/2 teaspoon ground sage
- 1/2 teaspoon dried thyme, crushed
- 1/4 teaspoon ground ginger
- 1/4 teaspoon ground cinnamon

CHILI:

- 4 tablespoons olive oil
- 4 pounds boneless sirloin, cut in 1/2-inch cubes
- 2 onions, finely chopped (about 1 1/2 cups)
- 1 1/2 cups water
- 1 can (8 ounces) tomato sauce
- 1 chicken bouillon cube
- 1 beef bouillon cube
- 1 square (1 ounce) semisweet chocolate, grated, for garnish

1. In a small bowl, combine all ingredients for spice mix and set aside.

2. In a large pot, heat 1 tablespoon oil, add ½ of the meat, and cook, stirring occasionally, until it is well browned on all sides. Remove meat and its juices to a large bowl; repeat, using another tablespoon of oil and remaining meat; remove to bowl.

3. In the same pot, heat remaining 2 tablespoons oil, add onions, and cook, stirring occasionally, until softened. Return meat to pot and add spice mix, stirring to coat meat. Add water, tomato sauce, and bouillon cubes; bring to a boil, then lower heat and simmer, uncovered, until sauce is thickened, about 20 minutes. Serve topped with grated chocolate.

MAKES 6 SERVINGS

The Evergreen Chiliheads' Hot and Spicy True Chili, 1989 winner

Kevin Wilson, Augsburg, Germany

Supported by Ronald and Carolyn Peters and Brian Bedard—
Evergreen symbolizes Washington, their home state—Sergeant Wilson
began competing in cookoffs in 1987 when he and Peters got into
an argument over who could make the best chili. Wilson earned a trip
to the World's Championship with this recipe, winner of the
European Regionals.

1/4 cup instant minced onion

1/4 cup water

2 tablespoons mild pure chile powder

2 teaspoons garlic powder

1 teaspoon ground cumin

1/2 teaspoon cayenne

1/4 teaspoon dried thyme

1/4 teaspoon curry powder

1/4 teaspoon ground nutmeg

1/4 teaspoon paprika

1/4 teaspoon black pepper

2 tablespoons vegetable oil

3 pounds beef tenderloin, cut in 1/2-inch cubes

2 cans (15 ounces each) tomato sauce

1 jar (8 ounces) mild, medium, or hot salsa picante

1. Soak onion in water and set aside. In a small bowl, mix the chile powder, garlic powder, cumin, cayenne, thyme, curry powder, nutmeg, paprika, and black pepper; set aside.

2. In a Dutch oven, heat oil and add beef $^1/_3$ at a time; sauté, until no longer pink, about 5 minutes. Remove meat to a bowl after it is browned; repeat with remaining 2 batches. When all meat is browned, return to the Dutch oven.

3. Drain onion; stir into meat along with spice mixture and cook, stirring, about 1 minute. Stir in tomato sauce and salsa, cover, and simmer about $1^1/_2$ hours.

MAKES 6 SERVINGS

Wasco Bob Chili, 1988 winner

〰️

Bob Nelson, Wasco, California

Bob, who owns a men's clothing store, won with this recipe after only a year on the chili cookoff trail. His cooking prowess, however, goes back to his army days, and he does most of the cooking at home for his family and friends.

2	tablespoons vegetable oil
3	pounds lean beef chuck, finely diced
1/2	cup instant minced onion
1/3	cup mild pure chile powder
2	tablespoons ground cumin
1	tablespoon paprika
1	teaspoon dried oregano
1	teaspoon garlic powder

3/4	teaspoon salt
1/8	teaspoon dried marjoram
1/8	teaspoon dried thyme
1/8	teaspoon ground sage
2	cups chicken broth
1/2	can (3/4 cup) beer
1	can (8 ounces) tomato sauce
1 1/2	teaspoons sugar
1/4	teaspoon black pepper

1. In a Dutch oven, heat oil over medium heat. Add 1/3 of the beef and cook, stirring, until no longer pink. Transfer to a bowl using a slotted spoon; repeat with remaining meat.

2. Return meat to the Dutch oven and add onion, chile powder, cumin, paprika, oregano, garlic powder, salt, marjoram, thyme, sage, chicken broth, beer, and tomato sauce. Bring to a boil, then lower heat and simmer, partially covered, for 1 1/2 hours, stirring occasionally.

3. Stir in sugar and black pepper just before serving and serve with a dollop of sour cream if desired.

🍴 MAKES 6 SERVINGS

Barnstormers' Chili, 1987 winner

⚯

Richard and Tammy Rutherford, Palmdale, California

The Rutherfords compare themselves to the barnstormers of yesteryear who appeared at county fairs giving exhibitions of stunt flying and parachute jumping. Local chili cookoffs are the Rutherfords' arena, and they make quite a chili—spicy, but not overly so, cooked in a tomato-beer base with a touch of tequila.

¹/₃ cup instant minced onion	¹/₂ teaspoon dried oregano, crushed
2 teaspoons instant minced garlic	¹/₂ teaspoon salt
6 tablespoons water	¹/₂ teaspoon black pepper
2 tablespoons vegetable oil	¹/₄ teaspoon ground coriander
3 pounds boneless top round, sirloin, or chuck, cut in ¹/₂-inch cubes	¹/₄ teaspoon dried marjoram, crushed
³/₄ cup mild pure chile powder	¹/₈ teaspoon ground cloves
1 can (12 ounces) beer	¹/₈ teaspoon dry mustard
1 can (8 ounces) tomato sauce	¹/₈ teaspoon cayenne
2 tablespoons ground cumin	¹/₂ to 1 cup beef broth
	1 tablespoon tequila

continued

1. In a small cup, combine onion, garlic, and water set aside to soften, about 10 minutes.

2. In a large skillet, heat oil, add ½ of the meat, and cook, stirring until no longer pink, about 5 minutes. Using a slotted spoon, remove meat from pan. Add remaining beef and cook until no longer pink; return reserved meat to the skillet and lower heat to medium. Add softened onion and garlic mix, stir, and cook 5 minutes.

3. Stir in chile powder to coat meat, then stir in beer, tomato sauce, cumin, oregano, salt, black pepper, coriander, marjoram, cloves, mustard, and cayenne. Bring to a boil, then lower heat and simmer, covered, until meat is tender, about 1 hour. Add enough beef broth to thin sauce to desired consistency; remove from heat and stir in tequila.

MAKES 6 SERVINGS

Good as Gold Chili, 1986 Winner

༄

Rick Christman, Mobridge, South Dakota

Although beef is the most popular meat for chili, Rick uses chicken, a favorite in South Dakota, for a different yet flavorful twist.

1/3	cup water	1	teaspoon dried oregano, crushed
1/4	cup instant minced onion		
2	teaspoons instant minced garlic	1	teaspoon soy sauce
		1	teaspoon Worcestershire sauce
1/2	cup vegetable oil		
1 1/2	pounds boneless, skinless chicken breast	3/4	teaspoon salt
		1/2	teaspoon paprika
1	can (15 ounces) tomato sauce	1/2	teaspoon cayenne
1/2	can (3/4 cup) beer	1/4	teaspoon turmeric
1/2	cup chicken broth	1/8	teaspoon ground sage
2	tablespoons mild pure chile powder	1/8	teaspoon dried thyme, crushed
2	teaspoons ground cumin	1/8	teaspoon dry mustard

1. In a small cup, combine water, onion, and garlic; set aside to soften, about 10 minutes.

2. In a large skillet, heat oil; add chicken a few pieces at a time and sauté until golden brown, about 5 minutes on each side.

continued

Remove and drain on paper towels. When cool enough to handle, cut into $1/4$-inch dice and set aside.

3. Pour off all but about 2 tablespoons oil from the skillet; add softened onion and garlic and cook, stirring, until golden, about 5 minutes. Add tomato sauce, beer, chicken broth, chile powder, cumin, oregano, soy sauce, Worcestershire sauce, salt, paprika, cayenne, turmeric, sage, thyme, mustard, and chicken; mix well. Bring to a boil, lower heat, and simmer, covered, until sauce thickens, about 20 minutes, stirring occasionally.

MAKES 3 TO 4 SERVINGS

Bischoff's Chili, 1985 winner

Norb Bischoff, Fort Thomas, Kentucky

Norb, who thrives on scuba diving and competing in chili cookoffs, sometimes varies the spices in this intriguing chili. He never uses tarragon and dill in the same batch, as they're both so assertive.

2	tablespoons vegetable oil	$2^1/4$	cups water
1	pound marrow bones	$1/4$	cup instant minced onion
2	pounds beef sirloin, round, or chuck, cut in $1/4$-inch dice	$2^1/2$	tablespoons mild pure chile powder
1	can (29 ounces) tomato sauce	1	tablespoon light brown sugar

1½	teaspoons garlic powder	¼	teaspoon black pepper
1	teaspoon ground cumin	⅛	teaspoon ground allspice
1	teaspoon dried oregano, crushed		pinch of cayenne
¾	teaspoon dried tarragon, crushed	2	bay leaves

1. Heat oil in a large pot and add bones. Brown on all sides for about 5 minutes; remove and set aside.

2. Add ½ of the beef to the same pot and cook until no longer pink. Remove with a slotted spoon to a bowl and repeat with remaining beef.

3. Return reserved beef and bones to the pot and add remaining ingredients. Bring to a boil, lower heat, and simmer 2 hours, stirring occasionally and adding more water if needed. Remove bay leaves and bones before serving.

MAKES 4 SERVINGS

White Lightning Chili, 1984 winner

@

Ron Outten, Saskatchewan, Canada

Outten's past includes careers as a nurse, a corrections officer, and a chef. The champ usually makes this zippy recipe in huge portions, but it's been scaled down here.

2	tablespoons vegetable oil	1	tablespoon ground cumin
1	large green bell pepper, chopped (about 2/3 cup)	2	teaspoons dried oregano
2	stalks celery, chopped (about 1/2 cup)	1 1/2	teaspoons salt
		3/4	teaspoon instant minced garlic
2	pounds lean ground beef	1/2	teaspoon Italian seasoning
1	can (12 ounces) beer	1/2	teaspoon dry mustard
1	can (15 ounces) tomato sauce		pinch of cayenne
1/4	cup instant minced onion	1	bay leaf
3	tablespoons mild pure chile powder	1	tablespoon tequila

1. Heat oil in a chili pot and sauté pepper and celery with beef until vegetables are soft and meat is no longer pink.

2. Stir in beer, tomato sauce, onion, chile powder, cumin, oregano, salt, garlic, Italian seasoning, mustard, cayenne, and bay leaf

and bring to a boil. Lower heat and simmer, covered, about 2 hours, until thickened, adding water if needed. Just before serving, stir in tequila and remove bay leaf.

MAKES 4 SERVINGS

Survival Chili, 1983 winner

Don and Jan Campbell, Washington, D.C.

Don, a lieutenant colonel in the Air Force, developed this recipe while stationed at the Pentagon. He called it survival chili because he kept his chili ingredients in a special kit he called his survival kit.

2   tablespoons vegetable oil
2½ pounds beef chuck, cut in
     ½-inch cubes
1   can (12 ounces) beer
1½ cups water
1   can (8 ounces) whole
     tomatoes, crushed
1   can (8 ounces) tomato sauce
1   can (4 ounces) chopped green
     chiles, undrained
1   small green bell pepper,
     chopped (about ½ cup)

¼   cup instant minced onion
4   teaspoons mild pure chile
     powder
1½ teaspoons ground cumin
1   teaspoon salt
½   teaspoon dried oregano,
     crushed
½   teaspoon instant minced
     garlic
½   teaspoon paprika
½   teaspoon black pepper
pinch of cayenne

continued

1. Heat oil in a large saucepan and add ½ of the meat; sauté until it is no longer pink. Remove with a slotted spoon, set aside, and repeat with remaining meat.

2. Return all meat to the saucepan and add remaining ingredients. Bring to a boil, lower heat, and simmer, uncovered, for 3 hours, stirring occasionally and adding more water if needed.

MAKES 6 SERVINGS

ICS Guru Chili

Wish I had time for one more bowl of chili.

—ALLEGED DYING WORDS OF KIT CARSON

In the land of chili, there is a method to all our madness. Perhaps the best way to explain it is to use the always handy basketball team comparison. If the International Chili Society were a basketball team, the all-time lineup for a "Gurus of the Game" squad would consist of

Center:	*C. V. Wood*
Forwards:	*Carroll Shelby, Robert Petersen*
Guards:	*Jim West, Tom Deemer*
Sixth Man:	*Ormly Gumfudgin*

The first time these guys were together was during the first California State Championship in 1974 at the Balboa Bay Club in

Newport Beach. Maybe not together, but at least they were all there.

Until his death in 1992, Woody was perhaps the most important man in ICS history. Without his uncanny ability to "get it done at all costs," the ICS probably wouldn't exist. While the organization flourished around Woody's efforts, Shelby and Petersen remain the power forwards, always looking for the ball to put in the winning points. And the guys responsible for moving the ball up the floor are West and Deemer, a pair of Newport Beachers. West is the guy who dives for loose balls and goes where not many others would dare to go. Where that is exactly is a secret he refuses to divulge. Nonetheless, West is the guy who has kept the group going for more than twenty years. And as the sixth man, Ormly is the ICS historian, keeper of the keys, so to speak, and teller of tales. In the ICS newspaper, Ormly's "Chili con Carnival" is a compilation of factoids and fictionoids from the chili world. His sign-off? Warmly, Ormly. Warmly, here are the recipes of the Gurus of the Game.

Carroll Shelby, Beverly Hills, California
ICS Board of Governors

A friend once said of Carroll Shelby, "He wants to be the best, and he wants to do it fast." After serving as a flight instructor during World War II, Shelby turned to chicken farming to support his family. In 1951 he woke up to find four thousand chickens dead of limberneck disease. "I decided if I was going to go broke, it might as well be at something I like to do," he says. That turned out to be driving race cars. In his trademark bib overalls and black cowboy hat, Shelby went on to become one of the world's best-known and most successful drivers.

When a heart ailment forced him off the track in 1960, he developed and built the legendary Shelby Cobra, the car that beat Ferrari and won the GT class of the World's Manufacturers' Championship. He also launched dozens of other successful ventures and enterprises, including a cattle-breeding operation, a tire distributorship, and several radio stations. After two open-heart surgeries, Shelby underwent a successful heart transplant operation in 1990 and subsequently started the 'Shelby Heart Fund' to help other transplant patients. Along the way he found time to start the International Chili Society, which has raised more than $40 million for charity through 1994. Although chili, like rocks and rattlesnakes, was part of his life while growing up in Texas, he never paid much attention to it until the cookoffs started.

"I didn't know anyone who didn't like chili," he says. "My mom and daddy both cooked chili and I remember it vividly. They put their own personality into it back then, the way people do now. I cooked chili at home because I enjoyed it, but I didn't get into it until we started putting the cookoffs on [in 1967]." Since then, Shelby has eaten a lot of chili, having attended and judged every World's Championship. Although he says C. V. Wood (page 29) and Truett Airhart (page 120) rank as two of the finest chili cooks he's ever known, Shelby neatly sidesteps the question "What's the best chili you've ever tasted?" with this response: "Actually, I hope I haven't tasted it yet." Actually, we might add, his own chili is right up there.

ICS GURU CHILI

Carroll Shelby's Chili

⁊

8	ounces kidney suet
1	pound round steak, cubed
1	pound chuck, cubed
1	can (8 ounces) tomato sauce
1	can (12 ounces) beer
¼	cup pure hot New Mexico chile powder
3	cloves garlic, minced
1	small onion, minced (about ½ cup)
1	heaping teaspoon dried Mexican oregano
½	teaspoon paprika
1	heaping teaspoon salt
1	teaspoon ground cumin
⅛ to 1	teaspoon cayenne
12	ounces Monterey Jack or goat cheese, shredded
½	teaspoon cuminseeds

1. In a large pot, melt suet over medium heat, then remove any unrendered fat. Stir in meat and cook, stirring frequently, until it loses its reddish color.

2. Stir in tomato sauce, beer, chile powder, garlic, onion, oregano, paprika, salt, and cumin powder. Bring to a boil, then lower heat and simmer, covered, 1 hour.

3. Stir in cayenne to taste, then simmer 2 more hours.

4. Lower heat, then stir in cheese and cuminseeds and simmer very gently for 30 minutes, stirring to make sure the cheese

doesn't scorch. Serve with grated Cheddar cheese, chopped onions, and pinto beans on the side.

¶¶₱ MAKES 4 TO 6 SERVINGS

Jim West, Newport Beach, California
ICS Executive Director

One evening back in 1972, Bill Medley of the Righteous Brothers and Jim West, his manager, were relaxing over a game of eight-ball as they discussed Bill's upcoming six-week gig in Lake Tahoe. Suddenly West looked across the pool table at the singer and blurted, "I can't go with you. I can't handle the road trips anymore." Lifelong friends, the two parted amicably, with West heading back to his roots in Orange County. Soon afterward, he became the entertainment director at the Balboa Bay Club in Newport Beach, an advisory position that left him free to do other things, like stage rodeo events with Larry Mahan and promote rock concerts in the area.

The BBC became the site for the California Chili Cookoff two years later, and when Carroll Shelby and C. V. Wood decided they needed some help in managing the burgeoning world of chili cookoffs, they naturally turned to West, who was hired in 1976 as the executive director of the ICS. Working with sponsors such as Pepsi and Hunt-Wesson, West and the rest of the board of governors were able to put the ICS on a path that would enable cookoffs

ICS GURU CHILI

to raise millions of dollars for charities around the country—and allow the participants to have a lot of fun doing so.

"That's the whole point," says West. "It's not so much about who makes the best chili, but who has the most fun. The guy with the fake arrow stuck through his head is more what we're about than the guy trying to make a perfect bowl of red."

Jim West's Texas Range Chili

4 pounds tri-tip, cut in ³/₈-inch cubes

2 large sweet onions, diced

6 cloves garlic, minced

4 tablespoons ground cumin

20 tablespoons (1¹/₄ cups) commercial chili powder, Gebhardt's brand preferred

2 cans (13³/₄ ounces each) chicken broth

1¹/₂ teaspoons dried oregano

2 tablespoons paprika

1 tablespoon brown sugar

1 can (4 ounces) diced green chiles, drained

1 can (15 ounces) tomato sauce, Hunt's brand preferred

1 tablespoon cider vinegar

1 cup water

salt to taste

1. Working in batches, cook tri-tip in a large skillet along with onions, ¹/₂ of the garlic, and 2 tablespoons cumin until meat is no longer pink. Stir in 10 tablespoons chili powder and let simmer for 30 to 40 minutes.

2. Meanwhile, in a chili pot, combine chicken broth, remaining garlic, remaining 2 tablespoons cumin, remaining 10 tablespoons chili powder, oregano, paprika, brown sugar, chiles, tomato sauce, cider vinegar, and water. Bring to a boil, then lower heat and simmer 30 minutes.

3. Add meat to sauce and simmer 1 hour, stirring occasionally. Add salt to taste and adjust consistency with water or, if thickening is needed, with a little arrowroot. If heat needs a boost, add 2 tablespoons chili powder mixed with water as a paste. Be HUMBLE when you serve this chili!

MAKES 8 TO 10 SERVINGS

Robert "Pete" Petersen, Beverly Hills, California
ICS Board of Governors

In 1948 Petersen published the first issue of *Hot Rod* with a press run of five thousand. From that beginning, he became the world's leading publisher of special-interest consumer magazines and books. He is founder and chairman of the board of Petersen Publishing Company, which is headquartered in Los Angeles and has offices in New York, Detroit, Chicago, Atlanta, Denver, and Dallas and publishes *Motor Trend, Guns and Ammo, Golfing, 'Teen, Pro Football, Sport,* and more than seventy other titles.

In June 1994, Petersen opened the Petersen Automotive Museum, a 300,000-square-foot museum that celebrates the automobile. Located on the corner of Wilshire and Fairfax, it is the premiere automotive museum of its type and is administered by the Natural History Museum of Los Angeles County. Involved with numerous civic and charitable affairs, Petersen, who also owns Petersen Aviation, was the shooting sports commissioner at the 1984 Los Angeles Olympics and developed a world-class shooting facility out of a dairy farm in Chino, California, in less than six months. After the Olympics he got the venue donated to the county of San Bernardino and now operates Petersen's Prado Tiro Olympic Shooting Park.

Because of his great love for cooking, and through his friendship with Carroll Shelby, Tom Deemer, Bill Ray, and C. V. Wood, Petersen and his wife, Margie, became involved with the International Chili Society. Their presence graces ICS cookoffs throughout California, and his presence on the board of governors ensures that the organization will continue to raise millions for charity well into the 21st century.

Petersen's Hot Rod Chili

〰

4	pounds London broil, cubed		salt and black pepper to taste
2	tablespoons olive oil	1	can (15 ounces) tomato sauce,
2	large Maui onions, chopped		Hunt's brand preferred
	(2 cups)		juice of 1 lime
4	teaspoons minced garlic	1	teaspoon Tabasco sauce
1	cup commercial chili powder,	1	can (12 ounces) beer
	Gebhardt's brand preferred	2	cans ($13^3/_4$ ounces each) beef
2	tablespoons ground cumin		broth
$1^1/_2$	teaspoons paprika	1	can (18 ounces) green chiles,
$^1/_2$	teaspoon dried oregano		drained and minced

1. Heat oil in a large skillet, add beef, 1 cup onions, and 2 teaspoons garlic, and sauté until meat is no longer pink. Stir in $^1/_2$ cup chili powder, 1 teaspoon cumin, $^1/_2$ teaspoon paprika, the oregano, salt, and black pepper. Simmer over low heat for 30 minutes.

2. Meanwhile, in a large pot, combine tomato sauce, lime juice, Tabasco, beer, and $1^1/_2$ cans beef broth. Stir in remaining 1 cup onion, 2 teaspoons garlic, $^1/_2$ cup chili powder, 1 tablespoon cumin, and 1 teaspoon paprika. Simmer 30 minutes.

continued

3. Stir meat mixture into sauce and add green chiles. Stir well, bring to a boil, then lower heat and simmer, partially covered, 2 hours, adding remaining beef broth if necessary. Adjust seasonings, serve, and ENJOY!

¶¶ MAKES 8 TO 10 SERVINGS

Ormly Gumfudgin, La Crescenta, California
ICS Official Historian

In the fall of 1967, Ormly was quietly working as the recreation director for a firm of aerospace engineers and writing a column titled "Warmly, Ormly" when he got a call from a family friend. On the other end of the line was Carroll Shelby, who asked, "Wanna go to a chili cookoff?" Ormly (born Clarence Forman) had never heard of a chili cookoff but, being the amicable sort that he is, readily agreed. "I knew if I went to Texas with Carroll Shelby, I'd have something to write about in my newspaper column," he says. He was right.

That long weekend in Terlingua changed Ormly's life. "I was forty-five years old then, and now I'm practically seventy-two," he says. "And I've been writing about chili ever since." After the ICS became an actual entity in the mid-1970s, Ormly was appointed official historian of the society and began writing a regular column for the ICS newspaper. Tall and lean, with a distinctive white beard, he makes a special point to attend any and all cookoffs to which he is invited, and with his stovepipe hat covered with chili pins, he is an unmistakable figure. He's even more unmistakable if he brings along his bazooka (the instrument, not the weapon) and gets into a spoon-playing duet with Jim Parker of the Hard Times Cafe. So distinctive is his appearance, in fact, that he was selected as the chili poster boy when Pepto-Bismol started a campaign to make chili the official food of the United States, appearing in full cookoff regalia in front of the Capitol building on a Pepto-pink background.

"Every time we have a cookoff, it's more like a family reunion than any recreation of which I'm aware," he says. "The most intriguing chiliheads I know are Carroll Shelby for No. 1, followed by the rest of the crew—Roy Palmer, Burck Smith, Father Duffy, Fred Wieland, Harry Coleman, and my good buddy Madeline Sophie Gary, who just keeps cooking in spite of all the reverses she's suffered in life."

One of the highlights of Ormly's chili career was being selected to represent the state of California in the 1971 cookoff at Terlingua, to which he toted marinated antelope meat all the way from Los Angeles to Texas in a Tupperware container. Ormly thoughtfully included vitamins to help fight smog (although why he thought that was necessary in Terlingua, Texas, remains a complete mystery), and threw in some water chestnuts and dried mushrooms along with various Mexican ingredients to honor the ethnic groups that helped win the West. This prompted Shelby to call it "Chinese stew," claiming it bore as much resemblance to real chili as a goat does to a Brahman bull, but Ormly says his assistant, astronaut Scott Carpenter, and Shelby's two boys, Pat and Mike, loved it.

ICS GURU CHILI

Ormly's California Frontier Survival Chili

〜

safflower oil

5   pounds western antelope (or beef), cut in small cubes and marinated overnight in red wine

4   cloves garlic, minced

2   Bermuda onions, chopped (about 2 cups)

2   green bell peppers, chopped (about 1 cup)

2   small stalks celery, chopped (about ½ cup)

5   tablespoons salsa brava or any hot salsa

2   cans (12 ounces each) beer

1   cup sliced water chestnuts

large handful sliced Oriental mushrooms

2   cups canned small white onions, drained

½   teaspoon salt

1   teaspoon commercial chili powder

1   tablespoon freshly ground black pepper

2   teaspoons ground cumin

2   teaspoons dried oregano

2   teaspoons dried woodruff

½   cup wheat germ

½   cup dried kelp

2   capsules vitamin A

2   capsules vitamin E

2   capsules omega-3

2   tablespoons masa harina, made into a paste with a little water

1   pound Mexican cheese, grated (about 4 cups)

1. Cover the bottom of a large chili pot with safflower oil and set over medium heat. Add drained meat and cook about 15 minutes, until no longer pink. Add garlic, onions, bell peppers, and celery and cook another 20 minutes over low heat, until vegetables are softened.

2. Stir in 3 tablespoons salsa brava, wait a few minutes, then stir in beer, water chestnuts, mushrooms, small onions, salt, chili powder, black pepper, cumin, oregano, woodruff, wheat germ, and kelp; simmer 30 minutes. Add remaining 2 tablespoons salsa brava and simmer 2 hours, adding spring water if necessary.

3. Add vitamins and masa harina and stir like hell. Five minutes before serving, lace the cheese over the top and serve with a stoned wheat wafer. Minimum cooking time is 3 hours, but it's even better if you let it simmer all day.

⫙ MAKES 10 SERVINGS

Tom Deemer, Newport Beach, California
ICS Board of Governors

A close friend of the late Billy Martin, Tom Deemer is a past president of the Balboa Bay Club and one of the driving forces behind its longtime involvement with the International Chili Society.

Now retired as president of a local bank, he is best known in Orange County chili circles for having once assembled the largest

ICS GURU CHILI

chili-cooking team on the planet. In 1974, at the inaugural California State Championship at the BBC, Deemer collected 250 wannabe chiliheads at his bank and proceeded to march them down the main drag of the upscale oceanfront community toward the cookoff site by the club pool. The chief of police, a friend of Deemer's, happened by and mistakenly assumed there was some kind of radical protest march going on. As the marchers surrounded his car, he rolled up his windows and threatened to call in reinforcements and have Deemer arrested if they didn't start behaving in a more civilized fashion. They did and Deemer escaped incarceration.

An avid golfer and sports fanatic, Deemer converted the top floor of his mountainside home into a sports bar where he and buddies can be found watching *Monday Night Football*, drinking beer, and eating chili. His recipe follows.

Deemer's Sports Bar Demolition Chili

❧

1	pound bulk sausage	4 to 6	cloves garlic
2	pounds ground pork		kosher salt
3	large red onions, diced (about 4 cups)	1	can ($10^{1}/_{2}$ ounces) beef bouillon
3	pounds coarsely ground chuck	1	can (28 ounces) crushed tomatoes
$^{1}/_{2}$	cup mild pure chile powder	1	can (28 ounces) tomato puree
3	tablespoons ground cumin	1	tablespoon Worcestershire sauce
2	tablespoons dried oregano	1	teaspoon Tabasco sauce
2	tablespoons mole powder		pinch of monosodium glutamate
1	can (7 ounces) whole jalapeño peppers, stemmed, seeded, and minced (if available, use jalapeños marinated with oil and carrots)	1	ounce Mexican chocolate, grated, or 2 tablespoons Dutch process cocoa powder
			juice of 1 lime

1. In a large, thick-bottomed pot sauté sausage, pork, and onions until onions are translucent, stirring frequently to prevent scorching.

continued

2. Add beef and cook until no longer pink. Stir in chile powder, cumin, oregano, mole powder, and jalapeños.

3. Mince garlic cloves with about 1 heaping teaspoon salt to produce 2 tablespoons garlic-salt mixture. Add to meat and stir well.

4. Add bouillon, crushed tomatoes, tomato puree, Worcestershire sauce, Tabasco, and MSG and stir well. Bring to a slow boil, lower heat, and simmer, partially covered, 4 hours, adding water if necessary.

5. About 30 minutes before serving, mix chocolate or cocoa with lime juice and stir into chili. Adjust seasonings and simmer another 30 minutes.

🍴 MAKES 20 SERVINGS

ICS GURU CHILI

Chili Appreciation Society International (CASI) Chili

Any man that eats chili can't be all bad.
—Pat Garrett

George Haddaway, an airline man who was the editor of *Flight*, started the Chili Appreciation Society in 1951 with the stated purpose of improving the quality of chili in restaurants and spreading the word about Texas chili throughout the known universe. The original "chili" pod was formed in Dallas, where members would meet over a chili-themed lunch (jalapeño salad, chili, jalapeño corn bread, and so on) on a monthly basis. Wick Fowler, who once cooked chili for the troops in Vietnam, was the Chief Chili Cook for the Society, which sent out "approved" recipes to those in need of a real bowl of red.

It was these fun-loving types who sent Fowler up against H. Allen Smith in the original cookoff at Terlingua in 1967, and all things remained harmonious until 1974, when Frank Tolbert got annoyed at Carroll Shelby and C. V. Wood and booted the Californians out of the Society. CASI (the International was added after pods formed overseas) continued to hold an annual cookoff at Terlingua, with contestants accumulating points at approved cookoffs, but because the ICS had trademarked "World's Championship Chili Cookoff," they had to call their cookoff the "CASI Terlingua International Chili Championship."

In 1982 Tolbert got annoyed again, this time at the CASI officials who wouldn't let two European friends of his cook because they hadn't qualified. The next year Tolbert started his own cookoff in Terlingua on the same day as the CASI in memory of Wick Fowler. The cookoff continued after Tolbert died in 1984 and is called "The Original Viva Terlingua International Frank X. Tolbert-Wick Fowler Memorial Championship Chili Cookoff."

Despite the schism, the cookoff in Terlingua (the CASI TICC) remains "the Big One" to the multitude of chiliheads just north of the border down in Texas. Here are the championship recipes from that arid patch of land that no one ever heard of before 1967.

Jim's Chili

International Chili Championship
1994, Terlingua, Texas
Jim Hedrick, Roanoke, Virginia

Jim's secret ingredient, never before used in Terlingua, was a brand-new baseball cap. "The other kept blowing off in the wind on Friday, so I bought a new one," he explained. A native Virginian and lifelong chilihead, Hedrick is an assistant manager with the Norfolk Southern Corporation. He began cooking chili competitively in a local cookoff in 1991 after his daughter, Nikki, came in one day and said either start cooking or quit talking about it. He first qualified to cook in Terlingua in 1993, and, much to his surprise, won the whole thing the next year.

SPICE MIX #1:

3 tablespoons commercial chili powder

$\frac{1}{2}$ teaspoon black pepper

$\frac{1}{2}$ teaspoon white pepper

$\frac{1}{2}$ teaspoon ground cumin

$\frac{1}{2}$ teaspoon garlic powder

SPICE MIX #2:

3 tablespoons mild pure chile powder

1 tablespoon commercial Texas-style chili powder, McCormick's brand preferred

1 tablespoon cumin

1 teaspoon garlic powder

SPICE MIX #3:

2 tablespoons mild pure New Mexico chile powder

1 tablespoon cumin

CHILI:

3 pounds chuck, cut in small cubes

$\frac{1}{2}$ pound pork, ground

1 cup beef broth

1 cup chicken broth

1 can (8 ounces) tomato sauce, divided

1 can (4 ounces) mild green chiles, drained, seeded, deveined, and pureed

1 jalapeño pepper, seeded, deveined, and minced

1 teaspoon Tabasco sauce

1 teaspoon vegetable shortening

salt and black pepper to taste

continued

CHILI APPRECIATION SOCIETY INTERNATIONAL (CASI) CHILI

1. Combine spice mixtures in 3 separate containers, and set aside. In a nonstick skillet, cook chuck and pork until no longer pink. Drain off fat, and transfer meat to a chili pot. Add beef broth, chicken broth, $\frac{1}{2}$ cup tomato sauce, pureed chiles, jalapeño pepper and Spice Mix #1. Bring to a boil, lower heat, and simmer for $1\frac{1}{2}$ hours.

2. Using a little cooking liquid from the chili, make a paste of Spice Mix #2 and add to chili along with the remaining $\frac{1}{2}$ cup tomato sauce and the Tabasco sauce. Simmer 30 minutes.

3. Mix vegetable shortening with Spice Mix #3; add to chili and simmer another 30 minutes.

4. About 10 minutes before serving, correct seasoning with salt and pepper. Start drinking, and PARTY!

MAKES 8 SERVINGS

Cin-Chili Chili

International Chili Championship
1992 and 1993, Terlingua, Texas
Cindy Reed, Houston, Texas

Cindy is the first person, male or female, ever to win back-to-back titles at Terlingua. She had the lineage, though—her mother was the 1988 champion and her dad took second place the same year. The name of her chili team? Chili Dynasty, of course. Here is her "secret" recipe, the secret of which is, there is no secret. "Everyone cooks the same basic recipe," she explains. Here is her winning chili (different from the ICS-style chili), followed by those of other past Terlingua champions.

SPICE MIX #1:

1 tablespoon pure ancho or pasilla chile powder

2 teaspoons garlic powder

SPICE MIX #2:

1 tablespoon onion powder

1 tablespoon pure ancho or pasilla chile powder

2 teaspoons garlic powder

1 teaspoon instant chicken bouillon granules

1 teaspoon jalapeño powder

1 teaspoon white pepper

½ teaspoon cayenne

¼ teaspoon dried oregano

SPICE MIX #3:

5 tablespoons mixed New Mexico and ancho or pasilla chile powders

1 tablespoon paprika

1 packet Sazon seasoning (Goya brand) or 1½ teaspoons monosodium glutamate

1 teaspoon onion powder

continued

CHILI APPRECIATION SOCIETY INTERNATIONAL (CASI) CHILI

1	teaspoon garlic powder
1/2	teaspoon white pepper

SPICE MIX #4:

2	teaspoons ground cumin
1/8	teaspoon salt

CHILI:

cooking oil

2	pounds beef tender (chuck), cut in 3/8-inch cubes
1	can (8 ounces) tomato sauce
1	can (13 3/4 ounces) beef broth
3	cups spring water
2	whole serrano peppers

1. Combine spice mixtures in 4 separate containers and set aside.

2. In a heavy saucepan, heat oil and sauté beef until no longer pink. As meat cooks, sprinkle with Spice Mix #1.

3. In a bowl, combine tomato sauce, beef broth, and water with Spice Mix #2. Stir into beef and bring to a boil, then lower heat and let simmer for 1 1/2 hours with serrano peppers floating on top.

4. Stir Spice Mix #3 into chili, bring to a boil, lower heat, and simmer 20 minutes. Remove serranos when they are softened.

5. Add Spice Mix #4 and simmer for 10 more minutes.

MAKES 4 SERVINGS

Out-of-Sight Chili

International Chili Championship
1991, Terlingua, Texas
Doris Coats, Irving, Texas

SPICE MIX #1:

2   teaspoons onion powder

2   teaspoons garlic powder

1   teaspoon instant beef bouillon
    granules

1   teaspoon instant chicken
    bouillon granules

SPICE MIX #2:

2   tablespoons commercial hot
    chili powder, McCormick's
    Mexican-style preferred

2   tablespoons commercial
    Texas-style chili powder,
    McCormick's brand
    preferred

2   teaspoons ground cumin

½   teaspoon cayenne

½   teaspoon salt

½   teaspoon seasoned salt

½   teaspoon onion powder

¼   teaspoon white pepper

SPICE MIX #3:

2   tablespoons commercial chili
    powder

2   teaspoons paprika

¼   teaspoon salt

CHILI:

1   teaspoon solid vegetable
    shortening

2½ pounds chuck, cut in ⅜-inch
    cubes

1   can (13¾ ounces) beef broth

1   can (8 ounces) tomato sauce

1   cup water

continued

CHILI APPRECIATION SOCIETY INTERNATIONAL (CASI) CHILI

1. Combine spice mixes in 3 separate containers. Set aside.

2. Heat shortening in chili pot and add beef. Cook, stirring, until meat is no longer pink. Add Spice Mix #1, beef broth, tomato sauce, and water and cook, covered, over medium heat for 30 minutes.

3. Stir in Spice Mix #2 and bring to a rapid boil, stirring. Lower heat, cover, and simmer 45 minutes, adding water as necessary to keep liquid 1 inch above meat.

4. Stir in Spice Mix #3, lower heat a notch, cover, and simmer 30 minutes. Serve and enjoy with sides of pinto beans, chopped onions, and grated Cheddar cheese for a customized bowl of Texas red.

🍴 MAKES 4 TO 6 SERVINGS

Hi-Octane Chili

International Chili Championship
1990, Terlingua, Texas
Jerry Hunt, Shreveport, Louisiana

SPICE MIX #1:

1/4 cup instant minced onion

2 tablespoons pure mild chile powder

2 teaspoons instant beef bouillon granules

2 teaspoons instant chicken bouillon granules

1 teaspoon garlic powder

1/2 teaspoon monosodium glutamate

1 packet Sazon seasoning (Goya brand)

SPICE MIX #2:

1/4 cup pure mild chile powder

1 tablespoon ground cumin

1 tablespoon paprika

1 teaspoon salt

1 packet Sazon seasoning (Goya brand)

1/2 teaspoon black pepper

1/2 teaspoon onion powder

1/2 teaspoon garlic salt

1/2 teaspoon white pepper

SPICE MIX #3:

3 tablespoons pure chile powder

1 teaspoon ground cumin

1/4 teaspoon cayenne

CHILI:

1 tablespoon vegetable oil

3 pounds chuck, cut in 3/8-inch cubes

1 can (13 3/4 ounces) beef broth

1 can (8 ounces) tomato sauce

2 teaspoons jalapeño sauce

continued

CHILI APPRECIATION SOCIETY INTERNATIONAL (CASI) CHILI

1. Combine spice mixes in 3 separate containers and set aside.

2. Heat oil in a chili pot over medium heat and sauté meat until no longer pink. Stir in Spice Mix #1, beef broth, tomato sauce, jalapeño sauce, and water, if needed, to cover meat. Simmer, covered, 1 hour.

3. Stir in Spice Mix #2 and simmer another 45 minutes to 1 hour.

4. Add Spice Mix #3 and cook another 20 to 30 minutes, or until meat is tender.

MAKES 6 SERVINGS

Yahoo Chili

∾

International Chili Championship
1989, Terlingua, Texas
Barbara Britton, Mesquite, Texas

SPICE MIX #1:

2　tablespoons commercial Texas-style chili powder, McCormick's brand preferred

1　tablespoon hot pure chile powder

1　tablespoon onion powder

2　teaspoons instant beef bouillon granules

1　teaspoon instant chicken bouillon granules

1/2　teaspoon salt

1/2　teaspoon cayenne

SPICE MIX #2:

3　tablespoons commercial Texas-style chili powder, McCormick's brand preferred

1　tablespoon ground cumin

2　teaspoons garlic powder

1/4　teaspoon black pepper

SPICE MIX #3:

1　tablespoon hot pure chile powder

1　teaspoon ground cumin

1/2　teaspoon salt

1/2　teaspoon onion powder

1/8　teaspoon cayenne

CHILI:

1　teaspoon solid vegetable shortening

2 1/2　pounds beef chuck, mock tender, or round, cut in 1/2-inch cubes

1　can (8 ounces) no-salt tomato sauce

1　can (13 3/4 ounces) beef broth

2 1/2　cups water

continued

CHILI APPRECIATION SOCIETY INTERNATIONAL (CASI) CHILI

1. Combine spice mixes in 3 separate containers. Set aside.

2. In a 5-quart Dutch oven, heat shortening over medium heat and cook beef until no longer pink. Add tomato sauce, beef broth, and water and stir. Add Spice Mix #1, bring to a boil, lower heat, and simmer $1^3/_4$ hours.

3. Stir in Spice Mix #2 and simmer 30 minutes.

4. Stir in Spice Mix #3 and simmer 15 minutes.

🍴 MAKES 6 SERVINGS

Lynn's Chili

∞

International Chili Championship
1988, Terlingua, Texas
Lynn Hejtmancik, Marble Falls, Texas

SPICE MIX #1:

1 tablespoon paprika

1 tablespoon onion powder

2 teaspoons garlic powder

1/2 teaspoon white pepper

1/2 teaspoon black pepper

SPICE MIX #2:

1/4 cup no-salt added commercial chili powder

2 tablespoons commercial hot chili powder, McCormick's Mexican-style preferred

1 tablespoon ground cumin

1 teaspoon monosodium glutamate (optional)

1/2 teaspoon brown sugar

1/4 teaspoon dried oregano

CHILI:

3 pounds beef, cut in 3/8-inch cubes

3 tablespoons solid vegetable shortening

1 can (13 3/4 ounces) beef broth

2 beef bouillon cubes (or 2 teaspoons instant beef bouillon granules)

1 chicken bouillon cube (or 1 teaspoon instant chicken bouillon granules)

2 tablespoons plus 1 teaspoon jalapeño sauce

water

1 can (8 ounces) tomato sauce

flour or arrowroot

continued

CHILI APPRECIATION SOCIETY INTERNATIONAL (CASI) CHILI

1. Combine spice mixes in 2 separate containers. Set aside.

2. Add Spice Mix #1 to meat and mix well. Heat shortening in a chili pot over medium-high heat, add beef, and cook, stirring constantly, until meat is no longer pink. Stir in beef broth, bouillon cubes, and 2 tablespoons jalapeño sauce and add enough water to cover by an inch. Bring to a boil, lower heat, and simmer 2 hours, stirring every 10 minutes.

3. When meat is tender, skim off fat and stir in Spice Mix #2 along with tomato sauce and 1 teaspoon jalapeño sauce. Bring to a boil, taste, and simmer an additional 45 minutes.

4. About 10 minutes before serving, taste and adjust seasonings with salt, garlic, cayenne, and chili powder. If chili is too thin, mix a little flour or arrowroot with water to make a paste, add to chili, and simmer another 10 minutes.

MAKES 6 SERVINGS

Fat Dog Chili

❧

International Chili Championship
1987, Terlingua, Texas
David Henson, Mesquite, Texas

SPICE MIX #1:

3 tablespoons mild pure chile powder

1 tablespoon instant beef bouillon granules

2 teaspoons ground cumin

½ teaspoon cayenne

½ teaspoon instant chicken bouillon granules

¼ teaspoon crushed bay leaves

¼ teaspoon dried oregano

1 packet Sazon seasoning (Goya brand)

½ teaspoon salt

SPICE MIX #2:

3 tablespoons commercial chili powder

2 teaspoons ground cumin

½ teaspoon garlic powder

½ teaspoon monosodium glutamate

¼ teaspoon cayenne

⅛ teaspoon black pepper

⅛ teaspoon jalapeño powder

SPICE MIX #3:

2 tablespoons mild pure chile powder

1 teaspoon ground cumin

½ teaspoon garlic powder

½ teaspoon onion powder

CHILI:

½ small onion, minced (about 4½ tablespoons)

1 small clove garlic, minced

½ teaspoon salt

2 tablespoons solid vegetable shortening

2½ pounds beef, cut in ⅜-inch cubes

1 can (13¾ ounces) beef broth

1 can (8 ounces) tomato sauce

continued

CHILI APPRECIATION SOCIETY INTERNATIONAL (CASI) CHILI

1. Combine spice mixes in 3 separate containers. Set aside.

2. Grind or finely chop onion and garlic together with salt and set aside. Heat shortening in a large chili pot and brown beef, adding onion mixture as meat cooks. Stir in beef broth, Spice Mix #1, and $\frac{1}{2}$ can tomato sauce. Simmer 1 hour.

3. Stir in Spice Mix #2 along with remaining tomato sauce and simmer 30 minutes.

4. Add Spice Mix #3 and simmer an additional 20 minutes.

¶¶¶ MAKES 6 SERVINGS

Bobby's Chili

∽∾

International Chili Championship
1986, Terlingua, Texas
Bobby Aldridge, Shreveport, Louisiana

SPICE MIX #1:

1	tablespoon onion powder
1	tablespoon paprika
2	teaspoons garlic powder
2	teaspoons instant beef bouillon granules
1	teaspoon instant chicken bouillon granules
$^1/_2$	teaspoon cayenne
$^1/_4$	teaspoon black pepper
$^1/_2$	teaspoon monosodium glutamate (optional)

SPICE MIX #2:

5	tablespoons commercial chili powder, Gebhardt's brand preferred
1	tablespoon ground cumin
$^1/_4$	teaspoon white pepper

SPICE MIX #3:

$^3/_4$	teaspoon commercial chili powder, Gebhardt's brand preferred
1	teaspoon ground cumin
1	teaspoon garlic salt
1	teaspoon onion salt
$^1/_4$	teaspoon cayenne

CHILI:

2	teaspoons vegetable oil
3	pounds beef, cut in $^1/_4$- to $^1/_2$-inch cubes or coarsely ground
1	can (14$^1/_2$ ounces) beef broth, Swanson's brand preferred
	water
1	can (8 ounces) salt-free tomato sauce

continued

1. Combine spice mixes in 3 separate containers. Set aside.

2. In a chili pot, heat oil and cook meat over medium heat until no longer pink. Drain off fat. Add broth and 1 soup can of water, bring to a boil, and simmer 15 minutes. Add Spice Mix #1 and cook, stirring, for 45 minutes to 1 hour, stirring occasionally.

3. Stir in Spice Mix #2 and cook another 30 to 45 minutes, or until meat is tender.

4. About 15 minutes before serving, stir in Spice Mix #3 and simmer another 15 minutes.

MAKES 6 SERVINGS

Sporting Chili

Hey, wouldn't a hot bowl of chili go great right now?

—Astronaut Tom Stafford during
the 1975 *Apollo-Soyuz* linkup

Everyone knows that chili and sports go together like, well, chili and sports. What's a Super Bowl without chili? A Super Bowl without chili, that's what! From baseball to hockey, football to horse racing, basketball to professional wrestling (we are serious), these hot and hearty recipes are guaranteed, Joe Namath–style, to make any sporting event a memorable one, even if your team loses. Just ask those four-time Super Bowl losers, the Buffalo Bills, whose fans just love chili tailgate parties. While we had many more to choose from, the following recipes were rated the best by our panel of chili-tasting sports freaks.

Jimmy Johnson's Chili

This recipe comes from John Allen of Allen's Drug Store in Miami, Florida, near the campus of the University of Miami.

Jimmy Johnson was born and raised in Texas, played college football in Arkansas, coached at Oklahoma State and Miami, and then led the Dallas Cowboys to Super Bowl victories in 1992 and 1993. A true Texas chilihead, yes? Well, Jimmy swears by this Florida recipe, and he actually may have quit the Cowboys to temporarily reside in the Keys because he likes it so much. Perhaps his boat, Three Rings, *is moving up the intercoastal to Allen's now. Yeah, that's the ticket.*

5   pounds ground beef
2/3 cup commercial chili powder
1/4 cup crushed red pepper flakes
1   green bell pepper, finely chopped (about 2/3 cup)
1   small onion, finely chopped (about 1/2 cup)

3   cans (6 ounces each) tomato paste
3   cups tomato juice
2 to 3 cans (16 ounces each) red kidney beans, drained

1. In a large chili pot over medium-high heat, cook beef, stirring frequently, until no longer pink. Drain off fat. Stir in chili powder, red pepper flakes, green pepper, onion, tomato paste, and tomato juice and bring to a boil, then lower heat and simmer 1 hour.

2. Correct seasonings and add beans just long enough before serving to heat through.

MAKES 16 SERVINGS

Mother Staub's Chili

Rusty Staub, Le Grand Orange if you will, played right field and first base for the Montreal Expos and New York Mets, but he is just as well known for his culinary talents as the owner of Rusty's on Fifth in New York City. Of course, he took the plunge into chefdom only after growing up on Mom's bowl of red. The redhead is an announcer for the Mets and hosts a cable TV show, At the Plate.

2	jalapeño peppers	2	cups tomato puree
1	tablespoon olive oil	1	guajillo pepper, chopped fine
1	medium Spanish onion, diced (about ³/₄ cup)	1	can (16 ounces) dark red kidney beans, drained and rinsed
1	large green bell pepper, diced (about 1 cup)	10	ounces andouille sausage, grilled and diced
1	large red bell pepper, diced (about 1 cup)	2	scallions, white part only, chopped
2½	pounds lean ground beef	1	tablespoon chopped fresh cilantro
1	large clove garlic, minced		salt and black pepper to taste
1	tablespoon crushed red pepper flakes (chile caribe)		shredded Cheddar cheese and sour cream, for garnish
½	teaspoon cayenne		
1½	cups tomato sauce		

1. Under a flame broiler, roast jalapeños 6 inches from the flame, turning frequently with tongs, until their skins blacken and

continued

blister. Wrap in paper towels and let cool. Peel off skins, remove seeds, and chop fine. Set aside.

2. Heat olive oil in a heavy 6-quart pot over medium heat, add onion and green and red peppers, and sauté until onion is translucent.

3. Add ground beef and cook until no longer pink. Drain off fat from the meat mixture in a colander and set aside.

4. In the same pot, sauté garlic, red pepper flakes, and cayenne for 2 minutes. Add ground beef mixture and stir to combine. Add tomato sauce, tomato puree, roasted jalapeños, guajillo pepper, beans, and sausage. Lower heat and simmer 40 minutes.

5. Add scallions and cilantro and simmer another 5 minutes.

6. Salt and pepper to taste and serve garnished with shredded cheese and sour cream.

MAKES 8 TO 10 SERVINGS

Jockey Julie Krone's Lentil Chili

Simply put, Julie Krone is a superstar in the horse-racing world. She's won more races than any other woman—and many men, too—with her crowning achievement a victory in the 1993 Belmont Stakes aboard Colonial Affair. Since Julie has to watch her weight, as do all jockeys, she came up with this concoction that should please vegetarians everywhere.

4   cups dried lentils, washed and drained

6   cups water

4   large ripe tomatoes, peeled and chopped

2   cups finely chopped red Bermuda onion

12   (yes, 12) cloves garlic, minced

3 to 6 tablespoons mild pure chile powder

2   teaspoons ground cumin

2   teaspoons minced fresh thyme (or $\frac{1}{2}$ teaspoon dried)

2   teaspoons minced fresh parsley (or $\frac{1}{2}$ teaspoon dried)

1   teaspoon paprika

6   tablespoons tomato paste

2   teaspoons sea salt

plenty of freshly ground black pepper

2   tablespoons balsamic vinegar

crushed red pepper flakes to taste

shredded New York State Cheddar cheese, for garnish (optional)

1.   In a large pot, bring lentils and 6 cups water to a boil, then partially cover and simmer for 30 minutes.

continued

2. Stir in tomatoes, onion, garlic, chile powder, cumin, thyme, parsley, and paprika. Partially cover and cook for 1 hour, stirring occasionally and adding water as needed to keep the chili from drying out.

3. Stir in tomato paste, sea salt, and black pepper. Cover and simmer for another 30 minutes, or until lentils are soft.

4. Stir in balsamic vinegar and red pepper flakes and simmer another 10 minutes.

5. Serve garnished with grated cheese if desired.

MAKES 8 SERVINGS

Chili to Give the Devil His Due

Devil His Due has won more than $3.5 million in his racing career, but his owner, Edith Libutti of Mahwah, New Jersey, is just as proud of her mom's chili. Edie is always up for a good bowl of red, as witnessed by her participation as a judge and supporter of the Belmont Stakes and Saratoga Regional chili cookoffs. Just ask the cooks about her People's Choice award!

½ cup cooking oil or rendered
   pork fatback

3 scallions, chopped

3 green bell peppers, chopped
   (about 2 cups)

6 large cloves garlic, minced

2 pounds sirloin, diced

1 or 2 large cans (28 ounces each)
   Italian-style plum tomatoes

1 can (6 ounces) tomato paste

2 to 10 tablespoons mild pure
   chile powder (start off easy
   and add more)

1 tablespoon sugar

1 tablespoon paprika

3 bay leaves

2 teaspoons dried basil

1 teaspoon ground cumin

cayenne, salt, black pepper to taste

1 can (15 ounces) kidney beans,
   drained

chopped raw onion, for garnish

1. In a medium skillet, heat oil or fatback; add scallions, peppers, and garlic and sauté until soft. Drain off fat.

2. At the same time, in a large pot, brown sirloin over medium heat, stirring frequently.

3. Drain off fat, stir in onions and peppers, and return to the heat.

4. Add tomatoes, tomato paste, chile powder, sugar, paprika, bay leaves, basil, cumin, cayenne, salt, and pepper, stirring to mix. Simmer 1 hour.

5. Add kidney beans if desired, and simmer 10 more minutes. Serve topped with chopped raw onion.

MAKES 4 TO 6 SERVINGS

SPORTING CHILI

Steve Spurrier's Chili

We know what you're thinking—no, this isn't Gator bait. The football coach at the University of Florida and his wife, Jerri, host several parties during the year, and the theme is the same each time—chili, chili, and more chili. We present the coach's recipe.

3   pounds ground beef

2   large onions, chopped (about 2 cups)

1   green bell pepper, chopped (about ³/₄ cup)

1   red bell pepper, chopped (about ³/₄ cup)

1   can (6 ounces) tomato paste

2   cans (15 ounces each) stewed tomatoes

3   tablespoons Worcestershire sauce

8   tablespoons commercial chili powder

3   tablespoons mild pure chile powder

1   tablespoon sugar

salt, black pepper, monosodium glutamate to taste

1   can (16 ounces) red kidney beans, drained

2   cans (16 ounces each) chili beans, undrained

chopped scallions and grated Cheddar cheese, for garnish

1.   In a large pot over medium-high heat, sauté beef along with onions, green pepper, and red pepper until meat loses its pink color.

2. Drain off most of the fat and add tomato paste, stewed tomatoes, Worcestershire sauce, chili and chile powders, sugar, salt, black pepper, and monosodium glutamate. Simmer 1 hour.

3. Add kidney beans and chili beans, and simmer another 10 minutes. Serve with chopped scallions and cheese.

MAKES 10 TO 12 SERVINGS

Lou Holtz's Chili

⊙⊙

As a coach who's spent time in many states, the current Notre Dame football guru has sampled lots of chili. This is the one he started with and it's kept him and the rest of the Holtz family happy for years. For an Irish twist, cook up a batch on a Saturday and watch Notre Dame chase another national championship.

1	can (28 ounces) tomatoes, drained	1	tablespoon olive oil
1	can (8 ounces) tomato sauce	1½	pounds lean ground beef
1	can (8 ounces) V-8 juice	2	cloves garlic, crushed
2	tablespoons commercial chili powder	1	can (15 ounces) red kidney beans, drained
½	cup water		grated cheese, chopped onions, tortilla chips, for garnish

1. In a blender, puree tomatoes, tomato sauce, V-8, chili powder, and water.

2. Heat olive oil in a medium pot, add ground beef and garlic, and sauté until meat is no longer pink.

3. Stir in tomato mixture and simmer over low heat for 1½ hours, stirring often.

4. Add drained beans and simmer an additional 20 minutes. Serve topped with cheese, onions, chips.

MAKES 4 TO 6 SERVINGS

SPORTING CHILI

Bob Knight's Chili

૭ૐ

Everyone knows Bob Knight takes his basketball seriously. But what many people don't know is how seriously the Indiana University basketball coach takes his chili. He's so serious about chili that he didn't even get hot and bothered when we asked for his recipe. He simply said okay and sent it along—without any scholarship offers for the kids. We liked it so much that we gave it the ICS seal of approval.

3	pounds ground beef	1	can (28 ounces) whole tomatoes with their juice
1	large onion, chopped (about 1 cup)	2	bay leaves
2	cans (10½ ounces each) tomato soup	1	tablespoon sugar
1	soup can (10½ ounces) water	1	teaspoon hot pure chile powder
2	packages (1¾ ounces each) chili seasoning mix, such as McCormick's, or 4 to 6 tablespoons commercial chili powder	2	cans (16 ounces each) dark red kidney beans
			salt and black pepper to taste

1. In a large pot, brown ground beef and onion. Drain off fat.

2. Add tomato soup, water, chili seasoning mix, tomatoes, bay leaves, sugar, and chile powder. Simmer over low heat for 2 hours, checking on liquid and stirring often.

continued

3. Add kidney beans during last hour of cooking. Salt and pepper to taste.

🍴 MAKES 8 SERVINGS

Roger Clemens's White Chili

His pitches may be fast, but Roger Clemens and his wife, Debbie, were not too quick in divulging the family's once-secret recipe. After continuous harrumphing, they relented. Perhaps this light yet spicy concoction is what puts the zip in the Boston Red Sox pitcher's fastball. Our tasters thought so. After giving out the recipe, the Clemenses had their third child—Kasy Austin—on July 27, 1994.

1	pound dried white beans, soaked overnight	1	can (4 ounces) green chiles, drained and chopped
2	pounds boneless, skinless chicken breasts	2	teaspoons ground cumin
1½	quarts water	2	teaspoons dried oregano
2	cloves garlic, minced	½	teaspoon ground coriander
1	teaspoon salt		pinch of ground cloves
1½	medium onions, chopped (about 1 cup)		pinch of cayenne
1	tablespoon corn oil	4	ounces Monterey Jack cheese, grated (about ½ cup)
		4	scallions, sliced

1. Drain beans, rinse, and drain again.

2. In a large pot, simmer chicken breasts in water until cooked, about 20 minutes. Remove chicken from broth, cut into $\frac{1}{2}$-inch cubes, and refrigerate until needed.

3. To the stock, add beans, garlic, salt, and $\frac{1}{2}$ of the onions and bring to a boil. Reduce heat, cover, and simmer $1\frac{1}{2}$ hours, or until beans are very tender, adding water as needed.

4. Heat oil in a large skillet, add remaining onions, and sauté until translucent, about 5 minutes. Add chopped chiles, cumin, oregano, coriander, cloves, and cayenne, mixing thoroughly. Sauté over low heat for 20 minutes, then add skillet mixture to bean mixture.

5. Reheat chicken and divide among six bowls. Spoon chili on top and sprinkle with grated cheese and sliced scallions.

MAKES 6 SERVINGS

Cheli's Chili

Kinda cute, huh? There's nothing cute about Chris Chelios, the tough-guy defenseman for the Chicago Blackhawks. When he isn't roughing up opponents, Chris can be found at his new Chicago restaurant, Cheli's Chili Bar. He and childhood pal Tim Zwijack use their favorite recipe, the one Tim's mother devised when the kids were growing up.

3 pounds lean ground beef

3 medium onions, chopped (about 2 cups)

3 tablespoons chopped garlic

3 pounds ripe tomatoes, diced

2 cans (15 ounces each) tomato sauce

2 cans (15½ ounces each) chili beans, Brooks brand preferred

2 cans (15½ ounces each) dark red kidney beans, drained

1 can (10½ ounces) tomato soup

½ cup commercial chili powder

red pepper flakes to taste

1. In a large pot, sauté ground beef until no longer pink. Add onions and cook over medium-high heat until meat is browned; add garlic and cook several more minutes. Drain off fat.

2. Reduce heat, add tomatoes, and simmer 30 minutes.

3. Add tomato sauce, chili beans, and kidney beans, and bring to a low boil. Add tomato soup, chili powder, and red pepper flakes and simmer 15 minutes.

MAKES **12** SERVINGS

Joe Theismann's Chili

The former Washington Redskins quarterback, now a talking machine on ESPN on pro football weekends, also happens to be a chilihead. He serves chili in his Washington, D.C.–area restaurants. It's the only thing on the face of the planet that we know can keep him quiet for more than a few seconds.

2	tablespoons vegetable oil	$1/4$	cup mild pure chile powder
1	medium onion, diced (about $3/4$ cup)	2	teaspoons paprika
		1	teaspoon ground cumin
2	cloves garlic, minced	4	bay leaves
3	stalks celery, chopped fine	salt and black pepper to taste	
3	pounds lean ground beef	3	cans (16 ounces each) dark red kidney beans
1	cup chopped ripe tomato		
2	cans (8 ounces each) tomato sauce		

continued

1. Heat oil in a large pot, add onion, garlic, and celery, and sauté until soft. Add ground beef and cook until no longer pink, then drain off fat.

2. Add tomato and tomato sauce and simmer 30 minutes.

3. In a small bowl, mix together chile powder, paprika, cumin, and bay leaves, then add to chili. Add salt and pepper and simmer 30 minutes.

4. Add kidney beans and simmer 20 minutes, adding water if necessary.

🍴 MAKES 8 SERVINGS

Krimsky's Olympic Five-Ring Rattlesnake Chili

John Krimsky is neither athlete nor coach, but his chili recipe is as well known as the Dream Team. Krimsky is the marketing guru for the United States Olympic Committee, and his bowl of red is a blend of ingredients used by winners of the ICS Colorado Springs cookoff, hosted each year by the USOC at the Olympic training headquarters. A 1994 Wall Street Journal article was devoted to Krimsky's chili expertise when his group hosted Olympic corporate sponsors at the Winter Games in Lillehammer, Norway.

4	pounds extra-lean ground beef	2	tablespoons hot pure chile powder (or more to taste)
1	pound bulk pork sausage	1	tablespoon salt
3	cloves garlic, minced	1	tablespoon dried oregano
2	large onions, chopped (about 2 cups)	2	teaspoons ground cumin
		1/2	teaspoon cayenne or to taste
2	large green bell peppers, chopped (about 2 cups)	1	can (15 ounces) red kidney beans, drained
2	cans (6 ounces each) rattlesnake meat	1	can (15 ounces) pinto beans, drained
3	cans (15 ounces each) stewed tomatoes	1	can (15 ounces) Great Northern beans, drained
3	cans (15 ounces each) tomato sauce	1	can (15 ounces) black beans, drained
1	can Budweiser beer	1	can (15 ounces) chick-peas, drained
3	tablespoons pure maple syrup		cooked white rice (optional)
1/4	cup Worcestershire sauce		
3	tablespoons mild pure chile powder (or more to taste)		

1. In a large skillet over medium heat, brown ground beef, pork sausage, garlic, onions, and green peppers. Drain off fat and transfer to a 10-quart pot.

2. Drain and bone rattlesnake meat, making sure all fine bones are removed. Add meat to the large pot.

continued

3. Stir in stewed tomatoes, tomato sauce, beer, maple syrup, and Worcestershire sauce and bring to a boil.

4. Lower heat and add chile powders, salt, oregano, cumin, and cayenne. Simmer 1 hour.

5. Add drained beans and simmer an additional 45 minutes, adding water and/or more beer to maintain desired consistency. Adjust seasonings. Serve over cooked white rice if desired.

MAKES 16 TO 20 SERVINGS

Tony Esposito's Chili

Kick save and a beauty for the former Chicago Blackhawks' Hall of Fame goaltender. Our friends in Tampa, Florida, turned us on to Tony O's rendition of red, and we found we had to share it with everyone else. Tony, it should be noted, is the younger brother of Hall of Famer Phil Esposito, his boss with the Tampa Bay Lightning of the National Hockey League.

1	large onion, chopped (about 1 cup)	$^1/_2$	teaspoon dried oregano
2	cloves garlic, minced	$^1/_4$	teaspoon black pepper
$^1/_4$	cup olive oil	pinch of cayenne	
1	pound lean ground beef	1	can (6 ounces) tomato paste
3	tablespoons commercial chili powder	2	cans ($10^1/_2$ ounces each) beef broth
1	teaspoon salt	2	cans (16 ounces each) red kidney beans, drained

1. In a large saucepan, sauté onion and garlic in oil over medium heat. Add ground beef and cook until meat loses its pink color. Drain off fat and return to heat.

2. Add chili powder, salt, oregano, black pepper, cayenne, tomato paste, and beef broth and stir well. Bring to a boil, lower heat, partially cover, and simmer 45 minutes, stirring occasionally.

3. Add well-drained beans and simmer 15 minutes longer. Serve with crusty Italian bread and a salad.

MAKES 4 SERVINGS

Bo-Dine's Crockpot Chili

❀

Don't let his profession as a stock car driver fool you. Geoff Bodine is from Chemung, New York, and has been eatin' this tasty dish for years. A former Daytona 500 winner, Geoff is one of the most competitive drivers today on the NASCAR Winston Cup circuit. And he's been at it since 1982.

2	pounds ground sirloin	1	large green bell pepper, diced
1	can (28 ounces) crushed tomatoes	2	large onions, chopped
2	cans (8 ounces each) tomato sauce	2 to 3	cloves garlic, minced
1	bottle (16 ounces) ketchup	6	tablespoons commercial chili powder
1	can (16 ounces) light red kidney beans, drained	1/4	cup sugar
1	can (16 ounces) dark red kidney beans, drained	3/4	teaspoon celery salt
		1/2	cup red (sweet) vermouth

1. In a large skillet over medium heat, cook sirloin until no longer pink. Drain off fat.

2. Combine with remaining ingredients in a crock pot and cook at low temperature for approximately 5 hours. Serve with saltines.

🍴 MAKES 8 SERVINGS

Yokozuna's Sumo Samurai Chili

According to legend, and we do mean legend, Yokozuna's recipe dates back to times when the dish was reserved for the fiercest warriors before battle to give them extraordinary powers believed to come from the Buddhist god of fire. But the original recipe was not potent enough for the 368-pound World Wrestling Federation behemoth, and he and his manager, Mr. Fuji, made some adjustments. While Yokozuna has made opponents suffer, his tuna chili is quite refreshing.

4 tablespoons olive oil

12 fresh shiitake mushrooms (if only dried are available, soften them in water first), thinly sliced

$1/_2$ cup chopped scallions

3 cloves garlic, crushed

3 jalapeño peppers, diced

3 bay leaves, crushed

1 can ($14^1/_2$ ounces) crushed tomatoes

1 cup fish stock or clam juice

3 tablespoons plus 1 teaspoon commercial chili powder

1 pound fresh tuna steak or fillet

1 teaspoon paprika

1 teaspoon dried oregano

salt and black pepper to taste

soy sauce to taste

2 cups cooked white rice

2 tablespoons each chopped fresh cilantro and chopped black olives, for garnish

1. Heat 3 tablespoons oil in a medium saucepan over medium heat. Add mushrooms, scallions, garlic, jalapeños, and bay

continued

leaves and sauté for 3 minutes. Add tomatoes, fish stock, and 3 tablespoons chili powder. Bring to boil, reduce heat, and simmer 20 minutes.

2. Coat tuna with 1 tablespoon olive oil and rub with remaining chili powder, paprika, oregano, salt, pepper, and a splash of soy sauce. Grill or broil 3 to 5 minutes per side. Remove from heat, cut into cubes, and add to sauce. Simmer 5 additional minutes and remove from heat.

3. Serve over white rice with the garnish of chopped cilantro and black olives.

🍴 MAKES 4 SERVINGS

The Undertaker's Drop-Dead Chili

From Death Valley, of course, the Undertaker remains alive and kicking with this recipe. Also known as the Grim Reaper of the World Wrestling Federation, this 328-pound mammoth cooks up a bowl that is sure to wake the dead. He eats it cold, but you can try it hot. We did. We're awake.

5	dried New Mexico chiles, seeded and stemmed
1/2	cup beef broth
1/4	cup vegetable oil
1 1/2	pounds Black Angus steak, trimmed and cut in 1/2-inch cubes
salt and black pepper to taste	
4	cloves garlic, minced
1	medium red onion, finely diced (about 3/4 cup)
1	jalapeño pepper, diced
8	ounces ground Black Angus beef
1	tablespoon hot pure chile powder
2	teaspoons ground cumin
1/2	cup black olives, cut in half (optional)
3/4	cup stout or dark beer
1 1/2	tablespoons Worcestershire sauce
2	teaspoons dried oregano
1	can (20 ounces) black bean soup
sliced purple bell peppers, for garnish	

1. Thinking of your next opponent, crush peppers with hands into beef broth and set aside. In a large saucepan, heat oil over medium-high heat. Season beef with salt and pepper and brown in oil about 3 minutes.

2. Reduce heat to medium, add garlic, onion, and jalapeño pepper, and sauté 1 minute. Add ground beef and sauté 2 to 3 additional minutes, until meat is no longer pink, then drain off fat. Add beef broth with chiles, chile powder, and cumin. Bring to a simmer, then add black olives (if desired), stout, Worcestershire sauce, oregano, and black bean soup. Simmer 1 hour and serve topped with purple peppers.

MAKES 4 SERVINGS

Adam Bomb's Radioactive A-Bomb Chili

❧

A native of Three Mile Island, according to the World Wrestling Federation, Adam, or Mr. Bomb if you will, calls his recipe a nuclear firestorm. It's sure to make anyone who eats it glow. And it's good, too.

MAKE-AHEAD A-BOMBS

1	pound ground beef
1	egg
1	cup bread crumbs, moistened
½	teaspoon Tabasco sauce
	pinch of commercial chili powder
	pinch of cayenne
¼	cup chopped green chiles
¼	cup chopped scallions
½	cup shredded Monterey Jack cheese with jalapeños

RADIOACTIVE CHILI

2	tablespoons bacon drippings
1	large onion, coarsely chopped (about 1 cup)
1	pound ground beef
2	cans (8 ounces each) tomato sauce
1	can (6 ounces) tomato paste
½	cup beef broth
½	cup chopped jalapeño peppers
½	cup chopped green bell pepper
¼	cup commercial chili powder
¼	teaspoon garlic powder
	salt and black pepper to taste

1. Preheat oven to 350°F. Combine all ingredients for A-Bombs and roll into 1-inch balls. Bake in shallow pan for 20 minutes, until browned.

2. Melt bacon drippings in a large pot over medium heat, add onion, and sauté until softened. Add ground beef and cook until no longer pink. Drain off fat. Add remaining ingredients and bring to a slow boil. Reduce heat and simmer 1 hour.

3. Add A-Bombs and simmer an additional hour. Serve over rice, with plenty of water.

MAKES 6 SERVINGS

Bret Favre's Mother's Cajun Chili

This Cajun quarterback from Louisiana is a star with the Green Bay Packers. He'd better be, after they signed him to a five-year, $19-million contract in 1994. His mom made sure he grew up big and strong by serving him lots of this spicy chili. Our tasting-panel review? Touchdown!

2 pounds ground chuck

1 can (12 ounces) tomato juice, plus more if needed

1 can (10½ ounces) diced tomatoes with green chiles

1 green bell pepper, diced (about ¾ cup)

1 onion, chopped (about ¾ cup)

1 can (16 ounces) kidney beans

1 can (12 ounces) beer

4 to 6 tablespoons commercial chili powder

1 teaspoon salt

diced Cheddar cheese and Fritos, for garnish

1. In a large skillet over medium heat, cook beef until no longer pink. Drain off fat and transfer to a large pot along with the remaining ingredients except the garnishes. Bring to a boil, then lower heat and simmer 3 hours, adding more tomato juice if necessary.

2. Adjust seasonings and serve with Cheddar cheese and Fritos.

MAKES 4 SERVINGS

Randal Hendricks's Chili

❦

This guy is a walking American Express commercial. Randy's not known for his athletic talents (he's a pretty tough out in softball, we hear), but he and brother Alan are at the top of the baseball agent game. From Spring, Texas, they represent nearly ninety players, from Roger Clemens to Doug Drabek to Jeff Blauser to Chuck Knoblauch. Randy's the chilihead, though, and that's why we always liked him best. This recipe uses either beef or turkey. We prefer the turkey.

1½ pounds beef chuck or fresh turkey breast, cut in ³⁄₈-inch cubes

1 large sweet onion, diced (about 1 cup)

2 cans (15 ounces each) tomato sauce

1 cup water

2 tablespoons commercial chili powder

3 tablespoons chili sauce

2 tablespoons Worcestershire sauce

1 tablespoon brown sugar

1 tablespoon Tabasco sauce

salt to taste

1. In a chili pot over medium heat, sauté beef or turkey until no longer pink. Drain off fat.

2. Stir in onion, tomato sauce, water, chili powder, chili sauce, Worcestershire sauce, sugar, and Tabasco. Bring to a boil, then lower heat and simmer for at least 1 hour or up to 3 hours, until meat is tender. Add salt to taste and serve.

🍴 MAKES 4 SERVINGS

Political Chili

∞

Chili concocted outside of Texas is usually a weak,
apologetic imitation of the real thing. One of the first
things I do when I get home to Texas is have a bowl of red.
There is simply nothing better.

—LYNDON BAINES JOHNSON

$W\!hen$ *we first got the idea* for this book, we started off with the assumption that everyone has a chili recipe. This is not a true fact. The following people do not have chili recipes, or at least wouldn't share them with us: Hillary Rodham Clinton, David Letterman, Troy Aikman, Jerry Seinfeld, Liz Smith, Bernard Shaw, Chili Davis (for goodness' sake!), Senator Lawton Chiles, Mike Ditka, and Pat Riley. Just about everyone else did, including an astonishing number of our nation's leaders, from the Midwest to the Northeast and, of course, Texas. Their versions range from mildly liberal to red-hot reactionary, with the vast majority taking a nice, middle-of-the-road approach.

The Chili of President Bill Clinton

～ ～

*Somewhere in between the Jell-O Pineapple 7-Up Salad and the cauli-
flower topped with shrimp sauce (8 ounces frozen shrimp, 1 can cream of
shrimp soup, etc.), Bill Clinton consumed a bowl or two of red during his
years as the governor of Arkansas. Actually, we know he ate chili before
that because his mother, the late Virginia Kelley, loved chili as much as
she loved horse racing and even agreed to be a judge at the Saratoga
Regional Chili Cookoff in 1993. This recipe was adapted from* Thirty
Years at the Mansion *(Little Rock: August House, 1985), a collection
of recipes from Liza Ashley, head cook at the Arkansas governor's mansion since 1955.*

1	tablespoon unsalted butter	1	can (10½ ounces) tomato soup
1	pound lean ground beef		
1	medium onion, chopped (about ¾ cup)	1	tablespoon commercial chili powder (or more to taste)
2	cans (15½ ounces each) chili beans		salt to taste

In a large skillet, melt butter, add beef and onion, and sauté until
meat is no longer pink. Drain off fat; stir in remaining ingredients
except salt and simmer 1 hour. Salt to taste before serving.

🍴 MAKES 4 SERVINGS

Lyndon Johnson's Chili

Before Johnson became President in 1963, mainstream America viewed chili as a spaghetti-sauce-like concoction of ground beef, lots of tomatoes, and beans scented with chili powder. Once photos of Johnson eating some real Texas chili hit the wires, Lady Bird Johnson was swamped with requests for this recipe.

4	pounds lean beef, coarsely ground	1	teaspoon dried Mexican oregano
1	Texas-sized onion, diced (about 1 cup)	1	teaspoon cuminseeds, crushed
2	large cloves garlic, minced	1	can (16 ounces) crushed tomatoes
1/4	cup hot pure chile powder	2	cups water
2	tablespoons mild pure chile powder		salt to taste

1. In a large pot over medium heat, sauté beef until no longer pink. Add onion and garlic and cook until onion is translucent.

2. Add remaining ingredients, bring to a boil, lower heat, and simmer 1 hour.

3. Skim off fat, adjust seasonings with salt, and serve.

MAKES 8 SERVINGS

GOP* Chili

Former South Dakota Governor Walter D. Miller

What looked like just a cleverly written recipe for chili turned out to be one of the biggest hits with our tasting panel. The sun-dried tomatoes not only lent a rich, sweet taste to the finished product but prompted two liberals to switch party allegiance.

4 pounds GOP extra-lean, no-excess-fat meat (beef or pork, your choice)

1 teaspoon oil

1 stalk celery, chopped (Democrat celery—lots of strings attached)

2 large onions, chopped (causing big Democrat tears to go with the red faces)

6 jalapeño peppers, chopped

1 pound green bell peppers, chopped

1 cup beef stock (building a strong GOP foundation for this recipe)

2 quarts hot chili beans (because Republicans are out front, forging new paths)

2 quarts sun-dried tomatoes, drained and chopped

2 quarts tomato sauce (both as red as the Democrats' faces were after the 1994 elections)

3/4 cup hot pure chile powder (packing necessary punch to finish off the Democrats)

1/4 cup ground cumin (to balance the recipe like the GOP balances the budget)

1/4 cup garlic powder (to ward off Bram Stoker Democrats)

* Does not stand for Greasy Old Pan.

POLITICAL CHILI

2	tablespoons black pepper (A-CHOO! God bless the GOP!)	2	tablespoons cayenne (too strong for weak-willed Democrats' taste buds)

No preparation instructions are included because, just as in their view of the government, Republicans don't need excessive directions or regulations to ensure successful results.

For those accustomed to a little guidance, former governor Miller adds: Sauté beef in nonstick skillet until no longer pink, drain off fat, and set aside. In a big pot, heat a little oil and sauté celery, onions, jalapeños, and bell peppers until soft. Mix in beef stock, beans, tomatoes, and tomato sauce. Add spices and meat and simmer 3 hours. Refrigerate overnight, simmer another 3 hours, and serve.

MAKES 12 SERVINGS

Heartland Vegetable Chili

❧

Kansas Senator Nancy Landon Kassebaum

For those accustomed to big, beefy chilis, the satisfying taste of this simple vegetarian recipe will come as a surprise. For variety, Senator Kassebaum often uses different kinds of tomatoes. Crushed tomatoes in tomato puree, for instance, make a very rich broth.

2 tablespoons corn oil	2 good-sized carrots, chopped
1 large onion, chopped (about	(1 generous cup)
1 cup)	1 can (15½ ounces) chick-peas,
2 cloves garlic, minced	drained
2 to 3 tablespoons mild pure chile	1 can (15½ ounces) red kidney
powder	beans, drained
1 teaspoon ground cumin	1 can (28 ounces) tomatoes,
¼ teaspoon dried basil	undrained
¼ teaspoon dried oregano	
2 good-sized zucchini, chopped	
(2 generous cups)	

1. In a large pot, heat oil over medium heat and sauté onion with the garlic, chile powder, cumin, basil, and oregano, stirring frequently. Add zucchini and carrots and cook several minutes, again stirring frequently.

2. Stir in chick-peas, kidney beans, and tomatoes and bring to a boil, then lower heat and simmer 30 minutes, until liquid is reduced to desired consistency.

ꗨ MAKES 4 TO 6 SERVINGS

Blaine House Chili

Former Maine Governor John McKernan

This recipe quickly goes from zero to sixty with the addition of the jalapeños, which give it that back-of-the-throat heat that chiliheads seem to crave. The longer the peppers simmer, the hotter the chili.

2   pounds ground beef
1   large green bell pepper, chopped
1   large onion, chopped
1   can (15½ ounces) red kidney beans, drained
2   cans (14 ounces each) Del Monte Cajun stewed tomatoes
6   ounces medium-hot chunky salsa

1   can (6 ounces) tomato paste
2   tablespoons commercial chili powder
1 to 2   teaspoons Worcestershire sauce
10   jalapeño peppers (optional)
shredded cheese, chopped raw onions, diced fresh tomatoes, chopped black olives, for garnish

continued

1. In a large pot, sauté ground beef with green pepper and onion until meat is no longer pink. Drain off fat.

2. Add kidney beans, tomatoes, salsa, tomato paste, chili powder, and Worcestershire sauce and simmer $1\frac{1}{2}$ hours. If you like your chili hot, add the jalapeños before simmering.

3. Serve with cheese, onions, tomatoes, and black olives as toppings.

🍴 MAKES 6 SERVINGS

Classic Southern Chili

Mississippi Governor Kirk Fordice

The historic governor's mansion in Jackson, Mississippi, recently celebrated its 150th anniversary. Tommie Darras, who was born nearby in 1910, has served as resident chef for Governor Fordice and several other first families who have occupied the 1842 house. Chef Tommie holds a vast collection of the South's favorite dishes in his head, and Governor Fordice was gracious enough to slow him down long enough to get this chili in written form. We're glad he did.

5	pounds ground beef		salt and black pepper to taste	
2	large onions, chopped (about 2 cups)	1	quart water	
4	cloves garlic, chopped	3	tablespoons cornstarch, mixed with a little water	
3	heaping tablespoons mild pure chile powder (or more to taste)	2	cans (15½ ounces each) pinto beans, drained	
2	heaping teaspoons ground cumin	2	cans (15½ ounces each) Great Northern beans, drained	
1	heaping teaspoon cayenne	2	cans (15½ ounces each) red kidney beans, drained	
½	teaspoon dried oregano			

1. In a large pot over medium heat, cook ground beef, onions, and garlic until meat is no longer pink. Drain off fat.

2. Add chile powder, cumin, red pepper, oregano, salt, black pepper, and water. Simmer at least 1 hour, until chili has cooked down.

3. Add cornstarch and beans; cook an additional 20 minutes. Serve with toppings as desired—shredded cheese, Fritos, minced green onions.

MAKES 10 TO 12 SERVINGS

Mansion Chili

༄

Kentucky Governor Brereton C. Jones

This mild, tasty chili was a big hit with the under-ten and over-sixty-five crowd in our tasting panel.

1	pound ground beef	3 to 4 cups beef broth	
2	medium onions, chopped (about 1½ cups)	1 can (28 ounces) diced or crushed tomatoes	
½	green bell pepper, chopped (about ½ cup)	1 can (15½ ounces) red kidney beans, drained	
2 to 3	tablespoons mild pure chile powder	2 cups cooked elbow macaroni	
1	teaspoon ground cumin	6 ounces Cheddar cheese, grated	

1. In a heavy chili pot, brown ground beef and drain off fat. Add onions, green pepper, chile powder, and cumin and sauté 2 additional minutes. Stir in beef broth, tomatoes, and beans and simmer 45 minutes.

2. Serve over cooked macaroni and top with cheese.

🍴 MAKES 4 SERVINGS

Low-Fat Chili

☉

Illinois Governor Jim Edgar

When the Center for Science in the Public Interest came out with a report blasting the unhealthful qualities of Mexican food, the International Chili Society came right back with Governor Edgar's classic-tasting chili that proves you can have your chili and eat it too. There are just 325 calories per 1½-cup serving, with 4.5 grams of fat, 60 milligrams of cholesterol, and just 40 milligrams of sodium. Enjoy!

8   ounces lean buffalo or sirloin, coarsely ground

1   large onion, chopped (about 1 cup)

1   small green bell pepper, chopped (about ½ cup)

1   can (8 ounces) low-sodium tomato sauce

1   can (13¾ ounces) low-sodium beef broth

1   can (6 ounces) low-salt tomato paste

2   teaspoons no-salt commercial chili powder

1   teaspoon ground cumin

brown sugar to taste (1 tablespoon to start)

2   cans (15½ ounces each) dark red kidney beans, undrained

1. In a medium nonstick saucepan, cook beef, onion, and green pepper over medium heat until beef is well-done and onion and

continued

pepper are soft. Pour mixture into colander and drain, rinsing under hot water until beef loses oily feel when touched.

2. Add tomato sauce, beef broth, tomato paste, chili powder, cumin, brown sugar, and beans. Bring to a boil, lower heat, and simmer 1 hour.

MAKES 4 SERVINGS

Tennessee Chili

Tennessee Governor Ned McWherter

This recipe was a great favorite of Governor McWherter's mother, Lucille Golden Smith McWherter. A version of it won Honorable Mention in the 1988 Ladies' Home Journal chili cookoff.

2	teaspoons butter	1	clove garlic, crushed
3	pounds beef chuck, cut in 1/2-inch cubes (cut while partially frozen)	4 to 6	tablespoons mild pure chile powder
1	large onion, diced (about 1 cup)	2	bay leaves
		2	teaspoons dried oregano
1	green bell pepper, diced (about 1 cup)	2	teaspoons sugar
		1	teaspoon ground cumin
		1	teaspoon salt

½ teaspoon black pepper	1 can (15½ ounces) red kidney
1 can (15½ ounces) stewed	beans, drained and rinsed
tomatoes	1 can (8 ounces) tomato sauce
1 can (14½ ounces) beef broth	1 tablespoon cornmeal,
	dissolved in 1 cup warm water

1. Melt butter in a heavy chili pot over high heat, add beef, and cook until meat is no longer pink. Drain off fat. Lower heat and stir in onion, green pepper, and garlic. Cook until softened, about 5 minutes.

2. Stir in chile powder, bay leaves, oregano, sugar, cumin, salt, and black pepper and sauté about 2 minutes.

3. Add stewed tomatoes, beef broth, kidney beans, tomato sauce, and cornmeal mixed with water, raise heat, and bring to a boil.

4. Lower heat, cover, and simmer 1 hour; remove cover and simmer an additional hour. Discard bay leaves and garlic and serve.

MAKES 8 SERVINGS

Hot Chili

ᚖ

Minnesota Governor Arne H. Carlson

Chili is one of Governor Carlson's favorite dishes, especially during the cold Minnesota winters. He and his family enjoy making this recipe whenever they visit their lakeside cabin. It's hot and mildly spicy—just the cure for warming cold winter bodies.

2   pounds ground beef

1   medium onion, chopped (about ³/₄ cup)

2   cloves garlic, minced (about 2 teaspoons)

2   stalks celery, chopped (about 1 cup)

2   cans (15¹/₂ ounces each) spicy chili beans

2   cans (15¹/₂ ounces each) dark red kidney beans, drained

1   can (28 ounces) whole tomatoes

2   cans (8 ounces each) tomato sauce

1   teaspoon Tabasco sauce

2   tablespoons Worcestershire sauce

3   tablespoons commercial chili powder

1   teaspoon dry mustard

¹/₂   teaspoon cayenne

1   teaspoon black pepper

In a large pot, sauté beef over medium heat until no longer pink. Drain off fat. Add onion, garlic, and celery and sauté until vegetables are soft. Mix in remaining ingredients, stir thoroughly, and simmer 1 hour.

🍴 MAKES 6 TO 8 SERVINGS

Hot 'Zanta Chili

∞

Georgia Governor Zell Miller

This chili is rich, thick, spicy, and HOT! For those who have less adventuresome taste buds, Governor Miller recommends using fewer peppers or eliminating the seeds, which are the hottest part of the pepper. The whole jalapeños are used more for flavor than fire, but if you want extra heat, squeeze the juice from the simmered jalapeños into the chili.

1	teaspoon vegetable oil	3	jalapeño peppers, finely chopped (include ribs and seeds)
2	really large onions, preferably Vidalia, chopped (about 3 cups)		
		3	dried cayenne peppers, crushed (include seeds)
4	pounds round steak, cut in $1/_2$-inch cubes	4	cans (16 ounces each) hot chili beans
3	cans (16 ounces each) whole tomatoes	$1/_2$	cup plus 2 tablespoons commercial chili powder
2	cans (10 ounces each) diced tomatoes with chiles	1	teaspoon garlic powder
3	whole jalapeño peppers	1	can (28 ounces) tomato juice
		$1/_2$	can ($3/_4$ cup) beer

continued

1. Heat oil in a large pot over medium heat and sauté onions until softened. Add meat and cook slowly, stirring often, until no longer pink.

2. Place tomatoes, undrained, in a large bowl and crush with your hands, then add to meat along with whole and chopped jalapeños. Mix in cayenne peppers, chili beans, chili powder, garlic powder, tomato juice, and beer. Bring to a boil, then lower heat and simmer 1 hour.

3. Reduce heat to low and simmer another hour, stirring occasionally.

MAKES 10 TO 12 SERVINGS

Award-Winning Chili

ை

Texas Senator Phil Gramm

No controversy here— this chili is very simple, very classic, and very Texas.

1	pound beef, cut into sugar-cube size	2	cups water	
1	pound ground beef	$^{1}/_{4}$	cup hot pure chile powder	
1	small onion, minced (about $^{1}/_{2}$ cup), *or* 1 tablespoon dehydrated onion	1	tablespoon ground cumin	
		2	teaspoons paprika	
		1	teaspoon salt	
		1	teaspoon cayenne	
2	cans (8 ounces each) tomato sauce	2	cloves garlic, minced	
		3	tablespoons flour	

1. In a heavy chili pot, cook beef cubes, ground beef, and onion until meat is no longer pink. Drain off fat.

2. Add tomato sauce, water, chile powder, cumin, paprika, salt, red pepper, and garlic; simmer 1 hour.

3. Mix in flour and cook an additional 15 minutes.

MAKES 4 SERVINGS

Pedernales River Chili

∽∾

Former Pennsylvania Governor Bob Casey

This Keystone State version of the Texas dish is a favorite of not just Bob and Ellen Casey but the entire Casey clan, including their eight children and sixteen (at last count) grandchildren. The Pedernales River, in case you were wondering, is really in Texas, not Pennsylvania. This chili makes it seem like it's right around the bend.

4	pounds chuck, coarsely ground
1	large onion, chopped (about 1 cup)
2	cloves garlic, minced
6	tablespoons commercial chili powder
1	tablespoon cuminseeds
2	cans (10 ounces each) tomatoes with green chiles
1	teaspoon salt
2	cups hot water

1. In a heavy skillet, brown meat, onion, and garlic until meat is no longer pink; drain off fat.

2. Stir in chili powder, cuminseeds, tomatoes, salt, and hot water. Bring to a boil, then lower heat and simmer about 1 hour.

MAKES 6 TO 8 SERVINGS

Celebrity Chili

Write a chili cookbook.

—JAMES GARNER TO SALLY FIELD IN
THE MOVIE *MURPHY'S ROMANCE* WHEN
SHE ASKED HIM WHAT HE WANTED TO
DO WHEN HE GREW UP

One *of the reasons* the International Chili Society became famous is that famous people like chili too. A lot. In fact, the list of celebrities who have judged at the World's Championship Chili Cookoffs is almost as long as one of C. V. Wood's recipes and includes Ernest Borgnine, John Derek, Robert Mitchum, Harvey Korman, Tommy Lasorda, Rory Calhoun, Alex Trebeck, Wilt Chamberlain, Billy Martin, Michael J. Fox, Barry Corbin, and, of course, Joanne Dru and Jeanne Cooper. When it comes to chili, we found that famous people don't differ much from lesser-known chiliheads—all appreciate a good bowl of red.

Vanna White's Wheel of Fortune
C-H-I-L-I

Turn over the letters and call Vanna White R-E-D-H-O-T, as in a bowl of her red hot turkey chili. Vanna's recipe, most likely influenced by husband and restaurateur George Santo Pietro, turned out to be quite a dish with our tasting chiliheads.

1 tablespoon vegetable oil	1 can (13 3/4 ounces) less 2 tablespoons chicken broth
1 large onion, finely chopped (about 1 cup)	1 tablespoon flour dissolved in 2 tablespoons chicken broth
1 green bell pepper, diced (about 3/4 cup)	2 cans (16 ounces each) pinto beans, drained
2 pounds ground turkey	salt and black pepper to taste
1/4 cup commercial chili powder	Tabasco jalapeño sauce to taste
1 teaspoon ground cumin	
1/2 teaspoon garlic powder	
2 cans (8 ounces each) tomato sauce	

1. Heat oil in a large pot, add onion and pepper, and sauté until soft. Add ground turkey and cook, stirring frequently, until turkey is no longer pink. Drain off fat.

2. Stir in chili powder, cumin, and garlic powder and cook briefly. Add tomato sauce and chicken broth and simmer 1 hour over medium heat, stirring occasionally.

3. Stir in flour mixture and simmer another 40 minutes, then add beans and heat through. Add salt, black pepper and Tabasco jalapeño sauce to taste.

Judith Light's I'm the Boss Chili

The star of Who's the Boss *and* Phenom, *plus several made-for-TV movies, Judith still finds time to heat up a bowl of chili. In a 1993 interview, the actress said she loves doing different and risky things. Her recipe may be a tad different, but no risk is involved. In case you forgot, Judith first came to our attention as Larry's wife, Karen, in the soap opera* One Life to Live.

1 pound dried red kidney beans, soaked overnight and drained

2 tablespoons olive oil

4 pounds chuck, trimmed of fat and cut in ¹/₂-inch cubes

2 large sweet onions, diced (about 2 cups)

4 cloves garlic, minced

¹/₂ cup mild pure chile powder

2 tablespoons commercial chili powder

2 tablespoons ground cumin

1 teaspoon cayenne

1 teaspoon dried oregano

1 can (28 ounces) Italian plum tomatoes, crushed between hands, plus 1 can water

1 teaspoon freeze-dried instant coffee

salt and black pepper to taste

continued

1. In a large pot, cover drained beans with fresh water and bring to a boil. Lower heat and simmer 1 hour, until tender. Set aside.

2. Meanwhile, in another large pot, heat olive oil and sauté meat until no longer pink. Add onions and garlic and cook until soft, about 10 minutes. Drain off excess fat.

3. Stir in chile and chili powders, cumin, cayenne, and oregano, cook briefly, and add tomatoes. Simmer 2 hours, stirring occasionally and adding water as needed.

4. Stir in coffee granules and simmer another $1/_2$ hour. Add salt and black pepper to taste. Serve with drained beans on the side.

MAKES 6 SERVINGS

Robert Wagner's Chili

◠◠

The longtime actor who starred in Hart to Hart *from 1979 to 1984 is a chilihead from way back. Here's his version.*

1	tablespoon canola oil	1	can (29 ounces) tomato sauce
1	pound ground pork	1	can (13³/₄ ounces) chicken
2	pounds lean beef, cut in		broth plus additional water
	tiny cubes	¹/₂	cup commercial chili powder
2	medium onions, chopped	1	teaspoon cayenne
	(about 1¹/₂ cups)	2	cans (16 ounces each) dark red
2	cloves elephant garlic, minced		kidney beans, drained
2	stalks celery, chopped (about	1	can (15 ounces) Mexican-
	³/₄ cup)		style corn
2	red bell peppers, diced (about	2	tablespoons red wine vinegar
	1¹/₂ cups)		salt and black pepper to taste

1. Heat oil in a large pot and sauté pork until no longer pink. Then stir in beef and sauté until no longer pink, stirring frequently. Add onions, garlic, celery, and peppers and cook until onions are beginning to get translucent, about 5 minutes. Place mixture in a colander to thoroughly drain off fat.

2. Return meat to the pot and add tomato sauce, chicken broth, chili powder, and cayenne. Bring to a boil, then lower heat and simmer 2 hours, adding water if needed.

continued

3. Stir in kidney beans, corn, and vinegar, and simmer another 10 minutes. Add salt and black pepper to taste, and serve with sour cream and wedges of lime.

¶¶ MAKES 6 SERVINGS

Jeanne Cooper's Chili

What can you say about the Queen of the Soaps? Jeanne is a great supporter of the ICS and longtime judge at the World's Championship. Of course, that's provided she can break away from her role as the wealthy matriarch Katherine Chancellor-Sterling in The Young and the Restless. *She makes a mean chili too.*

4 pounds lean chuck, cut in $^3/_8$-inch dice

6 tablespoons mild pure chile powder

2 tablespoons ground cumin

2 teaspoons hot pure chile powder

$^1/_2$ teaspoon garlic powder

$^1/_2$ teaspoon cayenne

2 tablespoons lard

1 can (8 ounces) tomato sauce

1 can (12 ounces) dark beer

2 cans (13$^3/_4$ ounces each) beef broth or bouillon

2 tablespoons commercial chili powder

1 tablespoon brown sugar

1 teaspoon unsweetened cocoa powder

salt and black pepper to taste

1. Rub beef with mild chile powder, cumin, hot chile powder, garlic powder, and cayenne, then set aside in refrigerator for about 2 hours.

2. In a large pot, melt the lard over medium heat, then add spiced beef and cook until meat is no longer pink. Drain off fat.

3. Stir in tomato sauce, beer, and beef broth, then cover and simmer 2 hours. Stir in commercial chili powder, brown sugar, and cocoa powder and simmer an additional $\frac{1}{2}$ hour.

4. Adjust seasonings with salt and black pepper, adding more cayenne if desired, and serve with tortilla chips and chili beans on the side.

MAKES **6** SERVINGS

Corbin Bernsen's Lawless Grilled Chili

∽

Best known for his portrayal as the womanizing Arnie Becker in L.A. Law, Corbin is the son of Jeanne Cooper. But he has his own version of red, which he says impresses the ladies when he adds the eggplant and mushroom. Nice going, Arnie, it worked with our female tasters.

continued

2	pounds sirloin steak, well trimmed	3	jalapeño peppers, diced
1	large eggplant, cut lengthwise in $^1/_2$-inch slices and rubbed with oil	1	heaping teaspoon flour
		$^1/_4$	cup commercial chili powder
		1	teaspoon ground cumin
1	large portobello mushroom, rubbed with oil (optional)	1	can (8 ounces) tomato sauce
		1	can ($13^3/_4$ ounces) beef broth plus water as needed
1	tablespoon extra-virgin olive oil		salt and black pepper to taste
1	large sweet onion, chopped (about 1 cup)		

1. Grill steak, eggplant, and mushroom, if desired, over medium-hot coals about 6 minutes per side, then refrigerate for 1 hour, until meat is firm.

2. In a large pot, heat olive oil, add onion and peppers and sauté over medium heat until soft, then stir in flour and cook briefly, stirring. Add chili powder, cumin, tomato sauce, and beef broth and simmer 1 hour.

3. Meanwhile, with a very sharp knife to minimize tearing, dice beef, eggplant, and mushroom into bite-sized cubes and stir into tomato mixture. Simmer 10 minutes, add salt and black pepper to taste, then serve with wedges of Italian bread brushed with olive oil, grilled, and spread with goat cheese.

🍴 MAKES 4 SERVINGS

Roger Smith's Chili

✆✆

Marriage to the glamorous Ann-Margret—what more could a man want? A good bowl of chili, naturally. We've loved her since we first saw her in Bye Bye Birdie. *And we thought she was just as great in* Grumpy Old Men. *Didn't you? Oh, this is Roger's recipe. We didn't forget, it's just that . . . Right, right. Roger Smith, 77 Sunset Strip, great TV show. Great chili. Really.*

2 tablespoons unsalted butter	1 can (13¾ ounces) chicken broth
1 large onion, finely diced	
3 pounds ground pork *or* ½ pork and ½ sausage	2 cans (16 ounces each) pinto beans, drained
½ cup commercial chili powder	1 jar (8 ounces) salsa—mild, medium, or hot to your taste
2 cans (10 ounces each) diced tomatoes with green chiles	salt and black pepper to taste

1. In a large pot, melt butter and sauté onion until translucent. Stir in ground pork or pork and sausage and sauté until no longer pink. Drain off fat.

2. Stir in chili powder, cook briefly, stirring, and then add tomatoes and chicken broth. Simmer 1 hour.

3. Stir in pinto beans and salsa and simmer an additional 10 minutes and add salt and black pepper to taste and serve with chips, shredded cheese, and chopped raw onions.

🍴 MAKES 8 SERVINGS

Jess Walton's
Young and Restless Chili

Jess, who won the 1991 Daytime Emmy as Outstanding Supporting Actress for her role as Jill Foster Abbott in The Young and the Restless, was born in Grand Rapids, Michigan, and grew up in Canada. She joined the cast of the popular soap opera in 1987, which is about when she perfected this classic recipe.

1 tablespoon bacon drippings	1 teaspoon hot Hungarian paprika
1 large onion, chopped (about 1 cup)	1 can (28 ounces) Italian plum tomatoes, crushed
4 cloves garlic, crushed	water as needed
1 pound ground beef	1 stick cinnamon
1 pound bulk sausage	2 cans (16 ounces each) red kidney beans, undrained
1/3 cup mild pure chile powder	salt and black pepper to taste
1 tablespoon cuminseeds, toasted briefly	
1 teaspoon dried Mexican oregano	

1. Heat bacon drippings in a large cast-iron skillet over low heat, add onion and garlic, and sauté until soft, about 10 minutes. Stir in beef and sausage and cook until meat is no longer pink. Add chile powder, cuminseeds, oregano, and paprika and cook briefly. Drain off fat and transfer meat to a chili pot.

2. Stir in tomatoes and simmer 1 hour, adding water if necessary. About 20 minutes before serving, add cinnamon stick and continue to simmer.

3. Add undrained beans and heat through. Remove garlic, add salt and pepper to taste, and serve with warm flour tortillas and fresh tomato slices sprinkled with chopped cilantro.

MAKES 6 TO 8 SERVINGS

Marilu Henner's Evening Shade Vegetarian Chili

෧ඏ

She drove a cab in Taxi, *had a baby on* Evening Shade, *also played in
such films as* The Man Who Loved Women *and* Cannonball Run
II, *and hosted her own talkshow, but Marilu still manages to spend time
in the kitchen. A vegetarian, she experimented with her chili recipe and
came up with another winner. Fortunately for us, she didn't include it in
her tell-all autobiography* By All Means Keep On Moving.

1   cup spicy Bloody Mary mix,
    such as Tabasco brand

1   cup coarse bulgur

2   tablespoons olive oil

2   onions, diced (about 1½ cups)

2   cloves garlic, minced

2   large stalks celery, chopped
    (about 1 cup)

½   cup commercial chili powder

1   tablespoon pure hot chile
    powder

1   teaspoon dried Mexican
    oregano

1   can (28 ounces) crushed
    tomatoes

2   cups water

1   yellow bell pepper, diced
    (about ¾ cup)

1   red bell pepper, diced
    (about ¾ cup)

4   jalapeño peppers, diced
    (about ⅓ cup)

2   packages (10 ounces each)
    frozen Italian green beans

2   cans (16 ounces each) red
    kidney beans, drained

2   cans (16 ounces each) chick-
    peas, drained

1   can (16 ounces) corn, drained

red pepper flakes to taste

salt and black pepper to taste

1. Pour Bloody Mary mix over bulgur and set aside to soak at least ¹/₂ hour.

2. Meanwhile, heat olive oil in a large Dutch oven, add onions, garlic, and celery, and sauté until softened. Stir in chili and chile powders and oregano, then add tomatoes and water. Bring to a boil, lower heat, and simmer over very low heat 30 minutes.

3. Add bell peppers and jalapeños and simmer 20 more minutes. Add frozen green beans and soaked bulgur and simmer another ¹/₂ hour, stirring frequently and checking to make sure bulgur doesn't stick to the bottom of the pot and scorch, which it does easily.

4. Add beans, chick-peas, and corn and simmer another 15 minutes, stirring frequently.

5. Stir in red pepper flakes to taste (start with 1 teaspoon and rev it up from there), season with salt and pepper to taste, and serve with chopped raw onion.

MAKES 8 TO 10 SERVINGS

Darrien Iacocca's Chili

∽

The former wife of former Chrysler Corporation baron Lee Iacocca is a devout chilihead. Her recipe is as sleek and upscale as a brand-new Concorde and comes equipped with standard features such as roasted garlic, tequila, and Dutch cocoa, which make the ride on this chili a luxurious experience.

1	whole head of garlic, rubbed with oil	1	tablespoon cuminseeds, toasted briefly and crushed
6 to 8	whole dried California chile peppers	1	teaspoon dried oregano, preferably Mexican
4	cups hot water	1	teaspoon cayenne
2	teaspoons leaf lard	1	can (8 ounces) tomato sauce
3	pounds sirloin tip, cut in little cubes	2	cans (13 3/4 ounces each) beef broth
1 1/2	ounces tequila	1	tablespoon Dutch-process cocoa
1/4	cup high-grade commercial chili powder, Gebhardt's brand preferred		hot sauce to taste
			salt and black pepper to taste

1. Preheat oven to 350°F. Wrap garlic loosely in aluminum foil and bake about 45 minutes, then remove and let cool. Meanwhile, toast chile peppers briefly until they start to smell really good (about 1 minute), then remove from heat and

plunge into boiling water. Let stand (off heat) about 40 minutes, then scrape the pulp from the chiles into a small bowl. Squeeze the roasted garlic into the same bowl and smash into a paste.

2. In a large skillet, melt lard and brown meat in it over medium heat, then flambé with tequila. Don't stand over it or you'll scorch your eyebrows. Stir in chili powder, cuminseeds, oregano, and cayenne, then add tomato sauce and beef broth and bring to a boil. Lower heat and simmer 1 hour.

3. Stir in roasted garlic and chile pulp and cocoa and simmer another hour, adding water if needed.

4. Add hot sauce, salt, and pepper to taste and serve with warm sourdough bread and a lentil salad on the side (see page 328).

¶¶ MAKES 6 SERVINGS

Sandy Duncan's True Tyler, Texas, Chili

❀

Last time we looked, Sandy Duncan was standing next to a large purple dinosaur and singing, "I love you, you love me, I know I make great chili…" This simple and delicious recipe is not one you'd serve to Barney the Dinosaur. You might, however, want to offer a few Wheat Thins along with it.

2 tablespoons corn oil	1 can (13¾ ounces) beef broth
2 pounds lean top round, coarsely ground	1 cup ketchup
	3 cloves garlic, minced
5 teaspoons pure chile powder, mild or hot to your taste	1 medium red bell pepper, diced (about ¾ cup)
1 teaspoon ground cumin	1 medium onion, diced (about ¾ cup)
1 teaspoon salt	
½ cup beer	

1. In a large skillet, working in 2 batches, heat oil and brown meat in it until no longer pink. Drain off fat and set meat aside. Meanwhile, dissolve chile powder, cumin, and salt in the beer and let stand for 10 minutes.

2. Mix beef broth and ketchup together in a medium saucepan. Add beef and beer mixture and bring to a slow boil. Add garlic, lower heat, and simmer 30 minutes, stirring occasionally.

3. Add red pepper and cook another 10 minutes.

4. Add onion and cook for another 20 minutes.

MAKES 6 SERVINGS

James Garner's Sooner Chili

What a year it was for James Garner in 1994. Big Jim starred in Maverick, CBS reopened The Rockford Files, and his chili recipe was a smashing success with our tasters. He's a chili lover from way back, though—appearing on screen with Sally Field, he told her his ambition was to write a chili cookbook. Sorry.

3	pounds chuck, ground	1/4	cup commercial chili powder
1	large onion, chopped (about 1 cup)	2	teaspoons brown sugar
		2	teaspoons black pepper
2	green bell peppers, chopped (about 1 1/2 cups)	1/2	teaspoon garlic salt
		1/4	cup honey
1	can (28 ounces) whole tomatoes, drained and chopped, with liquid reserved	1	teaspoon Tabasco sauce

continued

1. In a large skillet, cook meat over medium-high heat until no longer pink. Using a slotted spoon to allow fat to drain back into the skillet, transfer meat to a medium saucepan.

2. In the same skillet in remaining fat, sauté onion and bell peppers over low heat until softened, about 20 minutes. Drain off fat and add vegetables to beef mixture.

3. Sauté tomatoes briefly in the skillet and add to meat mixture along with reserved tomato liquid. Stir in remaining ingredients and bring to a slow boil.

4. Reduce heat, cover, and simmer 3 hours, stirring frequently.

MAKES 6 TO 8 SERVINGS

Marylou Whitney's Debutante Chili

Marylou Whitney (Mrs. Cornelius Vanderbilt Whitney), socialite, racing enthusiast, and collector of doll houses, is probably the only person we know who was decorated by the Spanish government's Order of Isabella la Católica. When last seen, she was skipping down the road toward one of her famous parties in Saratoga Springs, arm in arm with the Tin Man and Dorothy, dressed as the Good Witch Glenda. You might expect her chili to be, well, frou-frou, but it's not. It's really, really good. Eat it while wearing a large hat.

1   pound dried pinto beans, soaked overnight in water to cover
$\frac{1}{2}$ cup butter or margarine
2   onions, chopped (about 1 cup)
2   cloves garlic, minced
1   can (7 ounces) diced green chiles
3   pounds coarsely ground sirloin or top round
1   pound bulk pork sausage
2   tablespoons flour
1   can (4 ounces) pimientos

2   cans (28 ounces each) tomatoes
4   large stalks celery, chopped (about 3 cups)
8   ounces mushrooms, sliced
1   large red bell pepper, chopped (about 1 cup)
1   large green bell pepper, chopped (about 1 cup)
1   bottle (12 ounces) chili sauce
$\frac{1}{4}$ to $\frac{1}{2}$ cup commercial chili powder
1   tablespoon salt

continued

1. Drain soaked beans, cover with fresh water, and bring to a boil. Lower heat and simmer 2 to 3 hours, or until tender. Drain.

2. Meanwhile, in a large pot, melt butter or margarine over medium heat. Add onions, garlic, and green chiles and sauté until softened. Add chopped sirloin and cook until meat is no longer pink.

3. In a medium skillet, cook sausage thoroughly. Drain off fat and add sausage to meat mixture. Blend in flour, then add beans and remaining ingredients with a little water if needed. (The mushrooms release liquid, so don't add much.) Bring to a boil, lower heat, and simmer about 40 minutes, adding water if necessary. Adjust seasonings and serve.

MAKES **12** SERVINGS

Chili by the Pros

I adore chili.

—JAMES BEARD

For some mysterious reason, many chefs don't get excited about chili. This we find very confusing, as some of the greatest chefs of our time were chili lovers, notably the late James Beard, whose musings about chili could inspire one to rush out and embrace a bowl of red. "There are very few aromas, or bouquets, if you will, that can touch the smooth, velvety bouquet of a good chili," he wrote in a piece contained in a collection called *Simple Foods* (New York: Macmillan Publishing Co., 1993)."There's no other bouquet of cooking food that has quite that penetrating provocativeness. It smells rich, yet it doesn't taste rich. It smells complicated, but it isn't. It smells divinely good and arouses the most urging longings. When you just can't stand it any longer, you rush into the nearest chili joint and have a bowl of canned chili with beans that gives you a momentary satisfaction, even though it has about as much good chili powder in it as you could put under the nail of your little finger. But no matter—it does something marvelous to your soul." Not get excited? Who couldn't, after reading that? This collection of recipes is from chefs around the country who find chili very exciting indeed.

James Beard's Chili

This recipe is adapted from the one he put forth in Simple Foods *and, in Beard's words, is simple, flavorful, and as authentic as any chili recipe can be. Just serve it with a bowl of beans and a bowl of rice or, if you'd rather, with good crackers or tortillas.*

8   ounces well-chilled suet or rendered beef fat

2   very large onions, chopped (about 2½ cups)

3   pounds top round, cut in ½-inch cubes

2 to 4 cloves garlic, finely chopped

3   tablespoons (minimum) commercial chili powder

1   tablespoon ground cumin

healthy dash of Tabasco sauce

1   can (28 ounces) tomato puree, thinned with beef broth or warm beer

salt to taste

1. Chop suet finely, put a small amount in a large skillet, and add onions. Over low heat, begin sautéing onions very gently, adding remaining suet as they start to soften. Cook very slowly until suet is rendered to a liquid and onions have practically melted into the fat.

2. Add meat and garlic and sauté over medium heat, shaking the pan thoroughly until everything mixes together. Don't rush it.

3. When meat has lost all its pink color, add a minimum of 3 tablespoons chili powder (we used 8 tablespoons and it was fine), cumin, and Tabasco. Cover the mixture with thinned tomato puree, cover, and simmer at the lowest possible heat for 2 to 2½ hours, stirring occasionally. As you stir, taste and correct the seasonings, since you and you alone know how you want your chili. Serve at once, or let cool and chill overnight.

MAKES 6 SERVINGS

The Frugal Gourmet's Texas Chili

〜

Jeff Smith, Seattle, Washington

*The immensely popular TV chef and best-selling cookbook author
remains convinced that chili was invented in 1840 in San Antonio,
where a blend of dried beef, beef fat, chili powder, and spices was pressed
into bricks and taken by prospectors to the California gold fields. This
fine version has no beans about it.*

4 ounces bacon, diced

2 pounds chuck, diced

3 onions, finely chopped (about
  2¹/₄ cups)

6 cloves garlic, minced

6 fresh jalapeño peppers,
  seeded, stemmed, and
  chopped

¹/₄ cup chili powder blend
  (see Note)

1 can (28 ounces) whole
  tomatoes with liquid

salt to taste

1. Heat a chili pot, add the bacon, and sauté until translucent.
   Add the meat and sauté over medium heat, adding onions, garlic, and jalapeños as the meat cooks.

2. Stir in chili powder, lower heat, and continue to cook until
   onions are translucent. Meanwhile, squish the tomatoes with
   your hands, and add to chili. Simmer 1 hour, adding water if
   needed, and correct seasonings.

Note: Smith makes his own chili powder blend in a spice grinder using 10 seeded, stemmed pasilla chiles, 2 seeded, stemmed ancho chiles, $^3/_4$ teaspoon ground cumin, 1 tablespoon dried oregano leaves, 1 teaspoon garlic powder, and 1 teaspoon salt.

MAKES 6 SERVINGS

Jamie's Chili

☙❧

Scott Cohen, chef at New York's Tatou Club

Jamie, who is Scott's wife, hails from Texas and refused to believe (at first) that anyone from New York could make decent chili. Scott spent a few days preparing this delectable version. After one taste, she promptly asked him to marry her. By the way, Scott recently moved over to New York's Stanhope Hotel.

1	pound dried red kidney beans, soaked overnight in water to cover	1	fresh poblano chile, seeded and finely diced
6	cups water	2	jalapeño peppers, seeded and finely diced
$3^1/_2$	teaspoons commercial chili powder	$1^1/_2$	teaspoons onion powder
4	dried ancho chiles, soaked, seeded, and finely diced	1	tablespoon garlic powder
		$^1/_2$	teaspoon ground cumin

continued

½   teaspoon freshly ground black   2   cloves garlic, minced
    pepper   2   cans (10 ounces each) stewed
salt to taste   tomatoes, finely diced
4   pounds coarsely ground beef   1   can (6 ounces) tomato paste
1   medium onion, finely diced   2   smoked ham hocks
    (about ¾ cup)

1. Drain beans and place in a large pot with the water, chili pow-
    der, and ancho chiles. Bring to a boil and simmer 2 hours.

2. Add poblano chile, jalapeños, onion powder, garlic powder,
    cumin, black pepper, and salt; simmer 3 hours.

3. Remove from heat, let cool to room temperature, and refriger-
    ate 8 hours or overnight.

4. In a large skillet, sauté ground beef until no longer pink. Add
    onion and garlic and sauté until soft. Remove from heat and
    drain off fat.

5. Add beef mixture to beans and stir in stewed tomatoes, tomato
    paste, and smoked ham hocks. Bring to a boil and simmer 2
    hours, adding water if needed. Adjust seasonings and holler,
    "Come and get it!"

🍴 MAKES 12 SERVINGS

Ouachita Mountain Buffalo Chili with Black-eyed Pea Relish

Chef John Bennett, Oklahoma City, Oklahoma

This dazzling chili and its enchanting accompaniment take a bit of work, but the effort is rewarded in every delicious mouthful. Bennett serves the relish on the side and spoons in some with each bite of the chili. For the ambitious, he suggests serving a salad of watermelon with julienned jícama, crystallized ginger, and dried strawberries sprinkled with balsamic vinegar and a splash of sesame oil. Chili heaven!

Chef's note:
In the wildlife preserve in the Ouachita Mountains in Oklahoma, the buffalo roam the range freely but are rounded up once a year for auction to preserve the herd and keep the range from being overgrazed. You may substitute lean beef, axis venison, or if you wish a gamier taste, blackbuck antelope.

continued

6 tablespoons JB's Chile Powder (recipe follows)

5 pounds buffalo chuck roast, well trimmed and cut in ¼-inch dice

8 ounces beef suet (kidney suet is best), cut in ¼-inch dice

2 tablespoons vegetable oil

2 large yellow onions, diced (about 2 cups)

6 cloves garlic, minced

1 tablespoon Spanish paprika

1 tablespoon dry-roasted cuminseeds, crushed between hands

1 tablespoon dried oregano, crushed between hands

1 tablespoon freshly ground black pepper

2 teaspoons sugar

2 quarts beef stock or bouillon

1 square (1 ounce) unsweetened chocolate

2 teaspoons Dutch process cocoa powder

salt to taste

Black-eyed Pea Relish (page 270)

1. Rub chile powder into meat and set aside to marinate about 2 hours.

2. In a large cast-iron skillet, render beef suet, add vegetable oil, and heat until very hot. Immediately add seasoned buffalo and cook until browned, stirring frequently.

3. Add the following ingredients one at a time, allowing each to cook several minutes before adding the next: onions, garlic, paprika, cuminseeds, oregano, black pepper, and sugar.

4. Transfer meat to a large chili pot and stir in beef stock, chocolate, and cocoa. Cover and simmer 2 hours, stirring occasionally. Test and continue to cook until meat is tender. Serve with Black-eyed Pea Relish.

JB's Chile Powder

¹/₂ cup dried red New Mexico chiles

¹/₂ cup dried ancho chiles

1 teaspoon dried chilitepin chiles (tiny and hot-as-hell)

1 dried chipotle chile

1 small dried habanero chile

Remove all seeds and place chiles briefly under the broiler to bring out their flavor. When cool, whirl in a spice grinder or food processor until powdered. Remove and sift through a fine strainer. Will keep in the freezer in an airtight container about 1 month.

MAKES ABOUT ¹/₂ CUP

Black-eyed Pea Relish

1 pound dried black-eyed peas, soaked overnight, then cooked until tender with ham hocks, onions, and garlic

1 medium red onion, very thinly sliced (about 3/4 cup)

4 scallions, chopped

4 cloves garlic, chopped

1 yellow tomato (if available), peeled, seeded, and chopped

1 red tomato, peeled, seeded, and chopped

assorted colored peppers (red, orange, purple, yellow), diced (about 1 cup)

juice of 3 limes (about 1/3 cup)

1 tablespoon brown sugar

1 cup shredded fresh basil leaves

1/2 habanero pepper, seeded and finely chopped, *or* 1 jalapeño pepper, seeded and finely chopped

1/2 cup Spanish or Greek olive oil

2 oranges, peeled, seeded, and diced

Combine all ingredients and taste. This relish should be served cool and is spicy and sweet with a hot aftertaste.

MAKES ABOUT 6 CUPS

Mike's Smoked Turkey and White Bean Chili

Mike Fennelly, Mike's On the Avenue, New Orleans

New Orleans is one of the great restaurant towns in the world, and its restaurant-goers are among the most sophisticated. If you're bold enough and creative enough to serve chili there, it had better be original. And good. This is.

1/2	cup finely chopped pancetta or bacon (about 6 slices)
1	tablespoon olive oil
1	tablespoon minced shallots
1	tablespoon finely chopped fresh cilantro
1	tablespoon finely chopped fresh tarragon
1	chipotle chile, seeded and finely chopped
2	bay leaves
2	teaspoons ground coriander
2	teaspoons ground cumin
3	large yellow onions, minced (about 3 cups)
1/4	cup dry sherry
6	cups chicken stock
2	cups fresh or frozen chopped green chiles
2	pounds smoked turkey, cut in 1/2-inch cubes (about 4 cups)
2	cans (16 ounces each) cannellini beans, drained
1/2	teaspoon kosher salt
2	teaspoons Worcestershire sauce
2	teaspoons cracked black pepper
3	tablespoons cornstarch dissolved in 1/4 cup water

continued

1. Heat a large saucepan over medium heat, add pancetta or bacon, and sauté for 5 minutes. Add olive oil and stir, then add shallots, cilantro, tarragon, chipotle chile, bay leaves, coriander, cumin, and onions. Sauté until onions are translucent, about 5 minutes, then drain off excess fat. Stir in sherry and cook 5 more minutes.

2. Add remaining ingredients except cornstarch, and simmer 30 minutes.

3. Stir in cornstarch to thicken. Serve with tortilla chips, guacamole, salsa, and grated Sonoma Jack cheese.

MAKES 8 SERVINGS

Chef Allen's Steak and Black Bean Chili

Allen Susser, Aventura, Florida

Scotch Bonnets are Susser's choice for this as well as other New World cuisine dishes. These beautiful chiles, whether red, yellow, or green, add a wonderful citrus, sweet heat to chili. Chef Allen, by the way, was the 1994 James Beard Award winner as the South's top chef.

1	pound black beans, soaked overnight in water to cover	2	large tomatoes, chopped (about 2½ cups)
6	cups water	1	tablespoon minced garlic
2	tablespoons salt	¼	cup commercial chili powder
1	large yellow onion	2	Scotch Bonnet peppers, seeded and finely diced
2	whole cloves	½	cup dry red wine
2	bay leaves	3	tablespoons lime juice
1	teaspoon dried thyme	3	tablespoons chopped fresh cilantro
3	tablespoons olive oil		salt to taste
1	large Bermuda onion, diced (about 1 cup)		
1	pound sirloin steak, cut in small dice		

continued

1. Drain black beans, place in a stockpot with 6 cups water, and add 1 tablespoon salt. Split yellow onion in half, stick each half with a bay leaf and clove, and add to the pot along with the thyme.

2. Cover and cook over medium heat for about 1 hour, until beans are just tender. Remove from heat and set aside.

3. In a large pot, heat olive oil over medium heat and add ½ of the diced onion. Sauté until onion is translucent, about 3 minutes. Raise heat, add the steak, and sauté until caramelized. Add tomatoes, garlic, chili powder, and Scotch bonnets and cook for 5 minutes. Drain black beans and add to the pot with red wine. Simmer 20 minutes.

4. To finish, combine remaining onion with lime juice and cilantro, add to the chili, and adjust seasonings with salt.

MAKES 6 SERVINGS

Señor Gringo's Chili del Norte

Scott Campbell, Vince & Eddie's, New York City

Campbell's twist on chili calls for the venison to be roasted, sliced, and served on top of the chili, not cooked in it. Different? Yes. Delicious? Absolutely!

6-rib loin of venison

2 teaspoons peanut oil

salt and black pepper

8 ounces black beans, soaked overnight in water to cover

4 ounces double-smoked bacon, diced (about 1/2 cup)

1 medium onion, diced (about 3/4 cup)

3 cloves garlic, minced

1 tablespoon ground cumin

2 tablespoons mild pure chile powder

2 tablespoons unsweetened cocoa powder

1 tablespoon ground coriander

1 tablespoon ground cinnamon

6 tomatillos, diced (about 1 cup)

2 cups veal stock (if unavailable, use chicken stock)

4 chipotle chiles

1 pasilla chile

1 ancho chile

1/4 cup raisins

1 teaspoon tomato paste

8 plum tomatoes, peeled, seeded, and diced

1/4 teaspoon black pepper

1 tablespoon white sesame seeds

1/4 cup sesame paste

4 corn tortillas, cut in thin strips and deep-fried; 1 sliced jalapeño pepper; 8 sprigs cilantro; 1 tablespoon sesame seeds; 2 tablespoons freshly diced tomato; 2 tablespoons cooked fresh corn kernels, for garnish

continued

CHILI BY THE PROS

1. Rub venison with oil, sprinkle with salt and pepper, and set aside in refrigerator.

2. Drain black beans, place in a stockpot with salted water to cover, and cook until done, about 1 hour. Remove from heat and set aside.

3. In a large pot, sauté bacon, onion, and garlic over medium heat until translucent. Add cumin, chile powder, cocoa, coriander, cinnamon, and tomatillos and sauté another 2 or 3 minutes.

4. Add veal stock, chipotle, pasilla, and ancho chiles, raisins, tomato paste, and plum tomatoes; simmer for 1 hour.

5. Add black pepper, sesame seeds, sesame paste, and drained black beans and cook another $\frac{1}{2}$ hour over medium heat. Remove the chiles.

6. Preheat oven to 450°F. In a large skillet or Dutch oven, sear venison, turning frequently, until browned all over. Roast for 25 minutes, until medium-rare. Remove from oven and set aside until ready to serve.

7. Ladle chili onto 6 plates, slice rack of venison, and place 1 chop atop each plate.

8. Garnish with tortilla strips, jalapeño slices, cilantro, sesame seeds, tomato, and corn arranged in an attractive pattern.

MAKES 6 SERVINGS

Mr. Food®'s Easy Chili

Mr. Food® is Troy, New York, resident Art Ginsburg, whose popular television and radio spots are seen all over the country. His recipes are uniformly straightforward, quick, and tasty. The breathtaking simplicity of this particular recipe belies its widely appealing flavor.

- 3 tablespoons oil
- 5 pounds ground beef
- 1 large onion, diced (about 1 cup)
- 1 tablespoon minced garlic
- 1 can (28 ounces) whole tomatoes, undrained
- 3 cups bottled barbecue sauce
- 3 tablespoons commercial chili powder
- 1 tablespoon salt
- 1 tablespoon hot red pepper sauce
- 1 tablespoon ground cumin
- 4 cans ($15^1/_2$ ounces each) red kidney beans, drained

1. In a large skillet, heat oil and sauté ground beef with onion and garlic until vegetables are soft.

2. Drain off fat and add tomatoes, barbecue sauce, chili powder, salt, hot pepper sauce, cumin, and kidney beans. Mix well and simmer for 1 hour, stirring occasionally.

3. Serve with warm tortilla chips and a side dish of jalapeños. "OOH it's so GOOD!!"™

MAKES 8 TO 10 SERVINGS

Mark Miller's Venison Chili

ⱺⱺ

Mark Miller, Coyote Cafe, Santa Fe, and Red Sage,
Washington, D.C.

*It's impossible to talk about chili without bringing up Mark Miller,
whose beautiful posters of chile peppers grace the walls of ICS executive
director Jim West. His book on chiles is the definitive edition, and some
of our testers thought his rendition of chili could well be the definitive
recipe. Miller toasts the cumin and oregano for 5 to 7 minutes in a 350°
oven to bring out the flavor before grinding.*

¼ cup rendered bacon fat or
   olive oil

2 large onions, coarsely
   chopped (about 2 cups)

8 cloves garlic, minced

8 jalapeño peppers, stemmed
   and minced

3 pounds shoulder of venison,
   diced

2 teaspoons salt

4 ounces canned chipotle chiles
   in adobo sauce

8 ounces hot pure New Mexico
   chile powder (about 1 cup)

2 tablespoons toasted ground
   cumin

2 tablespoons toasted ground
   Mexican oregano

1 pound Roma tomatoes,
   chopped

2 cups beef stock

1 bottle Mexican beer (preferably Bohemia or Dos Equis)

8 cups cooked black beans

1 cup sour cream, for garnish

½ cup finely chopped onion, for
   garnish

1. Heat bacon fat in a large skillet over medium heat. Add coarsely chopped onions, garlic, and jalapeños, lower heat, and sauté for about 20 minutes, stirring once or twice, until very tender.

2. Meanwhile, place meat and salt in a heavy 5-quart flameproof casserole or Dutch oven and brown over medium heat, stirring often, until meat is no longer pink, about 20 minutes.

3. Add sautéed onion mixture to the casserole and stir in chipotle chiles, chile powder, cumin, and oregano. Cook, stirring often, for about 5 minutes.

4. Stir in tomatoes, beef stock, and beer and bring to a boil. Lower heat and simmer, uncovered, for 1½ hours, stirring occasionally. Taste, correct seasonings, and continue to simmer another 30 minutes, or until the meat is tender and the chili is reduced to your liking. Stir in black beans and simmer for another 5 minutes. Serve with sour cream and finely chopped onion.

MAKES 6 TO 8 SERVINGS

Chris LaLonde's Turkey and Black-eyed Pea Chili

⁊⁊

Chris LaLonde, executive chef, Westin Hotel Galleria,
Dallas, Texas

LaLonde devised this recipe in the early 1990s for the lunch crowd at the Galleria, and it was an instant success. "We serve tons of it," he says. If you use the green beans, they add an interesting contrast to the turkey and black-eyed peas.

olive oil

1   pound coarsely ground turkey

2   large onions, chopped (about 2 cups)

2   large cloves garlic, chopped

1   pound dried black-eyed peas, soaked overnight in water to cover and drained

1   can (28 ounces) crushed tomatoes

1   can (10 ounces) diced tomatoes with green chiles

3   cups water

1   tablespoon salt

1   tablespoon coarsely ground black pepper

1/4   teaspoon dried oregano (or more to taste)

1   tablespoon ground cumin

1   tablespoon Worcestershire sauce

1   tablespoon mild pure chile powder

1   bay leaf

1   pound frozen green beans (optional)

1. In a large Dutch oven, heat a little olive oil over medium heat and brown turkey until it loses its raw look. Add onions and garlic and continue cooking until onions are softened. Add peas, crushed tomatoes, tomatoes with chiles, water, salt, pepper, oregano, cumin, Worcestershire sauce, chile powder, and bay leaf and bring to a boil. Lower heat and simmer, partially covered, for 30 minutes.

2. Add green beans and simmer an additional 30 minutes, or until peas are tender.

MAKES 8 SERVINGS

The Real McCoy

∽

The Manhattan Chili Co., New York City

After ten years in Greenwich Village, Bruce Sterman moved his first-rate chili restaurant to Broadway—Forty-third Street and Broadway, to be exact—in the summer of '94, where they serve ten different chilis from beneath a line of high-kicking chile pepper Rockettes. This recipe is one of the original favorites and is adapted from The Manhattan Chili Co. Southwest American Cookbook.

continued

1/4	cup olive oil	1/2	cup mild pure chile powder
2	large yellow onions, chopped (about 2 cups)	2	tablespoons ground cumin
8	cloves garlic, minced	2	tablespoons dried Mexican oregano
salt		1 1/2	teaspoons cayenne
4	pounds beef chuck, cut in 3/8-inch cubes	1	can (40 ounces) low-salt beef broth

1. Heat oil in large skillet over medium heat and gently sauté onions and garlic for 20 minutes, or until tender.

2. Meanwhile, heat a 5-quart Dutch oven over medium heat and sprinkle with salt. Add beef and cook, stirring often, until it is no longer pink.

3. Add sautéed onions and garlic to beef along with chile powder, cumin, oregano, and cayenne. Cook about 5 minutes, stirring frequently, and then stir in broth. Bring to a boil, lower heat, and simmer for 1 1/2 hours, adding water if necessary.

4. Correct seasonings with salt and simmer another 30 minutes.

MAKES 8 SERVINGS

Hard Times Cafe Vegetarian Chili

⸙

Fred and Jim Parker, Alexandria, Virginia

Fred Parker's mission? To make chili the official food of the United States. He certainly has our vote, and there's also a resolution pending in Congress with a bunch of whereases declaring chili be made America's dish. Fred does other things too, like promote the five chili parlors he, his brother Jim, and Barry Thompson run in Virginia and Maryland. This house specialty is one of Fred's favorites (and our tasting panel's too).

4   cups tomato sauce

1/2   can (6 ounces) tomato paste

4   ounces mushrooms, chopped (about 1 cup)

1   green bell pepper, diced (about 3/4 cup)

1   jalapeño pepper, seeded and diced

1   medium onion, chopped (about 1/2 cup)

2   teaspoons salt

1/3   cup mild pure chile powder

1   tablespoon ground cumin

2   teaspoons crushed red pepper flakes

2   teaspoons garlic powder

1   teaspoon dried oregano

scant 1/2 teaspoon ground allspice

1/4   cup water

1   cup textured soy protein (available in health food stores)

8   ounces spaghetti, cooked

2   tablespoons each chopped peanuts, grated Cheddar cheese, chopped onions, and hot pepper vinegar, for garnish

continued

1. In a Dutch oven over medium heat, combine all ingredients except soy protein, spaghetti, and garnishes. Mix well, then stir in soy protein and bring to a slow boil. Lower heat, cover, and simmer 2 hours, or until thickened. Remove from heat and refrigerate overnight.

2. Reheat chili and serve atop spaghetti. Garnish with peanuts, grated cheese, chopped onions, and hot pepper vinegar.

MAKES 4 SERVINGS

Cincinnati Chili

Cincinnati has more chili parlors per square inch than anyplace in the world, although it's hard to convince anyone who loves Texas-style chili that the thin, sweet stuff they serve up in the Buckeye State is actually chili. Nonetheless, none of the proprietors of various chili parlors we contacted were willing to part with their secret recipes. Here, in their stead, is a ubiquitous Cincinnati chili recipe that reflects the Middle Eastern origins of its developers.

kosher salt

1 pound ground chuck

1³/₄ cups chopped onions

2 cloves garlic, minced

1 cup barbecue sauce

1 cup water

¹/₂ ounce bitter chocolate, grated

1 tablespoon commercial chili powder

1 teaspoon black pepper

¹/₂ teaspoon ground cumin

¹/₂ teaspoon turmeric

¹/₂ teaspoon ground allspice

¹/₂ teaspoon ground cinnamon

¹/₄ teaspoon ground cloves

¹/₄ teaspoon ground coriander

¹/₄ teaspoon ground cardamom

1 teaspoon salt

tomato juice (optional)

garlic salt

8 ounces thin spaghetti, cooked, drained, and buttered

1 can (15¹/₂ ounces) red kidney beans, rinsed and drained

1 large onion, chopped (about 1 cup)

8 ounces Cheddar cheese, grated (about 2 cups)

continued

1. Sprinkle kosher salt on a large skillet and heat for a few moments; add chuck, $3/4$ cup onion, and garlic and sauté until meat is no longer pink. Drain well and transfer to a chili pot.

2. Stir in barbecue sauce, water, chocolate, spices, and 1 teaspoon salt and bring to a boil. Lower heat and simmer 30 minutes, adding tomato juice if mixture gets too thick. Adjust seasonings with garlic salt.

3. To serve classic "five-way" chili, layer spaghetti, chili, beans, remaining onion, and cheese. To complete the carbo overload, serve with oyster crackers on the side.

MAKES 4 SERVINGS

Chili Appetizers

Chili eaters is some of Your chosen people. We don't know why You so doggone good to us. But Lord God, don't ever think we ain't grateful for this chili we about to eat.

Amen.

—CLOSING TO A CHILI PRAYER
COMPOSED BY LEGENDARY RANGE COOK
MATTHEW "BONES" HOOKS

Good chili takes time. This can be a drawback if you suddenly are overcome with a burning desire for a bowl of red, your freezer is agonizingly empty of all that chili you stashed away last winter, and you don't happen to live within sprinting distance of the Hard Times Cafe or the Manhattan Chili Co. or some other such establishment. On the other hand, developing the steely fortitude to bide your time while a batch of chili is stewing is good for the soul and will no doubt come in handy in later life. (Just don't ask us when.) The three or so hours it takes to make up a pot of really good chili also provides an excellent opportunity to nosh.

While virtually all the chiliheads we know are fine cooks, not a single one is willing to expend a lot of energy on making up a plate of fancy appetizers as a prelude to a bowl of red. To begin with, doing things like carefully wrapping small fruits in prosciutto or mincing water chestnuts takes entirely too much time and effort. Moreover, it is possible to become totally involved in the preparations called for in making, say, crab wontons or mesquite-grilled bacon-wrapped olives and the next thing you know, the chili is bubbling away on top of an inch-thick layer of charred meat and even the dog won't touch it.

That doesn't mean chiliheads don't like to eat anything before they eat chili. Indeed, the rundown of pre-chili nibbling items is vast. This is doubly important if you are having a flock of chiliheads over to try out your new recipe. (Like migratory birds, chiliheads prefer to travel in large groups.) However, upon arriving at your home, they will immediately start hovering around that chili pot, lifting off the lid and smelling the chili and demanding to know when it's going to be ready. You could, of course, give in and have the chili ready to serve them right away, in which case it will disappear in about .07 microseconds and there goes your party. Far better to have the chili simmering sweetly on the back burner for an hour or so while your guests amuse themselves and others with various libations and assorted appetizers of the scoop, dip, and munch genus.

The key word here is simplicity. None of these recipes are difficult to prepare, all segue nicely to a bowl of chili, and for the most part, they leave you, the host, free to mingle with your guests, not stuck in the kitchen shuffling cookie sheets full of pastry puffs from the top to the bottom shelf and back again in the oven.

✦ Salsas ✦

Salsa, as we all know, was invented by chili cooks who wanted something to munch on while their chili was cooking. There are about a gazillion variations on the basic tomato-onion-cilantro-jalapeño-garlic mixture known alternately as pico de gallo, salsa fresca, and just plain salsa. Here are a few to get you started.

Debbie's Salsa

Debbie Fenton, Floral Park, New York

Debbie, who grew up on Long Island, fell for this salsa when she first tasted it at a friend's baby shower. The original recipe came from California, and it metamorphosed into something similar to this version as it migrated east. Debbie herself made a few more changes, and the result is always a hit.

3 large cans (28 ounces each) plum tomatoes, drained

1 medium red onion, chopped

½ bunch scallions

½ bunch fresh cilantro

1 can (4 ounces) jalapeño peppers, drained and chopped

4 cloves garlic

juice of 1 lime

dash of balsamic vinegar (optional)

1. Chop plum tomatoes and set aside.

2. In a blender or food processor, pulse red onion, scallions, cilantro, peppers, and garlic until coarsely chopped. Add lime juice and a dash of balsamic vinegar if desired.

3. Add tomatoes and let stand for a few hours or overnight to let the flavors blend.

MAKES ABOUT 8 CUPS

Colleen's Version of Debbie's Salsa

Colleen Freely, Floral Park, New York

Colleen, who used to light up Manhattan when she worked for CBS Sports (she is now the mother of two children, and New York is a tamer place for it), put her own touches on the basic recipe. It was good enough to win second place in the 1994 New York State Chili Championship.

3 cans (28 ounces each) Redpack crushed tomatoes (if you can't get Redpack, don't bother with the recipe)
1 medium red onion, chopped
½ bunch scallions, chopped

1 bunch fresh cilantro, chopped
4 fresh jalapeño peppers, diced
4 cloves garlic, minced
1 red bell pepper, diced
juice of 1 lime
salt and black pepper to taste

Stir all ingredients gently together and let them get acquainted for a couple of hours. Serve with nacho cheese–flavored chips and frozen strawberry margaritas.

MAKES ABOUT 10 CUPS

Colonel Roosevelt's San Juan Hill Salsa

❧

Dennis Roosevelt, Southbury, Connecticut

Shortly after starting his first chef's job following his graduation from the Culinary Institute of America, Dennis Roosevelt was asked by his French-speaking, Swiss-trained executive chef to "meeek uss soom chileee." Roosevelt hadn't the foggiest notion how to make chili but remembered a chili-cooking chef under whom he had studied named Jim Heywood. He dug out a copy of Big Jim's Hogbreath Chili (see page 102), and the recipe saved his job and started Roosevelt on the chili-cooking trail. Head of Team Durachili, Roosevelt developed this salsa after tasting dozens of salsas at various cookoffs that ranged from instant death to already dead. Now chiliheads from all over can enjoy a salsa that ICS advisory board member Jonathan Levine calls the "best salsa recipe in the whole world."

1   large green bell pepper, cut in ¼-inch dice (about 1 cup)

1   large red bell pepper, cut in ¼-inch dice (about 1 cup)

1   large Spanish onion, cut in ¼-inch dice (about 1 cup)

1   red onion, cut in ¼-inch dice (about 1 cup)

8   scallions, cut in ⅛-inch dice (about ½ cup)

2   Italian peppers, cut in ¼-inch dice (about ½ cup), or 1 can (4 ounces) chopped green chiles

4 really big tomatoes or 8 plum tomatoes, peeled, seeded, and coarsely chopped (about 2 cups)

6 cloves garlic, crushed

4 large jalapeño peppers, finely chopped

1 medium long hot pepper, finely chopped

1/4 cup finely chopped fresh cilantro

1/4 cup olive oil

1/4 cup red wine vinegar

juice of 1 lime

1 pint of your favorite commercial salsa

salt and black pepper to taste

Combine all vegetables and mix. Add oil, vinegar, and lime juice. Blend with prepared salsa and season with salt and pepper. Refrigerate for at least 1/2 hour.

MAKES ABOUT 10 CUPS

Mike's Salsa

Mike's On the Avenue, New Orleans

½ cup diced scallions (about 8)

½ cup diced red onion
(about ½ large onion)

8 cups finely chopped ripe
tomatoes (about 2½ pounds)

6 serrano chiles, finely chopped

½ cup finely chopped fresh
cilantro

¼ cup lime juice

2 tablespoons sugar

2 tablespoons kosher salt

Combine in a large bowl and toss together.

MAKES ABOUT 10 CUPS

Brown Dog's Salsa

Orv Balcom, Lomita, California

*Orv, a rock-and-roll musician in his youth, dabbled halfheartedly in
chili cookoffs until 1983, the year he overheard two young ladies in a bar
discussing which chili cooks would be at the next cookoff. "As I moved
into middle age, I missed the groupies," Orv said. "I thought chili cooking
might be the answer, so I sent in my one hundred dollars for a lifetime
membership. And that's how I got started." Most of these canned salsas
can be found in Mexican markets or in supermarkets, even in the
Northeast. If you can't find them, you can substitute jars of Paul
Newman's various salsas.*

2 medium tomatoes	1 can (10½ ounces) salsa ranchera
2 scallions	
2 jalapeño peppers	1 shot glass fresh lime juice
1 sprig fresh cilantro	1 shot glass Brown Dog's Chili Powder (recipe follows)
4 cans (10½ ounces) salsa casera	
1 can (10½ ounces) salsa verde	salt, ground cumin, Tabasco sauce to taste

Chop tomatoes, scallions, peppers, and cilantro. Combine with
canned salsas, lime juice, and chili powder and let stand 1 hour. Add
salt, cumin, and Tabasco to taste.

MAKES ABOUT 8 CUPS

Brown Dog's Chili Powder

∽

Combine ¼ cup ground pasilla chiles, ¼ cup ground California chiles, ¼ cup ground New Mexico chiles, ¼ cup ground cumin, ¼ cup paprika, 2 tablespoons ground oregano, 1 tablespoon ground coriander, 2 tablespoons garlic powder.

🍴 MAKES ABOUT 1½ CUPS

Timothy Schafer's Smoked Poblano, Black Bean, and Mango Salsa

∽

Creations Restaurant, Madison, New Jersey

Although this is meant to be served as an accompaniment to a main dish, we found it was terrific used as a dip with fresh vegetables.

1	roasted poblano chile, soaked and diced	1/4	cup honey
8	ounces dried black beans, soaked overnight and cooked until tender (or use 2 to 3 15-ounce cans)	1	teaspoon chopped fresh cilantro
		2	teaspoons cider vinegar
		1/2	teaspoon salt
			pinch of black pepper
1	medium ripe mango, peeled and diced		dash of Worcestershire sauce
			dash of Tabasco sauce
1/2	red onion, finely diced (about 1/2 cup)		

Combine all ingredients, then refrigerate to blend flavors.

MAKES ABOUT 5 CUPS

★ *Guacamole* ★

The yucky stuff you get out of cans bears little resemblance to the buttery fresh versions that follow. Use only the smaller, black-skinned avocados called Haas, or the smooth-skinned Calavos—both from California—as the green Florida ones are tasteless and watery. The trick here is to plan ahead—buy the avocados a couple of days in advance and let them ripen at room temperature until they squeeze nicely, like Charmin.

Mike's Guacamole

Mike's On the Avenue, New Orleans

6	shallots	1	large clove garlic, chopped
6	ripe avocados, peeled and coarsely chopped	1½	tablespoons chopped red onion
	juice of 2 limes	1	teaspoon black pepper
1	teaspoon kosher salt	2	tablespoons olive oil
10	dashes of Tabasco sauce		

1. In a 350°F oven, roast whole, unpeeled shallots for about 20 minutes. Let cool, then peel and chop.

2. In a medium-sized bowl, gently combine avocados, shallots, lime juice, salt, Tabasco, garlic, red onion, black pepper, and olive oil.

3. Serve with blue and white corn tortilla chips.

MAKES ABOUT 4 CUPS

World's Finest Guacamole

JoAnne Conley, Chairman, Gold Fever Chili Cookoff

"You can throw away all those other guacamole recipes you have collected," says JoAnne. "This is the only one you need!" Our testers were inclined to agree.

2   very large, very ripe avocados, peeled and cut in chunks

2   dead-ripe tomatoes, peeled, seeded, and chopped

1   bunch scallions, thinly sliced

1   can (7 ounces) peeled green chiles, finely chopped

4   ounces bacon, fried and crumbled

juice of ½ lime

Using a potato masher, combine all ingredients except lime juice until well mixed but still chunky. Just before serving, stir in lime juice.

MAKES ABOUT 2 CUPS

Easy Guacamole

꩜

Adapted from The Tabasco Brand Cookbook, *this simple recipe can be made hotter just by adding more Tabasco, eliminating the need to handle hot peppers.*

2   ripe Haas avocados, peeled
    and cut into chunks
1   small onion, minced (about
    ¹/₂ cup)

2   tablespoons lime juice
¹/₂   teaspoon Tabasco sauce
¹/₂   teaspoon salt

With a fork, mash avocados with onion, lime juice, Tabasco, and salt just enough to blend. Serve at once.

🍴 MAKES ABOUT 1 CUP

*   Dips   *

Tortilla or corn chips are great favorites of chiliheads, who were pioneers in developing dips that went beyond the old sour cream–onion soup varieties and also served to lay a good foundation for the upcoming chili. In case you were wondering (as we were) just why cheesy things seem to go so perfectly with chili, we found the answer in Jean Andrews's fascinating book, *Red Hot Peppers.* "Fat," she wrote, "takes hours longer than carbohydrates or proteins to digest, so stimulants such as alcohol take longer to affect someone who has eaten a fatty snack such as cheese before drinking." So eat some cheese before indulging in chili washed down with beer or margaritas!

Chili Dip

1 package (8 ounces) cream cheese, softened
1 cup chili
8 ounces sharp Cheddar cheese, shredded

2 jalapeño peppers, diced
1 large tomato, diced

1. Preheat oven to 375°F. Spread softened cream cheese in a small glass pie plate and cover with chili. Top with shredded cheese and bake for 10 minutes.

2. Top with diced jalapeños and tomato and serve with tortilla chips.

MAKES 12 SERVINGS

Maria's Hot Mexican Dip

∽

Maria Peluso, Floral Park, New York

Maria is better known for her Ragù Bolognese than any Tex-Mex specialty, but this dip pleases everyone north and south of the border.

1	package (8 ounces) cream cheese, softened	1½	cups chili
1	medium onion, chopped	8	ounces Monterey Jack cheese with jalapeños, shredded (about 2 cups)
1	green bell pepper, chopped		

1. Preheat oven to 350°F. Spread softened cream cheese over the bottom of a square baking dish or a pie plate.

2. Scatter onion and pepper evenly over cream cheese, then spread chili on top of that. Complete the layers with shredded Monterey Jack cheese. Bake for 20 minutes, serve with tortilla chips, and watch it vanish.

MAKES **12** SERVINGS

Classic Pickapeppa Spread

◠◡

Truett Airhart, Houston, Texas

Jim West described Truett Airhart as one of the great cooks of all time, and we had the pleasure of sampling his cooking one memorable evening at West's house in Newport Beach watching the New York Rangers nearly blow the Stanley Cup semifinals. Truett sent us to the store for some fresh peppers and the makings for this spread, which we had last tasted at our cousin's in South Carolina. It was as good as we remembered and neatly fulfilled all the requirements for a pre-chili nosh.

1   package (8 ounces) cream
     cheese

1   small bottle Pickapeppa sauce
     Triscuits or Wheat Thins

Put block of cream cheese in the middle of a plate and pour Pickapeppa sauce over it. (It will look like a rectangular chocolate sundae). Serve surrounded by crackers.

⑂ MAKES 8 SERVINGS

Chip Dip

∽

1 ripe medium Haas avocado

1 container (8 ounces) sour cream

1 can (4 ounces) whole green chiles, drained, seeded, and chopped

1 jar (15 ounces) salsa

8 ounces Monterey Jack cheese, grated (about 2 cups)

1. Peel and cut avocado into little cubes and spread over the bottom of a large glass pie plate or a wide, shallow glass bowl.

2. Carefully cover avocado with sour cream, then sprinkle chiles on top of sour cream and spread salsa on top of it all.

3. Top with grated cheese, refrigerate for 8 hours, and serve with tortilla chips.

MAKES 12 SERVINGS

Chili con Queso Dip

1994 World's Champion Cathy Wilkey, Seattle, Washington

Food snobs who turn up their noses at the use of Velveeta can use Cheddar cheese, but you lose some of that tacky authenticity that makes this special.

½ cup (1 stick) butter
1 bunch scallions, finely chopped
1 can green chiles, chopped
1 whole tomato, chopped

2 pounds Velveeta cheese, cubed
1 can (12 ounces) stewed tomatoes, Hunt's brand preferred

1. Melt butter in a skillet over medium heat, add scallions, chiles, and tomato, and sauté until scallions are softened. Stir in cheese and stewed tomatoes and cook over low heat until cheese is melted.

2. Transfer to an attractive crock (or an unattractive one if you're feeling cranky) and serve with tortilla chips.

MAKES 16 SERVINGS

A. H. Reamer Chili Co. Dip

❧❧

Bobbi Gaul, Irvine, California

*Bobbi made this dip up after complaining that her husband's version
was way too hot—he used jalapeño peppers instead of green chiles!*

8   ounces Monterey Jack cheese,
    grated (about 2 cups)

1   can (4 ounces) green chiles,
    drained and chopped, Ortega
    brand preferred

1   can (8 ounces) black olives,
    drained and chopped

4 to 5 tomatoes, chopped
    (about 3 cups)

1   bottle Italian salad dressing
    with cheese

1/4 cup chopped fresh cilantro

Mix all ingredients together and serve with tortilla chips.

🍴 MAKES **12** SERVINGS

Jim's Tex-Mex Hors d'Oeuvres

This recipe made the rounds through the ICS hierarchy in 1992, when Truett Airhart described it to Jim West, who described it to Sherre Mesker, who described it to Cheryl West. Kinda like telephone.

1   bunch scallions, chopped
$1/_4$ cup finely chopped jalapeño peppers
juice of 1 lime
1   package (3 ounces) cream cheese

1   container (8 ounces) sour cream
$1/_4$ cup salsa
$1/_4$ teaspoon cayenne
8 to 10 burrito-size flour tortillas

1. In a small bowl, mix chopped scallions with jalapeños and lime juice. In another bowl, mix cream cheese, sour cream, salsa, and cayenne.

2. Overlapping their edges, spread tortillas out on a very large table or a very clean floor. Spread the cream cheese–sour cream mixture over the tortillas right to the edges, then sprinkle the scallion-jalapeño–lime juice combo over that.

3. Working carefully, roll up tortillas into one long, narrow cylinder and freeze for $1/_2$ hour. Slice into bite-sized rounds and serve.

MAKES **12** SERVINGS

CHILI APPETIZERS

Cheesy Artichokes

〰

A bit more work but helpful if you're having the judges over the night before a cookoff and want to impress them.

1	can (14 ounces) artichoke hearts, drained	2	tablespoons Dijon mustard, plus extra for pie shell
1	tablespoon olive oil	1/2	cup grated Parmesan or Romano cheese
1	container (15 1/2 ounces) ricotta cheese	1	frozen deep-dish pie shell
4	eggs	8	ounces mozzarella cheese, shredded
1/4	cup chopped fresh flat-leaf parsley or cilantro		

1. Preheat oven to 400°F. Slice artichokes thinly and sauté briefly in olive oil. Set aside.

2. In a medium bowl, beat ricotta and eggs together with a fork until well mixed. Add parsley, mustard, and Parmesan cheese and stir until blended.

3. Brush bottom of the pie shell with mustard. Place artichokes in pie shell, pour cheese mixture over it, and top with shredded mozzarella. Bake 15 minutes at 400°F, then lower heat to 325°F and bake another 30 minutes. Serve in wedges.

🍴 MAKES **12** SERVINGS

Jalapeño Cheese Sticks

If you're serving a bunch of tender-mouthed individuals, use only 1 table-spoon chopped jalapeños and 2 tablespoons bell pepper. If, on the other hand, your guests have asbestos for taste buds, by all means substitute serrano or even (gasp) habanero peppers.

¼	cup solid vegetable shortening	2	tablespoons water
¾	cup all-purpose flour	3	tablespoons chopped jalapeño
¼	teaspoon salt		peppers
⅓	cup grated Cheddar cheese		

1. Preheat oven to 425°F. In a small bowl, using 2 knives or a pastry blender, cut shortening into flour and salt until mixture looks like small peas.

2. Mix in cheese and enough water to moisten dough, then stir in jalapeños. With hands, form dough into a ball.

3. Roll out dough on a floured surface between 2 sheets of wax paper until ¼ inch thick. Score dough lengthwise in half, then cut crosswise into strips about ½ inch wide and 4 inches long. Bake on a lightly oiled baking sheet for 12 minutes, or until golden brown.

MAKES 6 SERVINGS

Chile-Cheese Squares

∽

New Mexicans are very proud of the deep-fried dish called chiles rellenos, which, literally translated, means "death from instantly constricting arteries." This version isn't exactly Pritikin-approved, but at least you can eat it in peace.

2	cans (4 ounces each) chopped green chiles, drained	1	container egg substitute
2	cups grated reduced-fat Cheddar or Monterey Jack cheese	¼	cup half-and-half

1. Preheat oven to 350°F. Grease a 13 X 9-inch baking pan and spread chiles on the bottom. Sprinkle cheese evenly over chiles.

2. Beat egg substitute and half-and-half together, pour over chiles and cheese, and bake 30 minutes, or until top is lightly browned.

3. Let cool slightly and cut into small squares.

MAKES 6 SERVINGS

Quesadillas

૭૭

Most quesadillas we've encountered are huge, plate-sized affairs with cheese oozing out of the sides and are best tackled with a steak knife and fork. These, on the other hand, are small, neat, and very popular.

6   ounces Monterey Jack or American cheese with jalapeños, thinly sliced

8   small flour tortillas

Place about $3/4$ ounce cheese on $1/2$ of each tortilla, folding the other half over to make a half-moon. Heat a nonstick skillet, and toast the quesadillas for about 15 seconds on each side, or until cheese just melts. Cut each half-moon in 4 wedges and serve.

¶¶ MAKES 8 SERVINGS

Not by Chili Alone—Scrumptious Sides

It ain't corn bread without jalapeños.

—CARROLL SHELBY

Contrary to widespread public opinion, chiliheads do not live by chili alone. Sometimes they put eggs under their chili or heap chili in tacos and top it with shredded cheese, tomato, and lettuce or pile chili on top of hot dogs for one of the great taste treats of our time. But while chili, by its very nature, always commands center stage, it is gracious enough to allow room for supporting players. Show us a chilihead with a topnotch bowl of red, a plate full of warm, home-made corn bread, and a side of tangy coleslaw, and we'll show you one happy camper.

C. V. Wood's World-Class Tex-Mex Corn Bread

∽

The undeFEETed, undeniaBULL champion of corn breads.

1½ cups yellow cornmeal

¼ cup sugar

2 teaspoons salt

1 teaspoon baking powder

6 ounces Longhorn Cheddar cheese, grated (about 1½ cups)

2 large eggs, lightly beaten

1 can (12 ounces) Mexican-style corn, drained

¾ cup milk

¼ cup (½ stick) butter, melted

¼ cup corn oil

1 can (7 ounces) diced green chiles, drained

1. Preheat oven to 400°F. Grease a 9-inch square baking pan.

2. In a large bowl, mix together cornmeal, sugar, salt, and baking powder. In another large bowl, mix cheese, beaten eggs, corn, milk, melted butter, oil, and chiles. Add the dry ingredients and stir together until thoroughly blended.

3. Spread batter in baking pan and bake it on the top rack for about 45 minutes, or until top is just on the dark side of golden. ENJOY!

¶¶ MAKES 8 SERVINGS

West Virginia Governor Gaston Caperton's Corn Bread Muffins

༄

2 cups yellow cornmeal	2 large eggs, lightly beaten
1¼ cups all-purpose flour	2 cups buttermilk
5 tablespoons sugar	¼ cup vegetable oil
2¼ teaspoons baking powder	¼ cup chopped jalapeño peppers
1¼ teaspoons baking soda	(optional)
¾ teaspoon sea salt	

1. Preheat oven to 425°F. Grease 8 to 10 muffin cups or line with paper liners.

2. In a large mixing bowl, stir together cornmeal, flour, sugar, baking powder, baking soda, and salt. In a smaller bowl, stir together eggs, buttermilk, and oil.

3. Stirring well with a fork, add egg mixture to dry ingredients until thoroughly mixed. If desired, stir in jalapeños. Spoon into muffin cups and bake for 15 minutes.

MAKES 8 TO 10 SERVINGS

Eastern Corn Bread

⁓

This recipe comes via Robert Cacciola of the James Beard House, who adapted it from Chris Schlesinger and John Willoughby's corn bread in The Thrill of the Grill *(New York: William Morrow and Company, 1990) and serves it to rave reviews at the annual James Beard Invitational Chili Cookoff.*

4 cups sifted all-purpose flour	3 cups whole milk, at room temperature
2 cups sifted cornmeal	
1 1/2 cups granulated sugar	3 tablespoons vegetable oil
2 tablespoons baking powder	1/3 cup melted butter or margarine
1 teaspoon kosher salt	
4 large eggs, at room temperature	

1. Preheat oven to 350°F. Grease a 12 x 8-inch baking pan.

2. In a large bowl, mix together flour, cornmeal, sugar, baking powder, and salt. In another bowl, stir together eggs, milk, and oil. Add to dry ingredients, stir briefly, then add melted butter. Stir again until mixed.

3. Pour into greased baking pan and bake for about 1 hour, or until top is lightly browned and a knife inserted into the center comes out clean.

¶¶ MAKES **12** SERVINGS

Ann W. Richards's Jalapeño-Cheese Corn Bread

☙❧

Like the former Texas governor's hairdo, this light corn bread defies gravity.

1½ cups corn bread mix, such as Aunt Jemima

¾ cup milk

1 large egg

4 scallions, chopped (about ⅓ cup)

1 small can cream-style corn (about ½ cup)

4 fat jalapeño peppers, chopped (about ½ cup)

6 ounces Cheddar cheese, grated (about 1½ cups)

2 tablespoons vegetable oil

1 tablespoon sugar

bacon bits, chopped red bell pepper, minced garlic (as much or as many as you like)

1. Preheat oven to 425°F. Lightly grease a 12 X 8-inch baking pan.

2. Combine all ingredients in a large bowl and mix well. If desired, add bacon bits, chopped pepper, and/or minced garlic.

3. Pour into baking dish and bake for about 25 minutes, or until top is browned and a knife inserted into the center comes clean.

🍴 MAKES 8 SERVINGS

NOT BY CHILI ALONE—SCRUMPTIOUS SIDES

Carroll A. Campbell, Jr.'s Spoon Corn Bread

֍

From the former governor of South Carolina comes this smooth, almost creamy bread, a terrific side dish with the hottest, spiciest chilis.

3	cups milk		1	tablespoon baking powder
1	scant cup cornmeal		1	tablespoon butter, melted
3	large eggs, well beaten		1	teaspoon salt

1. Preheat oven to 400°F. Lightly grease a 1-quart glass baking dish.

2. Pour 2 cups milk into a saucepan, stir in cornmeal, and bring to a boil over medium-high heat, stirring constantly until it thickens to a mushy consistency.

3. Add remaining 1 cup milk, eggs, baking powder, melted butter, and salt and pour into the greased baking dish. Bake 32 minutes, or until firm.

🍴 MAKES 8 SERVINGS

Cathy Wilkey's Mexican Corn Brunch Bread

❦

1 cup (2 sticks) unsalted butter, at room temperature

1 cup sugar

4 large eggs

1 can (4 ounces) diced green chiles, drained

1 can (15 ounces) cream-style corn

4 ounces Monterey Jack cheese, shredded (about $1/2$ cup)

4 ounces Cheddar cheese, shredded (about $1/2$ cup)

1 cup flour

1 cup yellow cornmeal

4 teaspoons baking powder

$1/4$ teaspoon salt

1. Preheat oven to 350°F. Grease and flour a 13 x 9-inch baking pan.

2. In a large bowl, cream butter and sugar together. Add eggs one at a time, mixing thoroughly. Stir in chiles, corn, and cheeses and mix well.

3. Sift flour, cornmeal, baking powder, and salt over butter-egg mixture and blend in thoroughly. Pour into the baking pan, place in the oven, and lower heat to 300°F. Bake 1 hour.

🍴 MAKES 8 SERVINGS

Mexican Jalapeño Corn Bread

෧෨

Ermalee Hickel developed this recipe while shivering away as First Lady of Alaska.

3/4 cup milk

1 large onion, cut in chunks

2 large eggs

1 can (8 ounces) cream-style corn

1 tablespoon sugar

3 cups corn bread mix

1 can (4 ounces) whole green chiles, drained, seeded, and chopped

2 tablespoons chopped pimiento

1 can (8 ounces) whole-kernel corn

8 ounces Cheddar cheese, grated (about 1 cup)

1. Preheat oven to 425°F. Lightly grease a 13 X 8-inch baking pan and dust with a little cornmeal until lightly coated. Place in oven briefly until cornmeal is light brown. Remove and set aside.

2. Pour 1/2 cup milk into blender container, add onion chunks, and chop into large pieces. Add eggs, cream-style corn, sugar, and remaining 1/4 cup milk. Blend until fairly smooth.

3. Place cornmeal in a large bowl, and, using a fork, stir in blender mixture until just combined. Gently stir in chiles, pimiento, corn, and ²/₃ cup cheese.

4. Working quickly, spread batter in pan. Bake 20 to 25 minutes, until almost done.

5. Remove corn bread from oven and quickly sprinkle remaining cheese evenly over the top. Lower heat to 325°F, return corn bread to oven, and bake about 5 more minutes, or until cheese melts.

MAKES 12 SERVINGS

Janos Wilder's Blue Corn Bread

॰॰

Janos Wilder, Tucson, Arizona

Wilder serves French-inspired Southwest cuisine to rave reviews at his restaurant, Janos. The blue corn in this recipe gives the corn bread an earthy flavor. It's available by mail order if you can't find it in the gourmet section of your grocery, or you can substitute yellow cornmeal. Wilder triples this recipe and uses a dozen 5 x 3-inch loaf pans; we trimmed it down and used two 8-inch square baking pans.

1	medium to large onion, diced (about $^2/_3$ cup)	6	tablespoons unsalted butter, melted
1	teaspoon oil	4	jumbo eggs
1	cup blue cornmeal	$1^1/_3$	cups cold milk
$^1/_2$	cup bread flour	5	ounces Cheddar cheese, grated (about $^2/_3$ cup)
$^1/_2$	cup masa harina		
1	tablespoon sugar	1	can (7 ounces) diced green chiles, drained (about $^2/_3$ cup)
1	tablespoon baking powder		

1. Preheat oven to 375°F. Grease two 8-inch square baking pans thoroughly.

2. In a small skillet, heat oil over medium heat and sauté onion until softened. Set aside.

3. In a large mixing bowl, combine blue cornmeal, bread flour, masa harina, sugar, and baking powder.

4. In another bowl, mix butter, eggs, milk, cheese, chiles, and sautéed onions until thoroughly combined.

5. Pour into pans and bake 30 to 35 minutes, until tops are browned and a knife inserted in center comes out clean.

Buttermilk Biscuits

❧

2	cups flour	$^3/_4$	cup buttermilk
1	teaspoon salt	5	tablespoons solid vegetable
1	teaspoon baking powder		shortening
$^1/_2$	teaspoon baking soda	3	tablespoons melted butter

1. Preheat oven to 400°F. Sift flour, salt, and baking powder together in a small bowl. In a measuring cup, add baking soda to buttermilk and set aside for a few minutes.

2. Using a fork, cut shortening into dry ingredients until mixture is crumbly. Add buttermilk and mix until dough forms a ball.

3. Place dough on a floured surface and roll out until $^1/_2$ inch thick. Cut with a biscuit cutter (or a shot glass), place on an ungreased baking sheet, and bake for 10 minutes. Remove from oven, brush tops with melted butter and bake for another 5 minutes.

Lentil Salad

∾

1	pound dried lentils	3	tablespoons grainy Dijon mustard
1/4	cup chopped fresh cilantro	1	clove garlic, minced
1/2	small red bell pepper, chopped (about 1/4 cup)	1/3	cup red wine vinegar
1	small red onion, chopped (about 3/4 cup)	2/3	cup olive oil
			salt to taste

1. In a large saucepan, cover lentils with about 6 cups of water, bring to a boil, and simmer until tender, about 1 hour. Drain and let cool.

2. In a large bowl, mix lentils, cilantro, red pepper, and red onion. In a small bowl, mix mustard, garlic, and vinegar. Whisk in olive oil and add the vinaigrette to the lentils. Refrigerate until ready to serve and add salt to taste.

🍴 MAKES 12 SERVINGS

Renee's Lemon Coleslaw

〰️

Renee Rosenblatt, Lakewood, New Jersey

Renee, who happens to be Richard's mother and a good cook, closed up the kitchen when the youngest of her three sons went off to college. On special occasions (like the installation of a new pope) she will come out of retirement and put together a memorable meal. One of the highlights is this terrific coleslaw.

1	cantaloupe-sized head cabbage (about 2 pounds)	2	packets artificial sweetener
1	red bell pepper, finely diced (about 1 cup)		juice of 2 lemons
2	carrots, shredded	1/2	cup low-fat mayonnaise (or more as needed)
4	large scallions, finely chopped (about 1/2 cup)		salt and black pepper to taste

1. Using a long, sharp knife, shred cabbage finely, and then chop into smaller pieces. Place in a large bowl and mix in red pepper, carrots, and scallions. Sprinkle sweetener over cabbage and toss thoroughly. Squeeze lemon juice over cabbage and mix thoroughly. Refrigerate until ready to serve.

2. Just before serving, fold in mayonnaise to moisten, adding more if needed. Salt and pepper to taste.

🍴 MAKES 8 SERVINGS

Buttermilk Coleslaw

1 cantaloupe-sized head
cabbage (about 2 pounds)
juice of 1/2 lemon
2 teaspoons sugar

salt and black pepper to taste
1/2 cup mayonnaise (or more as
needed)
1/2 cup buttermilk

1. Using a long, sharp knife, coarsely shred cabbage and place in a large bowl. Squeeze lemon juice over cabbage, then sprinkle with sugar, salt, and pepper and toss gently.

2. In a small bowl, mix mayonnaise and buttermilk and blend well. Add to cabbage and refrigerate for about 2 hours before serving.

MAKES 8 SERVINGS

Sour Cream Coleslaw

⌘

1	cantaloupe-sized head cabbage (about 2 pounds)	1/4	cup cider vinegar
1	cup sour cream	2	tablespoons sugar
1/2	cup mayonnaise		dry mustard, salt, and black pepper to taste

1. Using a long, sharp knife, finely shred cabbage and let soak in water to cover for at least 30 minutes.

2. In small bowl, combine sour cream, mayonnaise, vinegar, and sugar. Add mustard, salt, and pepper to taste, starting with 1/2 teaspoon of each. Drain cabbage well and toss with dressing. Refrigerate for 2 hours before serving.

MAKES 8 SERVINGS

Lemon-Sour Cream Coleslaw with Fresh Dill

∾

1 cup sour cream

½ cup mayonnaise

½ teaspoon dry mustard

salt and black pepper to taste

2 tablespoons sugar

juice of 1 large lemon

1 tablespoon snipped fresh dill

1 cantaloupe-sized head cabbage (about 2 pounds)

1. Prepare the dressing by mixing together all ingredients except cabbage. Refrigerate several hours to let flavors blend.

2. When ready to serve, finely shred the cabbage and toss with dressing.

MAKES 8 SERVINGS

Bean Salad

✎

Beans are an integral part of chili cookery, but most purists insist they be served on the side. We find this cold garlicky bean salad a particularly refreshing accompaniment to chili.

2   cans (15 ounces each) beans (pinto, cannellini, navy, or even black beans)

1/2   red onion, chopped (about 1/2 cup)

1/2   large green bell pepper, chopped (about 1/2 cup)

2   tablespoons chopped flat-leaf parsley

1/2   cup olive oil

2   scant tablespoons red wine vinegar

1/2   teaspoon dry mustard

2   large cloves garlic, minced exceedingly fine or put through a garlic press

salt and black pepper to taste

1. In a large bowl, mix beans with onion, green pepper, and parsley.

2. Prepare vinaigrette dressing by mixing remaining ingredients together in a blender or a small screw-top jar.

3. Toss beans with dressing and refrigerate for several hours. Adjust seasonings with salt and pepper before serving.

🍴 MAKES 4 TO 6 SERVINGS

Ranch Salad

lettuce leaves

2 cans (15 ounces each) red kidney beans, drained

2 cans (15 ounces each) small white beans, drained

2 cans (15 ounces each) chick-peas, drained

1 large red onion, chopped (about 1 cup)

1 bunch scallions, white and tender green parts, chopped (about $\frac{1}{2}$ cup)

2 hot Italian peppers, chopped (about $\frac{3}{4}$ cup)

4 ripe tomatoes, chunked

2 to 3 large cloves garlic, minced

1 cup olive oil

$\frac{1}{4}$ cup red wine vinegar

1 teaspoon dry mustard

pinch of sugar

salt and black pepper to taste

1. Line a salad bowl with lettuce leaves. Mix beans with onion, scallions, peppers, tomatoes, and garlic and pile into the salad bowl.

2. Using a blender or a small screw-top jar, prepare vinaigrette by mixing remaining ingredients together. Pour over beans, stir gently, and serve.

MAKES 10 TO 12 SERVINGS

Jícama, Orange, and Avocado Salad with Poppy Seed Vinaigrette

⟡

lettuce leaves

8 ounces jícama, peeled and cut into small cubes

2 to 3 large oranges, peeled and sectioned

1 very ripe small Haas avocado, peeled, pitted, and cut in small cubes

1/4 cup olive oil

1 tablespoon lemon juice

1 tablespoon orange juice

1 teaspoon sugar

1/2 teaspoon poppy seeds

salt and black pepper to taste

1. Divide lettuce leaves among 6 salad plates. Arrange jícama, orange sections, and avocado over lettuce.

2. In a small screw-top jar, mix oil, lemon juice, orange juice, sugar, poppy seeds, salt, and pepper. Pour over vegetables and serve.

MAKES 6 SERVINGS

Afterburners—

Delectable Desserts

∞

Sugar in the gourd and honey in the horn; I was never so
happy since the hour I was born.

—UNKNOWN CHILIHEAD

*I*t is a proven fact that chiliheads like to end their chili-laced evenings with something sweet. (Judging by the response, so do our nation's leaders.) The trick is in the timing. Very few chiliheads like to go directly from chili to dessert, as this seriously cuts into the time spent swapping stories, gleaning hot new cooking tips, and drinking beer or margaritas or whatever. Generally speaking, folks will eat some chili, drink a beer, eat some more chili, drink a beer, and so on until the chili vanishes or the host does.

Eventually, though, usually before the sun rises (but not always), coffee is consumed and dessert is eaten. Crafty hosts sometimes lure chiliheads to the dessert bar even faster with the promise of Mexican coffee (with Kahlúa) or some other exotic *café du café avec liqueur*. Not always. But combined with the promise of these all-American desserts, you can't miss. Anyway, all these recipes can be prepared ahead and kept cold until it's time to eat.

Key Lime Pie

◎

4	large egg yolks	1	cup whipping cream
1	can (14 ounces) sweetened condensed milk	2	tablespoons confectioners' sugar
1/3	cup Key lime juice	1	teaspoon rum
1	prepared graham cracker pie shell		

1. Preheat oven to 350°F.

2. In a medium bowl, beat egg yolks for about 3 minutes. Add condensed milk and lime juice and beat until smooth. Turn into pie crust and bake 10 minutes. Chill.

3. In a small bowl, beat whipping cream with sugar and rum until stiff peaks form. Spread evenly over pie filling.

Variation: Reserve egg whites and whip until stiff with 1/3 cup sugar and 1 teaspoon rum. Working from the outside in, spread over unbaked lime filling and bake at 350°F for 15 minutes, or until peaks turn light brown.

🍴 MAKES 8 SERVINGS

Lemon Fluff

❦

Diane Schneider, New Hyde Park, New York

Dr. Schneider, a practicing psychologist who coached us through this book, is a very busy woman. Note the dazzling ease with which this delightful dessert is concocted.

1	package (3 ounces) lemon-flavored gelatin	1	container (8 ounces) refrigerated dessert topping
1	container (8 ounces) lemon yogurt		grated rind of 1 lemon

1. Prepare gelatin according to quick-set directions on package but refrigerate for only 15 minutes, or until just starting to set.

2. With a hand mixer, beat in yogurt until smooth and then fold in topping until well mixed. Stir in lemon rind and refrigerate 4 hours.

🍴 MAKES 8 SERVINGS

Tennessee Treats

〰

Tipper Gore, Washington, D.C.

When Vice President Al Gore and Tipper finish a bowl of chili, there's nothing they like better to finish off the meal than these toothsome treats.

2	cups packed dark brown sugar	$1/2$	teaspoon ground cinnamon
2	large eggs	$1/8$	teaspoon ground allspice
2	large egg whites	$1/8$	teaspoon ground cloves
2	tablespoons honey	$1/2$	teaspoon salt
1	teaspoon baking powder	$1/2$	cup raisins
$1/4$	cup boiling water	$1/2$	cup chopped dates
2	cups flour	$1/2$	cup chopped walnuts

1. Preheat oven to 350°F. Grease a 12 X 8-inch baking pan. In a large bowl, mix sugar, eggs, and egg whites until thoroughly blended. Add honey and stir until blended.

2. Stir baking powder in boiling water until dissolved, then add to sugar-egg mixture.

3. In another bowl, combine flour, spices, and salt, then stir into sugar-egg mixture. Add raisins, dates, and walnuts and mix in.

4. Pour batter into greased pan and bake for 30 to 40 minutes, or until a toothpick inserted in center comes out dry. Cut into squares while still warm.

MAKES 2 DOZEN SQUARES

AFTERBURNERS — DELECTABLE DESSERTS

Chocolate Chip Cookies

❦

Senator J. Robert Kerrey, Lincoln, Nebraska

Kerrey first tasted this recipe while governor of the Cornhusker State.

1	cup butter-flavored shortening	2¼	cups all-purpose flour
¾	cup granulated sugar	1	teaspoon salt
¾	cup brown sugar	1	teaspoon baking soda
2	large eggs	1	cup chopped nuts
2	teaspoons vanilla extract	1	package (12 ounces) chocolate chips

1. Preheat oven to 325°F. Cream shortening and sugars together, then add eggs and vanilla and beat well.

2. Sift flour, salt, and soda together in a small bowl, then stir into creamed mixture. Mix in nuts and chocolate chips and roll dough into 1-inch balls. Put balls 2 inches apart on an ungreased baking sheet and flatten with the bottom of a glass dipped in granulated sugar. Bake 10 minutes, then remove from oven (cookies will not look done). Let cool on baking sheet.

♟ MAKES 48 COOKIES

Kansas German Chocolate Pie

Former Governor Joan Finney, Topeka, Kansas

1	package (4 ounces) German sweet chocolate	3	tablespoons cornstarch
$\frac{1}{4}$	cup ($\frac{1}{2}$ stick) butter or margarine	$\frac{1}{8}$	teaspoon salt
1	can (12 ounces) evaporated milk	2	large eggs, lightly beaten
$1\frac{1}{2}$	cups sugar	1	teaspoon vanilla extract
		1	unbaked 9-inch pie shell
		$1\frac{1}{3}$	cups flaked coconut
		$\frac{1}{2}$	cup chopped nuts

1. Preheat oven to 375°F. In a small heavy saucepan (or microwave, following directions on chocolate package), melt chocolate and butter or margarine together, stirring occasionally. Stir in evaporated milk.

2. In a mixing bowl, combine sugar, cornstarch, and salt, then stir in eggs and vanilla. Add chocolate mixture to egg mixture and mix well. Pour into pie shell.

3. In a small bowl, combine coconut and nuts and sprinkle over pie filling. Bake for 25 minutes, then cover with aluminum foil and continue baking another 30 minutes. Let cool, then refrigerate at least 4 hours.

MAKES 8 SERVINGS

Chocolate Nuggets

Governor Bob Miller, Carson City, Nevada

6	ounces chocolate chips		pinch of salt
1	large egg	$^3/_4$	cup milk
$^1/_2$	teaspoon vanilla extract		

1. In a microwave-safe bowl, mix ingredients together. Microwave on high for 2 minutes.

2. Pour into a blender and blend for 1 minute. Pour into 4 demi-tasse cups and refrigerate at least 8 hours.

MAKES 4 SERVINGS

Baked Apple Crumble

⟲

Former Governor Lowell Weicker, Hartford, Connecticut

8	apples, peeled, cored, and thinly sliced	1/2	cup (1 stick) butter
3/4	cup sugar	3/4	cup uncooked oatmeal
3/4	teaspoon ground cinnamon	3/4	cup all-purpose flour
2	tablespoons water	1/8	teaspoon ground cloves
			whipped cream, for garnish

1. Preheat oven to 375° F. Grease a 9-inch pie plate.

2. Place apples in pie plate and sprinkle with 1/4 cup sugar, 1/2 teaspoon cinnamon, and water.

3. Cream together butter and 1/2 cup sugar; add oatmeal, flour, cloves, and 1/4 teaspoon cinnamon. Beat until well blended.

4. Spread oatmeal mixture on top of the apples and bake for 30 to 40 minutes. Garnish with whipped cream.

MAKES 8 SERVINGS

Big Apple Mousse

Former Governor Mario Cuomo, Albany, New York

2	pounds apples, New York State-grown preferred, peeled, cored, and sliced	3	tablespoons unflavored gelatin, softened in a little cold water
1½	cups packed light brown sugar	5	cups (2½ pints) heavy cream
1	stick cinnamon	½	cup granulated sugar
	juice of ½ lemon	1	tablespoon Calvados or apple brandy (optional)
1	cup water		

1. Place apples, brown sugar, cinnamon stick, lemon juice, and water in a heavy saucepan and bring to a boil. Lower heat, cover, and simmer until very tender, about 15 to 20 minutes.

2. Remove cinnamon stick and add softened gelatin to apples; mix well. Using an electric mixer, whip apples until soft peaks form. Refrigerate until needed.

3. In a cold bowl, whip heavy cream at high speed until it begins to thicken. Stop mixer, add granulated sugar and Calvados, and continue to whip until soft peaks form.

4. Fold apples into whipped cream, mix well, and refrigerate until ready to serve.

MAKES 12 SERVINGS

Apple Cake

❧

Governor Bill Weld, Boston, Massachusetts

1½ cups vegetable oil

2 cups sugar

1 teaspoon vanilla extract

2½ cups all-purpose flour

2 teaspoons baking powder

1 teaspoon baking soda

2 teaspoons ground cinnamon

4 to 6 apples, peeled, cored, and chopped (about 3 cups)

1. Preheat oven to 350°F. Grease an 8-inch square baking pan.

2. In a large bowl, mix all ingredients together. Spread into the pan and bake 1 hour. Let cool and cut into squares.

🍴 MAKES 12 SERVINGS

Lemon Chiffon Pie

Maryjean Wall, Lexington, Kentucky

Maryjean is an accomplished horsewoman and award-winning writer who has a talent for ferreting out great eateries in out-of-the-way places. They all have one thing in common—sensational desserts. Here is one of her favorites.

1 tablespoon unflavored gelatin	3/4 cup sugar
1/4 cup cold water	1 1/2 teaspoons grated lemon rind
4 large eggs, separated	1 prepared graham cracker
juice of 4 to 6 lemons (about 1/2 cup)	pie shell

1. In a small bowl, sprinkle gelatin over cold water and allow to soften.

2. Meanwhile, in a heavy-bottomed pan, mix egg yolks, lemon juice, and 1/2 cup sugar. Stirring well, cook for several minutes over low heat, until mixture thickens. Add gelatin, stir until dissolved, and then add 1 teaspoon lemon rind. Remove from heat and allow to cool.

3. In a cold metal bowl, beat egg whites with a hand-held mixer until they start to froth. Add remaining 1/4 cup sugar and beat until stiff peaks form. Fold in cooled lemon mixture, pour into pie shell, sprinkle with remaining 1/2 teaspoon lemon rind, and refrigerate, covered, for several hours or overnight.

MAKES 8 SERVINGS

Lemony Rice Pudding

This recipe was inspired by the terrific rice pudding once served to the press corps before home games at Giants Stadium.

5	cups milk	1	teaspoon grated lemon rind
3	tablespoons sugar	$\frac{1}{2}$	teaspoon pure lemon extract
pinch of salt		$\frac{1}{2}$	cup rice

1. Preheat oven to 275°F. In a heavy saucepan, mix milk, sugar, salt, lemon rind, and lemon extract and heat until just boiling.

2. Stir in rice, let simmer a few seconds, and then pour mixture into a nonstick 2-quart casserole. Cover tightly and bake 1½ hours, or until rice is very soft.

MAKES 12 SERVINGS

Cherry Cream Cheese Pie

This recipe was handed down from my mother, Kathleen Kellner, who served it to moans of pleasure after one of her famous holiday feasts. We tried it on a tableful of chili tasters. They moaned too.

1   cup whipping cream
1/3   cup confectioners' sugar
1   package (8 ounces) cream cheese, softened
1   package (3 ounces) cream cheese, softened

1   prepared graham cracker pie crust
1   can (16 ounces) pitted cherries, drained

1. In a cold bowl, beat whipping cream with sugar until it forms soft peaks. In another bowl, beat cream cheese until fluffy, then fold into whipped cream with a rubber spatula.

2. Scrape mixture into the pie shell and refrigerate several hours. Top with cherries.

MAKES 8 SERVINGS

Sour Cream Lemon Custard Pie

This recipe was adapted from Marilyn Moore's wonderful The Wooden Spoon Dessert Book *(New York: HarperCollins, 1990). Its tart, lemony flavor is a perfect punctuation to a sizzling hot bout with chili.*

1   unbaked 9-inch pie shell (purchased or homemade)

1   cup sugar

1/4 cup cornstarch

3   large egg yolks

1   cup milk

juice of 4 to 6 lemons (about 1/2 cup)

1/4 cup (1/2 stick) unsalted butter, softened

1   container (8 ounces) sour cream

1   cup heavy whipping cream

3   tablespoons confectioners' sugar

1. Preheat oven to 400°F. Bake pie shell for 15 minutes. Remove and let cool.

2. In a heavy saucepan, mix together sugar and cornstarch, then place over medium heat and quickly add egg yolks and milk. Stir in lemon juice and cook until mixture is thickened, about 5 minutes. Remove from heat and stir in softened butter a little at a time. Let cool to room temperature, stirring occasionally, and then stir in sour cream.

3. Spoon mixture into the pie shell and refrigerate several hours. Just before serving, whip together cream and sugar until it forms soft peaks and spread over pie filling.

MAKES 8 SERVINGS

AFTERBURNERS — DELECTABLE DESSERTS

Chili Cocktails

I make it a rule never to drink by daylight and never to

refuse a drink after dark.

—H. L. MENCKEN

If there is one given about chili, it's that you have to have something to wash it down. The first thing that comes to most people's minds is a beer. Well, actually, more than just a beer—or two. We're talking lots and lots of frosty-cold, long-necked beers, pulled from a galvanized tin bucket with bits of ice still clinging to the bottle, sliding off only as you pop off the cap and tilt it up to your lips... but that's another story. The thing about beer, in addition to just plain tasting great with chili, is that it contains (surprise!) alcohol, which seems to cut through the burning sensation triggered by capsaicin. Capsaicin is the chemical in chiles that gives chili powder, and thus chili, its heat. The sensation of having consumed a perfectly blended bowl of chili with that nice, smooth, front-to-back warmth and then cooling off with an ice-cold brew goes beyond words. For those who don't drink, it was a great day indeed when breweries decided to come out with nonalcoholic beer. Soft drinks are OK, but water merely spreads the capsaicin around your mouth and down your gullet.

If truth be known, the best remedy for the heat of chili is milk, although for the life of us we can't picture your basic chilihead swigging down a nice, cool glass of milk after a bowl of red. Sometimes, though, chiliheads get a hankering for something other than beer, not so much during the consumption of chili, but while preparing chili, cleaning up after having prepared chili, reading about chili, talking about chili, or even just thinking about chili, which pretty much covers most of the day (and night). In those instances, various libations involving tequila or rum seem to work best, although one diehard martini drinker we know refuses to drink anything but martinis with chili. The same person also eats bologna and cream cheese sandwiches at every opportunity, so take it from there.

Classic Margarita

❦

½ ounce Triple Sec	crushed ice	
2 ounces tequila	1 lime slice	
juice of ½ lime (if you can get your hands on Key limes, so much the better)	salt	

Shake Triple Sec, tequila, and lime juice with crushed ice. Rub the rim of a 3-ounce glass with a slice of lime, then dip rim into a plate of salt. Strain margarita into the glass.

🍴 MAKES 1 SERVING

Gold Margarita

❧

$1/2$ ounce Cointreau   juice of $1/2$ lime

2   ounces gold tequila

Shake Cointreau and gold tequila with lime juice, then pour over ice.

¶¶ MAKES 1 SERVING

Blue Margarita

❧

1   lime slice   2   ounces tequila

salt $3/4$ ounce blue curaçao

$3/4$ ounce Cointreau   juice of $1/2$ lime

Rim edge of a cocktail glass with lime slice and dip in a plate of salt.
In a cocktail shaker, mix Cointreau, tequila, curaçao, and lime juice
with ice cubes, shake, and strain into the glass.

¶¶ MAKES 1 SERVING

Pacific Rim Margarita

⤾

¹/₂ ounce Cointreau	¹/₂ ounce Midori melon liqueur
2 ounces tequila	juice of ¹/₂ lime

In a cocktail shaker, mix all ingredients with ice cubes, shake, and strain into a glass.

🍴 MAKES 1 SERVING

Chita Margaritas

⤾

Via Chita Rivera via Sardi's.

1 can (6 ounces) frozen limeade	6 ounces tequila
6 ounces beer	6 ice cubes

Mix all ingredients in a blender until slushy and serve in the stemmed, saucer-shaped glasses people mistakenly use to serve champagne in.

🍴 MAKES 4 SERVINGS

Long Island Iced Tea

❦

For the younger set—over twenty-one, under thirty.

½ ounce vodka	½ ounce Triple Sec
½ ounce gin	2 ounces lemon juice
½ ounce white rum	splash of Coca-Cola
½ ounce tequila	

Stir liquors and lemon juice together in a tall glass, fill with ice, and top off with a splash of cola.

🍴 MAKES 1 SERVING

Slammer

ⓢ

*We first encountered Slammers at the Jockey Club Chili Cookoff in
Miami back in 1986. Richard liked them so much—and they went down
so easily—he was virtually useless the remainder of the afternoon.
He did, however, rouse himself in time to judge the Miss Chili
Pepper contest. Richard always rouses himself in time to judge
the Miss Chili Pepper contest.*

1½ ounces tequila   splash of lemon-lime soda

Pour tequila into a 2-ounce shot glass and top with soda. Cover
with a napkin and bang the glass on the table until it's fizzy. Drink
in one gulp.

🍴 MAKES 1 SERVING

Primal Scream

ଡ଼ଡ଼

A distant, much less civilized relative of the Slammer.

³/₄ ounce Kahlúa   splash of club soda

³/₄ ounce tequila

Pour Kahlúa and tequila into a shot glass and top with soda. Cover with a napkin and bang the glass on the table until it fizzes (3 times ought to do it). Drink in one gulp. Scream.

MAKES 1 SERVING

Bloody Maria

ଡ଼ଡ଼

1¹/₂ ounces tequila   juice of ¹/₂ lime

6   ounces tomato juice   ¹/₄ teaspoon seasoned salt

2   dashes Tabasco sauce   freshly ground black pepper

2   dashes Worcestershire sauce   lime wedge, for garnish

Mix all ingredients except lime together and pour over cracked ice in a tall glass. Garnish with lime.

MAKES 1 SERVING

Mayan Punch

❧

Make this punch when you have a crowd around and don't feel like spending the evening hunched over a blender.

1	bottle (1.75 liters) tequila	4	cups sweetened iced tea
1/2	cup lemon juice		cinnamon stick
1/2	gallon pink grapefruit juice cocktail	1 1/2	ounces bitters

Mix all ingredients in a punch bowl and float a block of ice in the center.

¶¶ MAKES 40 SERVINGS

Island Tequila Cocktail

❧

1 1/2	ounces tequila	3	ounces freshly squeezed orange juice
1/2	ounce grenadine		juice of 1/2 small lemon

Stir ingredients together in a mixing glass and pour over ice in a tall glass.

¶¶ MAKES 1 SERVING

Tequila Sunrise

⊘⊘

1½ ounces tequila

½ ounce fresh lime juice

2 ounces orange juice

2 dashes grenadine

lime wedge, for garnish

Mix tequila, lime juice, and orange juice in a tall glass. Add ice to the brim. Pour in grenadine and let it sink to the bottom. Don't stir. Garnish with lime.

🍴 MAKES 1 SERVING

Firehouse Chili Margaritas

⤜

Richard King, Clinton, Virginia

Richard originally hails from Luckenbach, Texas, where, he says, "Everyone is someone, especially on a Sunday afternoon." The only thing we really know about Luckenbach is that Willie Nelson mentioned it in a song and the late, great Hondo Crouch bought the town just so he could have someplace to drink. Anyway, Richard likes to wander around chili cookoffs with this concoction in a fire extinguisher, squirting it into the mouths of chiliheads brave enough to give it a try. They always come back for a second, uh, squirt.

4 cans (6 ounces each) frozen
   limeade
1 bottle (1.75 liters) tequila

1 bottle (a fifth) Triple Sec

Mix limeade according to package directions, then add tequila and Triple Sec. Have fun! Don't drive!

MAKES **16** SERVINGS

Alabama Slammer

❧

Cindy Mullaney, Phoenix, Arizona

After a couple of these, Cindy strolls up to the microphone and sings "Love Shack" during karaoke night at the local tavern.

¹/₂ ounce Southern Comfort	3 ounces orange juice
¹/₂ ounce vodka	¹/₂ ounce grenadine

Fill a tall glass with ice cubes and add Southern Comfort and vodka. Stir in orange juice and then add grenadine until drink turns red. Stir. Drink. Sing.

🍴 MAKES 1 SERVING

Daiquiri

❧

2 ounces rum	2 teaspoons superfine sugar
³/₄ ounce lime juice	

Shake ingredients with ice cubes and strain into a cocktail glass. For a frozen daiquiri, blend ingredients with 4 or 5 ice cubes until slushy.

🍴 MAKES 1 SERVING

Frozen Strawberry Daiquiri

✺

2	ounces rum	6	big, ripe strawberries
3/4	ounce lime juice	6	ice cubes
2	teaspoons superfine sugar		

Put ingredients in a blender and mix until slushy. Serve in a cock-tail glass.

🍴 MAKES 1 SERVING

Frozen Banana Daiquiri

✺

3/4	ounce lime juice	1/2	small banana
2	teaspoons sugar	6	ice cubes
2	ounces rum		

Put all ingredients in a blender and mix until drink is slushy. Serve in a martini glass. If you want to annoy your guests, serve with one of those tacky small bamboo umbrellas.

🍴 MAKES 1 SERVING

Long Island Margaritas

෧෧

1   can (6 ounces) frozen limeade   1   can (6 ounces) water

1   can (6 ounces) tequila   1/2   can (3 ounces) Triple Sec

Put in a blender with ice filled to the top and blend to desired slushy consistency.

🍴 MAKES **6** SERVINGS

Sangria

෧෧

4   oranges   1/4   cup brandy

2   lemons   1   bottle (16 ounces) seltzer

1   bottle (1.5 liters) red wine   ice

1/3   cup sugar

1. Juice 3 of the oranges and cut the fourth into wedges. Juice 1 of the lemons and cut the other into slices.

2. In a large bowl, mix juices together with wine, sugar, and brandy; stir well. Add fruit, mix well, and pour into a couple of pitchers. If you have time, allow it to chill and add seltzer before serving; if not, add ice and seltzer and serve immediately.

🍴 MAKES **12** SERVINGS

CHILI COCKTAILS

✳ Sangria Wine ✳

Jerry Jeff Walker

Friends come for Saturday night
Man it's nice to make up some Sangria wine
It's organic and it comes from the vine
It's also legal and it gets you so high
Yeah, and I love that Sangria wine
Love to drink it with old friends of mine
yeah, I love to get drunk with friends of mine

CHORUS:
Oh, I love Sangria wine
Oh I love Sangria wine

Start with some wine
Get some apples and brandy and sugar just fine
Old friends always show up on time
That's why you add sparkling Burgundy wine
Yeah and I love that Sangria wine

Repeat CHORUS

In Texas on a Saturday night
Everclear is added to the wine sometimes
Some nachos, burritos and tacos
Who knows how it usually goes, it goes

Repeat CHORUS

continued

CHILI COCKTAILS

Yeah and I love that Sangria wine
Just like I love old friends of mine
To tell the truth when they're mixed with the wine
That's why I blend in the lemons and limes
Yeah, and I love that Sangria wine

Beth's Version of Jerry Jeff's Sangria

Beth Tooni, Trumbull, Connecticut

1 bottle (1.5 liters) California red wine	$1/3$ cup sugar
$1^1/_4$ cups orange juice	2 to 3 apples, peeled, cored, and sliced
$1/3$ cup brandy	

Combine all in a pitcher and serve in tall glasses with ice.

MAKES 12 SERVINGS

Chili Sources

✦

✶ *Recommended Chili Books* ✶

The Best from New Mexico Kitchens, by Sheila McNiven Cameron
(Santa Fe: New Mexico Magazine, 1978).

Book of Chili, by Jackie French (Sydney, Australia: Angus & Robertson,
1994).

A Bowl of Red, by Frank X. Tolbert (Dallas: Taylor Publishing
Company, 1953).

Chile Pepper Fever, by Susan Hazen-Hammond and Eduardo Fuss
(Stillwater, MN: Voyageur Press, 1993).

The Chili Cookbook, by Norman Kolpas (Los Angeles: HPBooks–
Price Stern Sloan, 1991).

Chili Lovers' Cook Book, compiled by Al Fischer and Mildred Fischer
(Phoenix: Golden West Publishers, 1984).

Chili Madness, by Jane Butel (New York: Workman Publishing, 1980).

Cooksource, by Isabelle Tourneau (New York: Doubleday, 1990).

Coyote Cafe, by Mark Miller (Berkeley: Ten Speed Press, 1989).

Coyote's Pantry, by Mark Miller and Mary Kiffin (Berkeley: Ten
Speed Press, 1993).

The El Paso Chile Company's Burning Desires, by W. Park Kerr and

Michael McLaughlin (New York: William Morrow and Company, 1994).

The El Paso Chile Company's Texas Border Cookbook, by W. Park Kerr and Norma Kerr (New York: William Morrow and Company, 1992).

The Food Lover's Handbook to the Southwest, by Dave DeWitt and Mary Jane Wilan (Rocklin, CA: Prima Publishing, 1992).

The Great Chile Book, by Mark Miller, with John Harrisson (Berkeley, CA: Ten Speed Press, 1991).

The Great Chili Book, by Bill Bridges (New York: Lyons and Burford, 1981).

Green Chili, by Bette Shannon (Tucson: Treasure Chest Publications, 1981).

Hot and Spicy Chili, by Dave DeWitt, Mary Jane Wilan, and Melissa T. Stock (Rocklin, CA: Prima Publishing, 1994).

The International Chili Society Official Chili Cookbook, by Martina and William Neely (New York: St. Martin's Press, 1981).

Just North of the Border, by Dave DeWitt and Nancy Gerlach (Rocklin, CA., Prima Publishing, 1992).

The Manhattan Chili Co. Southwest American Cookbook, by Michael McLaughlin (New York: Crown Publishers, 1986).

More of the Best from New Mexico Kitchens, by Sheila McNiven Cameron and staff of *New Mexico Magazine* (Santa Fe: New Mexico Magazine, 1983).

New Mexico Cookbook, by Lynn Nusom (Phoenix: Golden West Publishers, 1990).

The Pepper Garden, by Dave DeWitt and Paul W. Bosland (Berkeley, CA: Ten Speed Press, 1993).

Peppers, by Amal Naj (New York: Alfred A. Knopf, 1992).

Red Hot Peppers, by Jean Andrews (New York: Macmillan Publishing, 1993).

The Tabasco Brand Cookbook, by Paul McIlhenny, with Barbara Hunter (New York: Clarkson Potter Publishers, 1993).

The Whole Chile Pepper Book, by Dave DeWitt and Nancy Gerlach (Boston: Little, Brown and Company, 1990).

OTHER CHILI-READING MATERIAL

Bull Cook and Authentic Historical Recipes and Practices, by George Leonard Herter and Berthe E. Herter (Waseca, MN: Herter's Inc., 1960).

The 27 Ingredient Chili Con Carne Murders, by Nancy Pickard (New York: Delacorte–Bantam Doubleday Dell Publishing Group, 1993).

★ *Magazines, Newsletters, Newspapers, and Pamphlets* ★

The Chile Institute Newsletter
P.O. Box 30003
Department 3Q, NMSU
Las Cruces, NM 88003
505-646-3028

Chile Pepper (Spicy World Cuisine) Magazine
P.O. Box 4278
Albuquerque, NM 87196

Goat Gap Gazette (newspaper)
5110 Bayard Lane, #2
Houston, TX 77006
713-667-4652

International Chili Society Newspaper
P.O. Box 2966
Newport Beach, CA 92663
714-631-1780; 714-631-1786 (fax)

Terlingua Trails (newsletter)
Ken Large, editor
727 West Dormard
Midland, TX 79705
800-442-8688

* ✪ r g a n i z a t i o n s *

American Spice Trade
   Association Information
   Bureau
928 Broadway
New York, NY 10010
212-420-8808

Chili Appreciation Society
   International (CASI)
Hut Brown, executive director
1516 Prairie Drive
El Paso, TX 79925
915-772-2379

International Chili Society
Jim West, executive director
P.O. Box 2966
Newport Beach, CA 92663
714-631-1780; 714-631-1786 (fax)

International Connoisseurs of
   Green & Red Chile
P.O. Box 3467
Las Cruces, NM 88003

* E v e n t s   a n d   F e s t i v a l s *

Buffalo Wallow Chili Cookoff
Custer County Chamber of
   Commerce
447 Crook Street
Custer, SD 57730
605-673-2244

CASI Terlingua International
   Chili Championship
Terlingua, TX
915-772-2379

Chili and Bluegrass Festival
201 West 5th Street, Suite 450
Tulsa, OK 74103
918-583-2617

Goldstar Chili Fest
   Downtown Council
300 Carew Tower
441 Vine
Cincinnati, OH 45202
513-579-3191

Hatch Chile Festival
Hatch, NM 87937
505-267-4847

International Chili Society
World's Championship Chili
   Cookoff
Reno, NV 89520
714-631-1780; 714-631-1786 (fax)

Jalapeño Festival
Jalapeño Festival Association
P.O. Drawer 1359
Laredo, TX 78042-1359
210-726-6697

Macho Man Pepper Eating
   Contest
Palestine, TX 75802
1-800-659-3484

National Fiery Foods Show
Albuquerque, NM 87103
505-873-2187

The Original International
   Tolbert/Fowler Memorial
   Championship Cookoff
Terlingua, TX 79852
903-874-5601

Prairie Dog Chili Cookoff and
   World Championship of
   Pickled Quail-Egg Eating
Trader's Village
2602 Mayfield Road
Grand Prairie, TX 75052
214-647-2331

The Red Mile Chili Cookoff
P.O. Box 420
Lexington, KY 40585-0420
606-252-0752

Return of the Chili Queens
   Festival
City of San Antonio
514 W. Commerce Street
San Antonio, TX 78207
512-299-8600

Taste of Cincinnati
   Downtown Council
300 Carew Tower
441 Vine
Cincinnati, OH 45202
513-579-3191

WROK/WZOK Annual Chili
   Shoot-out
3901 Brendenwood Lane
Rockford, IL 61107
815-399-2233

✳ *Mail-Order Sources* ✳

There are hundreds of mail-order houses specializing in chiles, chili and chile powder, spices, salsa, and other hot and fiery ingredients. Here's the list we've compiled from a variety of sources.

Bueno Foods
2001 Fourth Street NW
Albuquerque, NM 87102
505-243-2722
fresh and dried chiles, spices

Casados Farms
P.O. Box 1269
San Juan Pueblo, NM 87566
505-852-2433
chile pods, powders, spices

The Chile Institute
P.O. Box 30003, Dept. 3Q
Las Cruces, NM 88003
505-646-3028
chile pepper research, pamphlets

The Chile Shop
109 East Water Street
Santa Fe, NM 87501
505-983-6080
chile apparel, art, pottery, ristras

Chile Today–Hot Tamale Inc.
Commerce Center Drive
2227 U.S. Highway 1, #139
North Brunswick, NJ 08902
908-360-0036
chile-of-the-month club, packaged chiles, ristras, smoked chiles

The Chili Pepper Store
1616 17th Street, #372
Denver, CO 80202
303-936-9309
chile peppers, chili blends, spices

Coyote Cocina
1364 Rufina Circle, #1
Santa Fe, NM 87501
800-866-4695
chili powders, dried chiles, Coyote Cafe line of hot sauces, salsas, and books

Don Alfonso Foods
P.O. Box 201988
Austin, TX 78720-1988
800-456-6100
chili powders, seeds, books, posters

El Guapo
631 S. Anderson Street
Los Angeles, CA 90023
213-261-7205
whole chile peppers

The El Paso Chile Company
El Paso, TX 79901
915-544-3434
chiles, chile products, Indian folk art

Gold Star Chili, Inc.
5204 Beechmont Avenue
Cincinnati, OH 45230
800-643-0465
chili mix

Hi-Co Western Products
1806 West Main Street
Mesa, AZ 85203
602-834-0149
chili mix, spices, chile peppers

Hot Stuff Spicy Food Store
227 Sullivan Street
New York, NY 10012
800-466-8206
canned, dried, and ground chiles, hot sauces, salsas

International HOT STUFF Inc.
905 North California Avenue
Chicago, IL 60622
800-505-9999
hot sauces from around the world

Los Chileros
P.O. Box 6215
Santa Fe, NM 87502
505-471-6967
*Mexican chiles, chili powders,
salsas, chile jelly*

Mo Hotta–Mo Betta
P.O. Box 4136
San Luis Obispo, CA 93403
800-462-3220
*dried chilies, hot sauces, chile
apparel*

Monterrey Food Products
3939 Brooklyn Avenue
Los Angeles, CA 90063-1899
213-263-2143
*chile peppers, chile powders, dried
chiles, spices*

Nichols Garden Nursery
1190 North Pacific Highway
Albany, OR 97321-4598
503-928-9280
chile pepper seeds

Old Southwest Trading
   Company
P.O. Box 7545
Albuquerque, NM 87194
505-836-0168
chile peppers, salsas, chile apparel

Pendery's Spices
1221 Manufacturing
Dallas, TX 75207
800-533-1870
chili blends, salsas, spices, ristras

Salsa Express
P.O. Box 3985
Albuquerque, NM 87190-3985
800-437-2572
hot sauces, salsas

Santa Cruz Chili & Spice Co.
P.O. Box 177
Tumacacori, AZ 85640
602-398-2591
chili powders, chile pastes, salsas

Santa Fe Seasons
1590 San Mateo Lane
Santa Fe, NM 87501
505-988-1515
spices, salsas

Southwest America
1506-C Wyoming NE
Albuquerque, NM 87112
505-299-1856
chile pepper art

The Southwestern Flavor Co.
P.O. Box 315
Red River, NM 87558
chili powders, hot sauces, salsas

Stewart's Chili Co.
P.O. Box 574
San Carlos, CA 94070
415-571-8530
chili powders, Reno Red

Stonewall Chili Pepper
    Company
P.O. Box 241
Highway 290 E
Stonewall, TX 78671
800-232-2995
*chile peppers, chili powders,
salsas, seeds*

Suzie Hot Sauce
P.O. Box 1025
Huntingdon Valley, PA
    19006-1025
215-512-1708
salsa, spices, chile apparel

Tabasco Country Store
McIlhenny Company
Avery Island, LA 70513-5002
800-634-9599
chili mix, spices, Tabasco

Index

Adam Bomb's radioactive A-bomb chili,
  212–213
A. H. Reamer Chili Co. dip, 308
Aikman, Troy, 219
Airhart, Truett, 48, 120
  classic pickapeppa spread of, 305
  Truett's mother lode chili, 120–121
Alabama slammer, 367
Aldridge, Bobby, 185
Allegani Jani's hot pants chili, 39–40
Allen, John, 26, 188
Anderson, George and Starr, 136
Ann W. Richards's jalapeño-cheese corn
  bread, 321
antelope, in Ormly's California frontier
  survival chili, 162–163
apple(s):
  Beth's version of Jerry Jeff's sangria,
    370

Big Apple mousse, 347
  cake, 348
  crumble, baked, 346
artichokes, cheesy, 310
Ashford, Emmett, 43
Ashley, Liza, 220
Austin, Maria, 92, 93
Austin, Mike, 92
Austin red championship chili,
    106–107
avocado(s):
  easy guacamole, 302
  jícama, and orange salad
      with poppy seed vinaigrette,
      335
  Mike's guacamole, 300
  world's finest guacamole, 301
award-winning chili, 235
  New York, 122–123

Backdoor chili, 75–76
Balcom, Orv, 297
banana daiquiri, frozen, 367
barnstormers' chili, 141–142
Barry, Dave, 3
Battise, Fulton, 32
bay leaf, 7
bean(s), 7
    salad, 333
Beard, James:
    on chili, 259, 261–262
    chili of, 262–263
Beaty, Jim, 64
Bedard, Brian, 131
beef cuts, 5–6
beer, 9
Bennett, John, 267
Bernsen, Corbin, 245
Beth's version of Jerry Jeff's sangria, 370
Betty Flinchbaugh's award-winning chili,
        98–99
Big Apple mousse, 347
Bill Neale's chili, 119
Bischoff, Norb, 144
    chili of, 144–145
biscuits, buttermilk, 327
black bean, smoked poblano, and mango
        salsa, Timothy Schafer's,
        298–299
black-eyed pea:
    relish, 270
    relish, Ouachita Mountain buffalo
        chili with, 267–269
    and turkey chili, Chris LaLonde's
        280–281
Blaine House chili, 225–226
bloody Maria, 362
blue corn bread, Janos Wilder's, 326–327
blue margarita, 358
Bobby's chili, 185–186

Bob Knight's chili, 199–200
Bodine, Geoff, 208
Bo-Dine's crockpot chili, 208
books, recommended, 371–373
Borgnine, Ernest, 43, 239
bottom-of-the-barrel gang:
    mid-South heat wave chili, 130–131
    ram-tough chili, 61
"Bowl of Red" (song), 19–20
brandy:
    Beth's version of Jerry Jeff's sangria,
        370
    sangria, 368
Bret Favre's mother's Cajun chili, 214
Britton, Barbara, 179
Brockway, Sy, 29
Brody, Scott, 110
Brown, H. Jackson, Jr., xiii
brown dog's:
    chili powder, 298
    salsa, 297
buffalo:
    chili with black-eyed pea relish,
        Ouachita Mountain, 267–269
    or venison chili, George Faison's,
        100–101
bun burner chili shack, 92–93
buns burner chili, 132–133
Burton, Levar, 43
Burton, Richard, xix
Butterfield Stageline chili, 54
buttermilk:
    biscuits, 327
    coleslaw, 330
buzzard breath chili, 136–137

Cacciola, Robert, 320
Calhoun, Rory, 50, 239
Campbell, Carroll A., Jr., 322
Campbell, Don and Jan, 147

Campbell, Scott, 275
Canadian chili, 108–109
Caperton, Gaston, West Virginia
    Governor, corn bread muffins of,
    319
capital punishment chili, 51–52
Carlson, Arne H., 232
Carpenter, Scott, 26
Carroll A. Campbell, Jr.'s spoon corn
    bread, 322
Carroll Shelby's chili, 154–155
Carson, Kit, 149
Cartwright, Gary, 24
Casey, Bob and Ellen, 236
CASI (Chili Appreciation Society
    International), xix–xxiii, 169–170,
    378
Cathy Wilkey's Mexican corn brunch
    bread, 323
cayenne pepper, 7
Chamberlain, Wilt, 239
Chan, Warren, 108
Chasen, Dave, xix
cheese:
    A. H. Reamer Chili Co. dip, 308
    -chile squares, 312
    chili con queso dip, 307
    chip dip, 306
    classic pickapeppa spread, 305
    cream, cherry pie, 351
    dip, chili, 303
    -jalapeño corn bread, Ann W.
        Richards's, 321
    Jim's Tex-Mex hors d'oeuvres, 309
    Maria's hot Mexican dip, 304
    quesadillas, 313
    sticks, jalapeño, 311
cheesy artichokes, 310
Chef Allen's steak and black bean chili,
    273–274

Chelios, Chris, 202
Cheli's chili, 202–203
cherry cream cheese pie, 351
chile-cheese squares, 312
chile paste, 12, 101
chile peppers, 12, 13
    roasting of, fresh, 14
chile powder, 10–13
    brown dog's, 298
    JB's, 269
Chiles, Lawton, 219
chili:
    con queso dip, 307
    dip, 303
    to give the devil his due, 194–195
    H. Allen Smith, 25
    history of, xv–xix
    à la Woody, 30–31
    Woodruff DeSilva, 27–28
Chili Appreciation Society International
    (CASI), xix–xxiii, 169–170, 378
chili powder, 10–13
    brown dog's, 298
    JB's, 269
chilli man chilli, 37
Chinese parsley, 7–8
chip dip, 306
Chita margaritas, 359
chocolate:
    buzzard breath chili, 136–137
    chip cookies, 343
    Cincinnati chili, 285–286
    nuggets, 345
    pie, Kansas German, 344
    unsweetened, 10
    see also cocoa
Chris LaLonde's turkey and black-eyed
    pea chili, 280–281
Christman, Rick, 143
cilantro, 7–8

Cin-chili chili, 173–174
Cincinnati chili, 285–286
cinnamon, 10
classic margaritas, 357
classic pickapeppa spread, 305
classic Southern chili, 226–227
Clemens, Roger and Debbie, 200
Clinton, Bill, 220
Clinton, Hillary Rodham, 219
Coats, Doris, 175
cocoa, 10
    Darrien Iacocca's chili, 252–253
    Jeanne Cooper's chili, 244–245
    Ouachita Mountain buffalo chili with
        black-eyed pea relish, 267–269
    Señor Gringo's chili del norte,
        275–276
coffee:
    as chili ingredient, 10
    Judith Light's I'm the boss chili,
        241–242
Cohen, Jamie and Scott, 265
Cointreau margarita, 358, 359
Coleman, Harry, 161
coleslaw:
    buttermilk, 330
    lemon–sour cream, with fresh dill, 332
    Renee's lemon, 329
    sour cream, 331
Colleen's version of Debbie's salsa, 293
Colonel Roosevelt's San Juan Hill salsa,
    294–295
Conley, JoAnne, 301
Conrad, William, 43
Constantine, Janice, 32
Cooper, Jeanne, 239, 244, 245
    chili of, 244–245
Corbin, Barry, 239
Corbin Bernsen's lawless grilled chili,
    245–246

coriander, 7–8
corn bread:
    blue, Janos Wilder's, 326–327
    C. V. Wood's world-class Tex-Mex,
        318
    Eastern, 320
    jalapeño-cheese, Ann W. Richards's,
        321
    Mexican jalapeño, 324–325
    muffins, West Virginia Governor
        Gaston Caperton's, 319
    spoon, Carroll A. Campbell, Jr.'s, 322
corn brunch bread, Cathy Wilkey's
        Mexican, 323
cream cheese cherry pie, 351
cumin, 8
Cuomo, Mario, 347
custard pie, sour cream lemon, 352
C. V. Wood's world-class Tex-Mex corn
        bread, 318

Daiquiris, frozen, 366, 367
Darras, Tommie, 226
Darrien Iacocca's chili, 252–253
dates, in Tennessee treats, 342
Davis, Chili, 219
Debbie's salsa, 292
    Colleen's version of, 293
Deemer, Tom, 163–164
    in ICS history, 151, 152
    sports bar demolition chili of, 165–166
DeFrates, Joe, xxi, 32, 36, 55
DeFrates, Walt, 36
Derek, John, 239
DeSilva, Woodruff "Woody", 7, 26
    chili, 27–28
dill, lemon–sour cream coleslaw with
        fresh, 332
dip, 302–303
    A. H. Reamer Chili Co., 308

chili, 303
chili con queso, 307
chip, 306
classic pickapeppa spread, 305
Maria's hot Mexican, 304
distant cousin to Big Jim's hog-breath
    chili, 102–103
Ditka, Mike, 219
Doc's secret remedy, 79
Drexal, Fred, 53
Dru, Joanne, 43, 53, 124, 239
Duffy, Father (Grant McNiff), 38–39,
    69, 161
Duncan, Sandy, 254
Dunlap, Al, 38
Durkin, Tom, xiv–xv

Eastern corn bread, 320
easy guacamole, 302
Edgar, Jim, 229
elephant garlic, 8
Esposito, Tony and Phil, 206
Everett, Marge, 53
Evergreen chiliheads' hot and spicy true
    chili, 138–139

Faison, George, 100
fam-lee affair chili, 93–94
fat, 8
fat dog chili, 183–184
Favre, Bret, 214
Fennelly, Mike, 271
Fenton, Debbie, 292
Fessenden, Rick, 66
festivals and events, 374–376
Field, Sally, xvii, 237, 255
Finney, Joan, 344
firehouse chili margaritas, 365
Flinchbaugh, Betty and Dawson, 98
Fordice, Kirk, 226

Fore, Charlie, 110
Fowler, Wick, 7, 24, 26, 32
    as CASI chief cook, 169
    death of, 34
    in ICS history, xix, xxi, xxii
    2-alarm chili of, 33
Fox, Michael J., 239
Freely, Colleen, 293
Friedkin, Tommy, 26
frozen daiquiris, 366, 367
Frugal Gourmet's Texas chili, 264–265
Fuss, Eduardo, xvi

Garlic, 8–9
Garner, James, 237
    sooner chili of, 255–256
Garrett, Pat, 167
Gary, Madeline Sophie, 161
Gaul, Bobbi, 308
Gebhardt, William, xviii
Geller, Uri, 34
George Faison's venison chili, 100–101
German chocolate pie, Kansas, 344
Ginsburg, Art, 277
gold margarita, 360
good as gold chili, 143–144
GOP chili, 222–223
Gore, Tipper and Al, 342
Gramm, Phil, 235
grandma chili's green revenge, 94–95
grapefruit juice, in Mayan punch, 363
Griffith, Bob, 132
guacamole, 299
    easy, 302
    Mike's, 300
    world's finest, 301
Gumfudgin, Ormly, 7, 26, 151, 152,
    160–161
    Ormly's California frontier survival
        chili, 162–163

Haddaway, George, xix, 169
Hancock, Carol and Dave,
    48, 62
Hard Times Cafe vegetarian chili,
    283–284
Harold's chili, 58–59
Harris, LaVerne, 46
Hazen-Hammond, Susan, xvi
heartland vegetable chili,
    224–225
Hedrick, Jim, 170–171
Hejtmancik, Lynn, 181
Hendricks, Randal and Alan,
    215
Henner, Marilu, 250
Henson, David, 183
Heywood, Big Jim,
    102, 294
Heywood, Slim Tim, 102
Hickel, Ermalee, 324
hi-octane chili, 177–178
Holtz, Lou, 198
honey, 10
Hooks, Matthew "Bones,"
    287
hot chili, 232–233
hot 'Lanta chili, 233–234
Howard Windsor's chili, 35
Hudspeth, Dusty, 60
Hunt, Jerry, 177

Iacocca, Darrien, 252
iced tea:
    Long Island, 360
    Mayan punch, 363
ICS (International Chili Society), xiii,
    xiv, xxiii–xiv, 378
ingredients, 5–14
iron kettles, 14–15
island tequila cocktail, 363

Jalapeño:
    -cheese corn bread, Ann W.
        Richards's, 321
    cheese sticks, 311
    chile peppers, 13
    corn bread, Mexican, 324–325
James Beard's chili, 262–263
James Garner's sooner chili, 255–256
Jamie's chili, 265–266
Janos Wilder's blue corn bread, 326–327
Jay's chili, 44–45
Jazzabell's chili, 96–97
JB's chile powder, 269
Jeanne Cooper's chili, 244–245
Jess Walton's Young and Restless chili,
    248–249
jícama, orange, and avocado salad with
        poppy seed vinaigrette, 335
Jimmy Johnson's chili, 190
Jim Parker's competition chili, 118
Jim's chili (Hedrick), 170–172
Jim's Tex-Mex hors d'oeuvres (West),
    309
Jim West's Texas range chili, 156–157
Jockey Julie Krone's lentil chili, 193–194
Joe Theismann's chili, 203–204
Johnson, Arte, 50
Johnson, Dave, 48
Johnson, Jimmy, 190
Johnson, Lady Bird, 221
Johnson, Lyndon, xviii, 217
    chili of, 221
Jones, Brereton C., 228
JT's truckin' chili, 116–117
Judith Light's I'm the boss chili, 241–242

Kahlúa, in primal scream, 362
Kansas German chocolate pie, 344
Kassebaum, Nancy Landon, 224
KATJ chili kats' secret brew, 110–111

Kelley, Virginia, 220
Kerrey, J. Robert, 343
kettles, iron, 14–15
Key lime pie, 340
King, Richard, 365
Knight, Bob, 199
Knight, Carol, 134
Knight, Richard, 130, 134
Knudson, Margo, 66
Korman, Harvey, 239
Kowalchik, Sergei, 64
Krimsky, John, 204
    olympic five-ring rattlesnake chili of,
        204–205
Krone, Julie, 193

LaLonde, Chris, 280
Landis, Joe, 50
Lasorda, Tommy, 43, 239
lemon:
    chiffon pie, 349
    coleslaw, Renee's, 329
    fluff, 341
    island tequila cocktail, 363
    Mayan punch, 363
    rice pudding, 350
    sangria, 368
    –sour cream coleslaw with fresh dill,
        332
    sour cream custard pie, 352
lentil:
    chili, jockey Julie Krone's, 193–194
    salad, 328
Letterman, David, 219
Levine, Jonathan, 122, 294
Lewis, Don, 66
Libutti, Edith, 194
Light, Judith, 241
lime:
    frozen daiquiris, 366, 367

juice, 9
pie, Key, 340
tequila sunrise, 364
see also margarita
liquids, 9
Logsdon, Loretta, 94
Long Island iced tea, 360
Long Island margaritas, 368
Lou Holtz's chili, 198
low-fat chili, 229–230
Lyndon Johnson's chili, 221
Lynn's chili, 181–182

McKernan, John, 225
McNiff, Grant (Father Duffy), 38–39,
        69, 161
McNiff, Pancho, 41
McWherter, Ned and Lucille Golden
        Smith, 230
magazines, 373–374
Mahan, Larry, 155
mail-order sources, 376–379
mango, smoked poblano, and black bean
        salsa, Timothy Schafer's, 298–299
mansion chili, 228
margarita(s):
    blue, 358
    Chita, 359
    classic, 357
    firehouse chili, 365
    gold, 358
    Long Island, 368
    Pacific Rim, 359
Margo's chili, 67–68
Maria's hot Mexican dip, 304
Marilu Henner's Evening Shade
        vegetarian chili, 250–251
marjoram, 10
Mark Miller's venison chili, 278–279
Marshall, Peter, 43, 50

Martin, Billy, 239
Marylou Whitney's debutante chili,
    257–258
Mary of Agreda, Sister, xvii
masa harina, 9
Matlock, Mike, 110
Mayan punch, 363
meat cuts, 5–6
Medley, Bill, 155
Mencken, H. L., 353
Mesker, Ron, 124
Mesker, Sherre, 66, 124, 309
Mexican jalapeño corn bread,
    324–325
Mexican oregano, 9–10
Miami heat chili, 134–135
Mike's on the Avenue:
    guacamole, 300
    salsa, 296
    smoked turkey and white bean chili,
        271–272
Miller, Bob, 345
Miller, Mark, 12, 278
Miller, Walter D., 200, 222
Miller, Zell, 233
Mr. Food®'s easy chili, 277
Mitchum, Robert, 50, 239
Moore, Rick, 66
Mother Staub's chili, 191–192
mountain express chili, 84–85
mousse, Big Apple, 347
muffins, West Virginia Governor
        Gaston Caperton's corn bread,
        319
Mullaney, Cindy, 366
Mullin, James, 104

Neale, Bill, 119
Nelson, Bob, 140
Nelson, Willie, 62, 365

Nevada Annie's championship chili,
    46–47
newsletters and newspapers,
    373–374

Onions, 9
orange:
    Alabama slammer, 366
    Beth's version of Jerry Jeff's sangria,
        370
    island tequila cocktail, 363
    jícama, and avocado salad with poppy
        seed vinaigrette, 335
    sangria, 368
    tequila sunrise, 364
oregano, 9–10
organizations, 374
Ormly's California frontier survival chili,
        162–163
Ouachita Mountain buffalo chili with
        black-eyed pea relish,
        267–269
out-of-sight chili, 175–176
Outten, Ron, 146

Pacific Rim margarita, 359
Palmer, Roy, 161
paprika, 10
Parker, Fred and Jim, 118, 283
pasta:
    Cincinnati chili, 285–286
    Hard Times Cafe vegetarian chili,
        283–284
    mansion chili, 228
Pedernales River chili, 236
Peluso, Maria, 304
Pender, DeWitt Clinton, xviii
Pennington, Jay, 43
Peters, Ronald and Carolyn, 131
Petersen, Margie, 158

Petersen, Robert "Pete," 157–158
   hot rod chili of, 159–160
   in ICS history, 151, 152
Pfeiffer, Bill, 50, 55
Pickens, Slim, 50
pie:
   cherry cream cheese, 351
   Kansas German chocolate, 344
   Key lime, 340
   lemon chiffon, 349
   sour cream lemon custard, 352
Pierczynski, Ed, 4, 78, 83
Pierczynski, Mary, 83
Pietro, George Santo, 240
poblano chile peppers, 14
   smoked, black bean, and mango salsa,
      Timothy Schafer's,
      298–299
poppy seed vinaigrette, jícama, orange,
   and avocado salad with,
   335
pork, diced vs. ground, 58
Poston, Tom, 50
pots, 14–15
primal scream, 362
pudding, lemony rice, 350
punch, Mayan, 363
puppy's breath chili, 81–82

Qaddafi, Muammar, 64
quesadillas, 313

Raisins, in Tennessee treats, 342
ranch salad, 334
Randal Hendricks's chili, 215
rattlesnake chili, Krimsky's olympic five-
   ring, 204–205
Ray, Bill and Karen, 83
real McCoy, 281–282
Reed, Cindy, 173

relish, black-eyed pea, 270
   Ouachita Mountain buffalo chili with,
   267–269
Renee's lemon coleslaw, 329
Reno red, 49–50
rice pudding, lemony, 350
Richards, Ann W., 321
Riley, Pat, 219
Rivera, Chita, 359
road meat chili, 77–78
Robert Wagner's chili, 243–244
Robinson, Isabel, 96
Robinson, Randy, 76
Roger Clemens's white chili, 200–201
Roger Smith's chili, 247
Roosevelt, Dennis, 294
Rosenblatt, Renee, 329
Rudy's ancestral chili, 42–43
rum:
   frozen daiquiris, 366, 367
   Long Island iced tea, 360
Rutherford, Richard and Tammy, 141

Salad:
   bean, 333
   buttermilk coleslaw, 330
   jícama, orange, and avocado, with
      poppy seed vinaigrette, 335
   lemon–sour cream coleslaw with fresh
      dill, 332
   lentil, 328
   ranch, 334
   Renee's lemon coleslaw, 329
   sour cream coleslaw, 331
Salis, Chalio, 32
salsa:
   brown dog's, 297
   Colonel Roosevelt's San Juan Hill,
   294–295
   Debbie's, 292

salsa (*continued*)
  Debbie's, Colleen's version of, 293
  Mike's, 296
  Timothy Schafer's smoked poblano,
      black bean, and mango, 298–299
salt, 10
Sandy Duncan's True Tyler, Texas, chili,
      254–255
sangria, 368
  Beth's version of Jerry Jeff's, 370
"Sangria Wine" (song), 369–370
sauce, *see* salsa
Schafer, Timothy, smoked poblano, black
      bean, and mango salsa of,
      298–299
Schlesinger, Chris, 320
Schneider, Diane, 341
Schneider, Floyd, xx
Schofield-McCullough, Jani, 38, 39
Segesser, Philipp, xvi
Seinfeld, Jerry, 219
Señor Gringo's chili del norte, 275–276
Sespe Creek chili, 65–66
7/8 chili, 70–71
Shaw, Bernard, 219
Shelby, Carroll, 41, 87, 152–153, 161, 315
  in CASI history, xix, xx, xxii–xxiii, 151,
      152
  chili of, 154–155
Shotgun Willie chili, 63–64
Sierra, Jose, 32
Silverado Saloon chili, 124–125
Simmons, Jean, 90
Simmons, Jerry, 83, 90
slammer, 361
Smith, Burck, 161
Smith, H. Allen, 14, 17, 24, 127
  in CASI history, 169
  chili, 25
Smith, Jeff, 264

Smith, Liz, 219
Smith, Roger, 247
sour cream:
  coleslaw, 331
  –lemon coleslaw with fresh dill, 332
  lemon custard pie, 352
Southwest whiskey chili for a crowd,
      104–105
spaghetti:
  Cincinnati chili, 285–286
  Hard Times Cafe vegetarian chili,
      283–284
spices, 6–7
spoon corn bread, Carroll A. Campbell,
      Jr.'s, 322
Spurgeon, Hope and Monty, 69
Spurrier, Steve and Jerri, 196
Stafford, Kenton and Linda, 69
Stafford, Tom, 187
Staub, Rusty, 191
Sterman, Bruce, 281
Steve Spurrier's chili, 196–197
Stewart, Joe and Shirley, 48
Stillborn, Robert, 131
Stillwell, Hallie, xx
strawberry daiquiri, frozen, 367
survival chili, 147–148
Susser, Allen, 273
sweeteners, 10

Tarantula Jack's thundering herd
      buffalo-tail chili, 73–74
Taylor, Elizabeth, xix
Taylor, R. S., 89
tea, Long Island iced, 360
10 commandments of chiliheads, 89
Tennessee chili, 230–231
Tennessee treats, 342
tequila:
  bloody Maria, 362

cocktail, island, 363
Long Island iced tea, 360
Mayan punch, 363
primal scream, 362
slammer, 361
sunrise, 364
see also margarita
Theismann, Joe, 203
Thomas, Jerry and Patty, 116
Thompson, Barry, 283
thousand mile chili, 90–91
Tierney, Tom, xix
Timothy Schafer's smoked poblano, black
bean, and mango salsa, 298–299
Tokyo Tom's banzai chili, 131–132
Tolbert, Frank, xx, xxii, 32, 169–170
tomatoes, 10
bloody Maria, 362
Tony Esposito's chili, 206–207
Tooni, Beth, 106, 370
Tooni, S. Neal, 106
tortillas:
Jim's Tex-Mex hors d'oeuvres, 309
quesadillas, 313
traveling chiliheads' competition chili,
112–113
Trebeck, Alex, 239
tri-tip beef cut, 5–6
Truett's mother lode chili, 120–121
turkey:
and black-eyed pea chili, Chris
LaLonde's, 280–281
Randal Hendricks's chili, 215
smoked, and white bean chili,
271–272
Vanna White's Wheel of Fortune
C-H-I-L-I, 240–241

Undertaker's drop-dead chili, 210–211
Unser, Bobby, 43

Valdez, Rudy, 41
Valega, David, 74
Vanna White's Wheel of Fortune
C-H-I-L-I, 240–241
vegetarian chili, 114–115
Hard Times Cafe, 283–284
heartland vegetable chili, 224–225
Marilu Henner's Evening Shade,
250–251
venganza del Alamo, la, 56–57
venison chili:
Canadian, 108–109
George Faison's, 100–101
Mark Miller's, 278–279
Señor Gringo's chili del norte, 275–276
vinaigrette, poppy seed, jícama, orange,
and avocado salad with, 335
vinegar, red wine, 9
vodka:
Alabama slammer, 366
Long Island iced tea, 360

Wagner, Robert, 243
Walker, Jerry Jeff, 369
Wall, Maryjean, 349
walnuts, in Tennessee treats, 342
Walter, Phil, 72
Walton, Jess, 248
Ward, Barbara, 112, 114
Ward, Charlie, 64, 112, 114
Wasco Bob chili, 140–141
Weicker, Lowell, 346
Weld, Bill, 348
West, Jim, 66, 155–156
in ICS history, xxiii–xxiv, 151, 152
Jim's Tex-Mex hors d'oeuvres, 309
Texas range chili of, 156–157
West Virginia Governor Gaston
Caperton's corn bread muffins,
319

whiskey chili for a crowd, Southwest, 104–105
White, Vanna, 240
white lightning chili, 146–147
Whitney, Marylou, 257
Wick Fowler's 2-alarm chili, 33
Wieland, Fred, 92, 161
Wilcox, Dick, 32
Wilder, Janos, 326
Wilkey, Cathy, 4, 80, 307
    Mexican corn brunch bread of, 323
    puppy's breath chili of, 81–82
Wilkey, Doug, 80
Willoughby, John, 320
Wilson, Kevin, 138
Windsor, Howard, 35

wine, red:
    Beth's version of Jerry Jeff's sangria, 370
    sangria, 368
    vinegar, 9
Witts, Dave, xix, xx
Wood, C. V. "Woody," xxi, xxii–xxiii, 29, 34, 41, 55, 124
    chili à la Woody, 30–31
    in ICS history, 151, 152
    world-class Tex-Mex corn bread of, 318
woodruff, 6–7
world's finest guacamole, 301

Yahoo chili, 179–180
Yokozuna's sumo samurai chili, 209–210

Zwijack, Tim, 200